SLOW and STRENUOUS

Finding Peace in a Fast-Paced World

Copyright © 2025 by Peter A. Gierlach

All rights reserved. No part of this book may be reprinted, stored, or reproduced in any form nor may it be uploaded to any website, database, or language-learning model, or other depository, reclamation, or artificial intelligence system without consent of the author. For permission, please email pgierlach@protonmail.com

Printed in the United States of America
Published in 2025
Juneberry Woods Publications

First Edition 2025
10 9 8 7 6 5 4 3 2 1

ISBN-13: 979-8-218-75394-8

Cover design by Evan Lau

To Gabby

Thank you for always supporting me and making life so incredible. You are my light, my life, and my love—forever and always.

To Elliott

Thank you for bringing so much joy into our lives. Let's support, love, and appreciate one another with every beautiful moment we have together.

CONTENTS

Prologue: "You Good?" 1

The Slow Life 19

The Strenuous Life 31

Jumping In 37

The Changing Seasons 43

The Great Unplugging 57

A De-optimized Morning 87

Eating Dandelions 109

Facing My Fears 117

Off the Wagon 155

A Little Farther 161

The Meaning of Success 189

Slow Food 199

The Magic of Forest Bathing 231

Epilogue: A Life Worth Paying Attention To 265

Bibliography 277

Acknowledgments

This book would not have been possible without the love, help, support, and "heck yes" attitude of my friends and family.

First, Gab, I would like to thank you for your endless love, infinite patience, and continual support of all my crazy ideas. My life would be incomplete without you.

Evan, thank you for designing such an amazing cover and capturing the soul of this book.

I would like to express my gratitude to Mom, Michael, Callie, Tonya, Sue, and Jack for taking the time and effort to read through the manuscript, provide your feedback, and help me believe that this project was worth pursuing. Chatting with all of you inspired me to see it through.

Troy and Jake, thank you for that critical midnight chat that helped me realize what this book was actually supposed to be about. Without you two, it probably never would have seen the light of day. (Troy, I'm coming back to you...)

To my whole crew of friends, thank you for always being down to join in on these adventures, coming over for food, supporting me every step of the way, and for being the best damn people to go through life with.

Once again, Troy, thank you for jumping into a frozen lake, thru-hiking an entire wilderness range on a bum ankle, and making sure I didn't fall to my untimely death . . .just because I asked. You are the definition of an incredible friend.

Acknowledgments

Finally, I would like to thank everyone who loved and supported me during the difficult period that inspired this project. I would not have coped as well without you. You know who you are.

Prologue: "You Good?"

Her last words sent me on this journey.

I was already three months into the most difficult, challenging, exhausting period of my life when I received yet another blow. While standing at my kitchen counter in the middle of December, the phone rang. My heart dropped as soon as I saw the name on the screen. I knew that my parents were in Virginia and that a phone call would not mean good news. Fearing the worst, I answered my dad's call. Unfortunately, he confirmed my fears.

My grandmother, who we called Nanny, fell and had been rushed for medical care. While there, she'd caught COVID and developed a terminal infection. She was never going to leave the hospital.

This was the end.

Nanny was an incredible grandmother. The matriarch, rock, and heart of our entire family. She was the strongest person I knew. She worked tirelessly to create a better life for our family and vigorously defended the dignity of complete strangers. Sure, in her later years she drove the wrong way down a one-way street after ignoring our family's request to stop driving, and she refused out of pride to use her walker (resulting in multiple falls and fractures). But she was *Nanny*. Indestructible. Endlessly enduring. Unbeatable. At least, that's how she seemed. Father Time, though, always finds a way to win one way or another.

My dad asked me to call back through FaceTime so I could say my final goodbye. As I waited for him to pick up, the thought of

Prologue: "You Good?"

seeing her almost lifeless in what would become her deathbed made me shudder. I didn't know if I was strong enough to handle it.

If I ever needed to feel better about myself, the easiest and quickest way was to talk to Nanny. As a kid, when Mom and Dad were (rightfully) punishing me for something I'd done, a quick call to Nanny would lead to her scolding my parents for being too harsh. When her grandchildren felt insecure, uncertain, or that they were underachieving in life, Nanny would always remind us that we were worthy of love and affection just by being ourselves. She loved all of us wholeheartedly and unconditionally; a special type of love that we all strive for in our lives but rarely achieve, let alone have to give to others.

It's not often that you know you're about to have your last conversation with someone. A true chance to say goodbye, share what they meant to you, lay it all out on the table. Most of the time, death just happens suddenly, without giving us the chance to properly bid them farewell. But here I was, given the opportunity to confront death and speak to Nanny one last time. Not after I had been recently forced to plan for an even *more* devastating conversation that, mercifully, never happened.

* * *

Just a few months earlier, I thought I'd be saying goodbye to the love of my life.

Gabby and I met in graduate school, just after I had returned from a bit of world travel. Without that experience under my belt, I would have been too insecure to be in a relationship. But when Gabby walked into the restaurant for that first time (twenty-three minutes late—so late that the waitstaff was giving me looks that implied, "You sure you don't just want to order?"), it felt like I was meeting an old friend, even though we had just met. We talked for

Prologue: "You Good?"

hours at that table, and I knew I had to nail down a second date before we left. That initial conversation started in 2015, and it hasn't let up since. Together, we have built an incredible life full of adventure, unconditional love, and endless support for each other through our most difficult times. Without her, I have absolutely no idea where I would be in life. I was never more sure of anything than when I dropped to one knee and asked Gab to marry me.

Like all great marriages, ours was built on lies. On the morning of the proposal, I kept my normal routine and got ready for work. When Gab left before me, blissfully unaware of my scheme, I walked her out, kissed her goodbye, returned upstairs, and changed right back into pajamas. Without her knowing, I had taken the day off from teaching to prepare my proposal. Throughout the day I sent texts about my students misbehaving, what we were talking about at lunch, and how my workday was going. This was to make her believe I was at work when, in reality, I was setting up a timeline of photos in our apartment.

She had always been so sure that I couldn't surprise her with a proposal. But when she returned that Friday to see dozens of photos on the wall, which led to a video on my computer and finished with a request to turn around so she could see me on my knee, I shocked her. She cried tears of joy (I think) and said yes. From there I took her to a surprise dinner where both our families were waiting at the restaurant. It was the perfect day for the perfect woman.

A year later we were in the depths of wedding planning, wondering if we'd even be able to pull off the day. Needing a little break from the stress, we decided to head downtown to explore a food festival. What better way to spend an afternoon than strolling around sampling food trucks? At the time, Gab was dealing with some stomach discomfort that had lasted a few days. We didn't think

Prologue: "You Good?"

it was anything serious. She had been quite stressed with the wedding planning, and we assumed that the pain was either related to that or possibly some bad fish. Normal stuff.

Unfortunately, we were wrong.

Without warning, while walking up a set of stairs, Gab collapsed in pain. She could barely move as she clutched her stomach and began breathing heavily. We ducked into a museum to shelter from the hoards of people and an oncoming rain shower. After a few minutes of rest, we started walking toward the building's exit when she keeled over and crumpled into the closest seat she could find. It took almost half an hour just to get her up and into the car parked right outside.

Several hours later, in the emergency room, it was revealed that she had developed an extremely serious health condition that needed immediate attention. The fact that it wasn't caught before was due to an inexplicable combination of incompetence and incorrect assumptions. She needed a major and invasive surgery, along with a series of tests. After the operation, there was no guarantee she would be okay long-term. The final diagnosis could potentially be terminal, depending on what they found in the operating room.

For the two weeks before the surgery, we managed as best as we could while she existed in debilitating agony. The woman who was a constant source of sunshine, energy, and joy was suddenly bedridden and wincing in pain with every movement.

I was scared.

I didn't want to say it, or think about it, but there was a real possibility that this was the beginning of the end. Until the test results came back, all we could rely on for solace was the doctor's assessment that he didn't *expect* this to be a serious issue post-op.

Prologue: "You Good?"

Expect.

Well, a lot of unexpected things happen every day. How could I ever take solace in an expectation?

Finally, the day of her operation came. I, my parents, and my soon-to-be in-laws paced around the hospital all morning, waiting for a call from the surgeon. After a few hours that had felt like days, my phone rang. The surgeon was on the other end. Her operation was successful, but more tests needed to be completed. Ten agonizing days later, we found out the results had come back in our favor: She was going to be okay. We both breathed a long, tearful sigh of relief. This wasn't going to kill her. Not to say that the challenge was over: We were just beginning the long recovery where she had to essentially relearn how to stand, how to walk, and how to live once again.

Making sure Gab could survive each day of the recovery became my job. Full-time caretaking while working a full-time job was stressful, to put it lightly. Each morning I arrived late to work after helping her out of bed, supporting her to the couch, and setting up everything she could possibly need throughout the day within arm's reach.

For the most part this was all she needed, and I could stay at work without too much distraction. But this wasn't always the case. One day, while grading essays at my desk, I got a text from Gab that read:

Um, my incision is squirting out blood. What should I do?

I burst into my principal's office and told him a coworker would be covering the start of my class and I'd be back in thirty minutes, then sped home to bandage her up. While tossing out the blood-soaked gauze, I took a deep breath and asked:

"You good?"

Prologue: "You Good?"

"I think so."

"Okay. Love you, angel. Bye."

And out the door I went. Which was the last thing I wanted to do. I just wanted to be with her and take care of everything. But part of taking care of everything meant earning a paycheck, which felt harder and harder by the day as my teaching suffered due to the physical and emotional exhaustion I was experiencing. No matter how I looked at it, I felt like I was failing at my job and failing at my caretaking. There simply wasn't enough time in the day. Life was moving way too fast.

* * *

Thankfully, Gab started feeling a little better each day, and life became easier as a result. Eventually, she was able to move on her own, prep her own food, and become more independent. Once she was officially healed and fully cleared by the doctor, our attention turned to happier matters: We had a solid two weeks to finish planning our wedding before the big day arrived.

Fun? Absolutely.

Stressful? You betcha.

Good stress is still stress.

The planning gave Gab an opportunity to move forward from her health situation, to be active, to continue her healing. Decorations, food plans, seating charts—it all (temporarily) got our minds off the horror we had just been through. We didn't have time to process; there was a wedding to plan for more than a hundred people.

The night before the ceremony, we were in a conference room of a budget hotel with my in-laws, frantically putting together favors. It was coming down to the wire, and I was doing my absolute best to make sure the day went exactly as Gabby had been dreaming of

Prologue: "You Good?"

her entire life. Once the favors were done, we gave a collective sigh of relief. The preparation was officially done. The stressful part was over. All we had to do now was show up and enjoy the day.

Proclaiming victory, I left the conference room to go visit my family at the other hotel just across town (wedding favors safely ensconced in my car), celebrate the day to come, and finally relax for a bit.

I never made it.

I don't know if there's ever a good time to get into your first car crash, but I'm sure the night before your wedding isn't it.

My car was slammed into oncoming traffic by a driver who changed lanes without checking his blind spot. If he had, he would've seen me right next to him.

But hey, why not keep the crazy times rolling, right?

I was okay, although my car was totaled. Thankfully, I had dozens of family members and friends in the area to help me. My dad picked me up on the median, we moved the favors to Gabby's cousin's car, and my friend Jake agreed to be my chauffeur on the wedding day. I don't know if I've ever felt more grateful for the people in my life. Maybe the evening before your wedding *is* actually the best time for your first car crash.

That evening I couldn't sleep. In addition to the pre-wedding jitters, I kept imagining what would have happened if a car had come in the opposite direction. That could have been it. On the day before my wedding, it all could have been over. What a terrifying thought. But also, what a beautiful thing to still be here to experience the day.

Our wedding was perfect. Hands down the best day of my life. I'd do it again a million times and never get sick of it. We were surrounded by all our loved ones, most of whom were crying tears of joy (myself included). A double rainbow broke out among the fall

Prologue: "You Good?"

foliage while we were taking our photos after the ceremony. Our favorite music echoed into the night.

One of the highlights of the evening was reconnecting with my best friend from childhood. Growing up, the two of us were inseparable. We were constantly roaming around the neighborhood, going on adventures, getting up to no good. Over the years we saw each other less frequently, getting together only when we both happened to be in town for the holidays. And when Gab and I moved away, I hadn't seen him at all, until he appeared on the patio of the venue. I ran up for a hug and made sure to catch up with him throughout the night. At one point, he mentioned that he recently found at his parents' house an old picture of us , taken at a state fair when we were seven years old.

"Isn't it something? From those early days all the way to this. It all worked out, man. It all worked out," he said before hugging me.

Thanks to beautiful moments like that, our wedding was a reset. It felt like, after the dark times, Gab and I were finally getting back into the light.

That feeling continued for two weeks, and then, after a few years of searching and getting outrageously outbid, we finally had an offer accepted on a house. Once again, good stress is still stress. We scrimped together every penny to buy the home, and we made sure we could close the deal on time. We signed more papers than we ever had in our life, to the point where my signature devolved with each stroke. If we messed up, we could lose our dream house. We stressed over inspections, saving balances, taxes, and final negotiations. While we were in the thick of the paperwork gauntlet, we decided to treat ourselves to a day trip to Vermont to loosen up and relax a bit. A well-deserved getaway to escape the insanity.

Prologue: "You Good?"

We never made it.

* * *

While driving on a beautiful country highway in the foothills of the Green Mountains, my phone rang. On the caller ID appeared the name of my friend Jared. He and I text frequently, but we rarely speak on the phone. When Jared calls, something is usually wrong. I put that thought aside and hoped he had some good news to share. Maybe one of our friends was pregnant! Maybe he had started a new relationship he wanted to tell me about!

Sadly, Jared had the brutal job of informing me that my old friend, the one I reconnected with at my wedding, had committed suicide the night prior.

He was just at our wedding. We hugged. We reminisced on all the crazy things we did as kids: the adventures, the stupid games, the nights when we'd talk about what we wanted to do with our lives. He patted me on the shoulder. *It all worked out, man. It all worked out.* We then lamented that we hadn't stayed in touch as much as we would've liked. But hey, it happens. We'd make plans in a few weeks.

The opportunity never came. There were no signs. He just snapped, flipped a few tables, and grabbed his shotgun. A moment later, his existence was over.

I pulled over and broke down in tears while idling in an RV dealer's parking lot. Eventually, I slipped into the passenger seat so Gab could drive us home. We were speechless.

The shock was immense at his funeral. In moments of stories, overdue hellos, and occasional laughter, I forgot where I was at times. Eventually it would quiet down, and I'd look up to the front of the room. I'd see his hat on his urn, my stomach would twist, and I would be snapped back into the reality of the situation. I would

Prologue: "You Good?"

remember where I was and why I was there. Tears fell as I touched his urn for one final time. We would never go on another adventure together again.

The next day, at his parents' house, his mom came downstairs with a gift for me. It was wrapped in tissue paper, and she said she had recently found it while cleaning out some old boxes. She wanted me to have it. Something to remember him by. In my hands, I felt the curved wooden frame hiding beneath the thin paper. Slowly, and with a few tears welling, I unwrapped that old photo of us from the state fair.

At our wedding, he slipped out the door quietly, not wanting to make a scene. At one point I realized he had left and that I hadn't gotten the chance to say a proper goodbye.

That's okay. I'll see him soon.

* * *

It was just a few weeks later, as Gab and I were days away from closing on the house, that I received the call about Nanny. I didn't know how much more I could take. It was already the most strenuous time of my life, and this just added onto the pile. I knew I couldn't be selfish and run away. I had to confront the situation. This wasn't about me. None of the experiences of the previous three months were. I just had to manage them as best as I could.

On FaceTime, Nanny was as lucid as she had been in days. She remembered that Gab and I had just gotten married. She knew about the house. These moments of clarity were fleeting, and we felt lucky to be experiencing her at her best, such as it was.

I told her how much I loved her, how much she meant to me, to all of us, and that we have her to thank for where we are. She looked into the camera, smiled, and with the little strength she had left, spoke her final words to me:

Prologue: "You Good?"

"Oh, sweetie. You have such a beautiful life. Enjoy every precious moment."

The wisdom hit me like a ton of bricks.

It wasn't just that those would be the last words Nanny, whom I adored, would speak to me.

It was that I hadn't been really following her advice.

Nanny had great excuses not to enjoy every moment of her life. She grew up in poverty with parents who were good people but weren't ready to be parents. She had a difficult childhood. Moved around a lot. Took a while to get her bearings. But she stayed strong, remained tough, and through the years built a storybook life. An amazing husband. Five kids. Upward economic mobility. She lived out the ever-fleeting American dream. She *made* reasons to enjoy every moment. It was tough, but she built her beautiful life from the ground up. And appreciated it deeply because of that.

Up till that point, I had not been enjoying every moment of my life. To be completely honest, I didn't even feel like I was really living it.

Nanny was tough as nails and lived through adversity. She put herself into strenuous situations that weren't guaranteed to be successful. But through grit and belief, she made her vision a reality. To the end, she maintained that toughness, that grit, that *vision*.

But me?

Not even close.

To say I was tough as nails, living through adversity, and challenging myself to grow and create a difficult-to-achieve-but-fulfilling vision would be a vast overstatement. In reality, I had been sliding through life, coasting on cruise control, and getting all too familiar with the luxuries of the modern world.

And I don't think I'm alone.

Prologue: "You Good?"

* * *

In my adult years I have slipped into a seductively easy life. And how could I not? Our society is surrounded with abundance. Endless food, entertainment, consumption of anything and everything at any time, all at my fingertips for my own personal pleasure. Everything is designed to be as convenient as possible. Using our evolutionary predisposition to get the most out of resources with the least amount of energy, we can consume more than we'd ever need without so much as lifting a finger. I for one adore the fact that I can get fresh Chipotle delivered to my door while watching an infinite stream of entertainment on my comfy couch. Shouldn't this be heaven? Shouldn't we all be stoked about how easy our lives have become?

Apparently not.

Despite this tech-created luxury, on average we have less leisure time, are less healthy, feel more anxiety, and are more depressed than ever. The average American is riddled with health issues, lonely, and unhappy. Living an average life has become actively dangerous to our well-being. In spite of all the "time-saving" technology, over 80% of Americans claim to be "too busy" and wish their schedules were lighter. Rates of anxiety and depression have been increasing steadily at a concerning rate, even as it becomes easier to cover our basic hierarchy of needs. In theory, with more time and less effort to complete our daily tasks, we should have more time to exercise, eat well, and improve our overall health. Yet more than 40% of Americans are obese, and rates of heart disease and diabetes are increasing year after year. Mine is the first generation to have a *lower* life expectancy than the previous one.

In my opinion the root cause of these trends is simple. For years our society has been growing in two directions: faster and

Prologue: "You Good?"

easier. Almost every facet of society is untouched from these trends. The internet, especially, has made *everything* faster and easier. But instead of using the extra time for intentional leisure activities, or to improve health indicators, we face a deep societal pressure to cram as much as we can into our schedules in order to "be and do it all." At the same time, we are told that consuming more than ever before will make us happy and satisfied, and that the easy life is the solution to what ails us. Yet this comes at a great cost to our well-being and our planet.

Buying is faster. Shipping is faster. Throwing stuff out is faster. Travel is faster. Posting online is faster. Eating is faster. Dating is faster. And *all* of these, plus more, are easier than ever. And yet our world is moving in the *opposite* direction of where it should be.

If we are not flourishing in this environment, then clearly this fast, convenient, frictionless existence is flawed. After my call with Nanny, I realized how, despite this luxury, I was certainly not thriving. Maybe, just maybe, this system is not creating the happy and fulfilling life that it had promised; things are looking more and more like the film *Wall-E* every day–dystopian, desolate, where Earth has been robbed of all its resources and humanity has succumbed to the whims of convenience. And I'm pretty sure that movie was intended to be a warning, not a blueprint. The characters in that film had all the ease imaginable, and yet they were unhappy and unhealthy and unfulfilled. As that starts to become our reality, it's essential that we look critically at where we're headed and what it's doing to us. Perhaps fulfillment lies somewhere outside an easy life of convenience. It's entirely possible it lies closer to its opposite: a slower, more intentional lifestyle, one where thoughtful friction is seen as a way to grow, not an inconvenience to destroy.

Prologue: "You Good?"

A way of living that Nanny had prescribed to and had encouraged me to pay attention to.

* * *

Personally, I feel that we've been sold this idea that the quick and convenient options will allow us to live more fully. But the data doesn't add up. Instead, with each passing year, life feels more stagnant.

So how do we live with deeper meaning, greater purpose, more intention, and better attention, in a modern world that makes each of those more challenging to experience?

Let's be clear: I am not immune to falling prey to this lifestyle. I have been fully sucked into this easy world and am admittedly worse off for it. It just took Nanny's last words to make me recognize and accept this truth.

After I ended my talk with Nanny, you'd figure—given my experiences—that I'd be thinking a lot about death. But that wasn't the case. Instead, I found myself thinking intensely about *life*. And how, deep down, *I didn't feel like I was really living it*. Her words made me realize that I *wasn't* enjoying every precious moment, nor was I making the most of my life. And it's all because I fell into that trap of speed and convenience.

Ever since I began working full-time and "officially" leaving my childhood behind, I've subscribed to a fast and easy life. I've crammed as much as I could into my schedule. I've done my best to "keep up with the Joneses," whoever they are. I've let everything be done for me.

When distraction came knocking in the form of social media algorithms, I always welcomed it with open arms and repeatedly fell down the rabbit hole. Too many hours were spent mindlessly scrolling instead of talking to Nanny or my friends. My busy

Prologue: "You Good?"

schedule somehow became more important than spending time with loved ones. For some reason I let myself get preoccupied with jetting around the country on stressful trips when I had beautiful, wild, and rugged places to explore right here in my own backyard. I never mustered up the courage to do the really hard things that my younger self dreamed of. I was always looking for something else out there, somewhere, although everything I needed has been right here the whole time.

I was living a nice life, but it was on cruise control. Gliding through life is pleasant enough, albeit not very intentional. And without that intention, it's easy to get distracted by every new gadget that gets released and every promise that happiness is right behind the next paywall. As a result, time goes by in a blur, and it's hard to pay attention to each precious moment.

Why didn't I recognize that where I was, who I was, *was enough*? Why haven't I recognized my beautiful life for what it is and enjoyed every moment, like Nanny saw so clearly?

After much reflection, I settled on an imperfect but satisfying answer:

I was living too comfortably and moving too quickly to actually be able to live fully. I got caught up with "adulting," technology, and everything that came with it. I was always thinking about the *next* thing instead of focusing on the present. There was always more to do, more productivity to squeeze out of a day, better experiences to be had. After a while, keeping up that pace became exhausting. I watched *other* people live their lives to the fullest, and I eventually started to live vicariously through them. I'd watch stories of brave people embarking on grand adventures instead of going on them myself. I'd spend hours watching videos of people building their dream cabins in the woods rather than saving to purchase or build my own. I'd read articles by folks who shared their experiences of slowing down and living the cottage life, even though I continued to live a complicated life in the fast lane. Each video or article I saw would give me a burning sensation inside that screamed, *Yes! That! That's what you should be doing with your life, dude!*

Yet I remained on the couch. Too busy, too tired, too much of a stick-in-the-mud to make that thought a reality. My comfort zone remained firmly in place. I was too fatigued and insecure about my abilities to go out and live the life I actually wanted to—one that fostered presence, attention, and more intentional experiences.

* * *

Being busy is a convenient excuse for us to feel like we're doing important things, when in reality we're putting off the work that's *truly* important and makes us feel alive. Busy is what happens between those moments that inspire presence: getting married, seeing a grand vista, going on a big trip, becoming a parent. All these allow us to feel immersed in the moment. But what about all the time in-between? Should we just chalk up our everyday existence as a blur that can't possibly be inspiring? Is it not possible to keep our water at a healthy simmer on a day-to-day basis?

Before that call with Nanny, my answer to these questions was a resounding: "No. It's not possible. Welp, that's settled. Back to YouTube to watch others live their lives and do things that I can't do."

After that call, though, I couldn't let that be my answer anymore.

The mission became clear: I needed to break free of this trap. But exactly *what* needed to be done, and why, required a deeper understanding of why time started moving so fast to begin with. In

Prologue: "You Good?"

addition, I needed to uncover how to properly *use* the extra time and space I would create from slowing down to build an intentional life worth paying attention to.

The Slow Life

As I age, I get the sense that every year ends faster than the one before. Each season goes by before I am fully settled into its rhythm. Every month sprints to the finish line while I'm still getting ready to sit down and watch. And all the days blur together into one amorphous block of time, leaving me to wonder: *What did I even do, exactly?*

Usually, this realization creeps up a couple of times per year: the start (and end) of summer vacation, around my birthday, the holidays, and especially New Year's. Around each of those times, I look back to reflect on just how *quickly* time has gone, and how there is no sense of it slowing down. Then, once I settle in with this realization, I resolve to make time go slower and to savor each precious moment as if it were my last. *Maybe,* I think, *it is possible to reverse this pace and get back to appreciating long, drawn-out days, months, and years. Perhaps I can get a handle on this whole time thing and take it down a few notches.*

And yet, despite this motivation, the next stretch of time goes by even faster. At each checkpoint I am left scrambling more and more to put together the pieces and to try to figure out the formula of how to slow down this relentless train, even just a smidge. The answer to this conundrum lies in understanding why this manic pace exists in the first place.

There are multiple reasons for feeling as if time were flying by faster than it should. For one, as we get older, we get busier, more distracted, and steeped in monotonous habits. When this happens our brain becomes accustomed to being on autopilot, therefore we do not feel the need to be focused on the moment and ingest new information like we did when everything was new (like, say, when we were children experiencing the world for the first time). When we have already gone through a litany of summers and a half dozen "first days" of new jobs, and we will never again experience a first love, first kiss, first home, or first child, our brains often stop paying attention. Why use the energy processing something we have already experienced? Because of this, time tends to meld into a blur of dreary routine that the brain does not feel the need to be wholly present for. Where our attention goes, so goes our life (and our perception of it). The common wisdom, therefore, is that the less we feel the need to be fully immersed in, and attentive to, the present moment, the faster time flies. Whether this is because we are distracted, disinterested, or just going through the motions, the result is the same: Time appears to speed up.

In her book *Peak Mind*, Dr. Amishi Ja explains that our focus often functions like a flashlight: It can be pointed at only one thing at a time. When we are distracted and rapidly shift our attention from one stimulus to another—like when we are scrolling through a bunch of posts online—our flashlight quickly bounces back and forth in a variety of directions. It's like turning the beam toward a creepy corner in the basement, then immediately flashing it elsewhere. We don't give ourselves enough time to *see* what's being illuminated. Logically, if our attention is constantly being jostled around by outside forces, without enough time to fully focus on what it's directed toward, then we are never fully immersed in the present moment. It would seem that intentional focus on the present moment would be the elixir to our time problem. If we could just slow down and focus on one thing at a time, it could guarantee a slower perception of life.

Or maybe not.

Research by Professor Adrian Bejan indicates that there may be a physical component to the quickening pace of time that is inevitable. According to Bejan, our brains sense that time is passing whenever the current mental image it is processing differs from a previous one. Therefore, the more mental imagery we process (and the more novel situations we encounter), the more time seems to stretch since we are having a richer, more intensely present experience. As we get older, the brain increases in complexity, which means it takes just a bit longer for it to process new mental images. This means that we manage slightly fewer images as an adult than when we did when we were younger, a progression that continues with every year we get older. With fewer novel images per day, we have less references for what happened during a span of life, and time subsequently appears to speed up.

While the physical explanation seems a bit depressing to me (as it resigns us to an ever-increasing speed of life passing by and renders all attempts to stop it as futile), Professor Bejan does agree with Dr. Ja on one point: Constant distraction can also contribute to our sense of time passing by too quickly. Even if there are some unavoidable physical changes within our brains, the key to slowing down time is simply focused presence in unique situations that fully engage our attention. Simply put, we need to slow down enough to literally smell the roses and deeply immerse ourselves in life rather than wading through as fast as possible in shallow waters. Doing otherwise will make life feel like it's going by in a flash.

We need to do the exact *opposite* of what I'd been doing, which was coasting along in a comfortable routine.

These findings are not necessarily surprising. I remember

growing up and hearing the adults in my life always cautioning me that "it all goes so fast" and to "appreciate where you are now because it'll be over before you know it." With the typical arrogance that comes with youth, I ignored these dire warnings and went back to watching TV. But I only realize now, as my third decade has gone by in a blink, how true that counsel was. Suddenly, I find myself as the older man with curious wrinkles and maddeningly dark circles under my eyes, whose life has stealthily gotten a ways behind me. Now *I* am the one lecturing kids on the preciousness of the moments that they thoughtlessly squander—although doing so makes me a hypocrite. Even with this understanding of valuing these fleeting moments, I *still* recklessly waste my time.

Let's face it: It's hard not to. Our current society is *designed* for us to waste as much time as possible, much of it in the name of mindless, useless, needless consumption. Advertisements are constantly forcing themselves into our awareness. Days consist mainly of surfing the internet at warp speed, with each thought, post, or article warranting barely a second of our attention. I personally can't remember a single online post I read in, say, 2018. And yet I'm certain that I spent much of that year mindlessly scrolling through tens of thousands of them. It feels like time has vanished, simply because of the high level of distraction.

We can't just point the finger at Silicon Valley for our fleeting attention spans, though, because there are other pernicious factors at play. In *Four Thousand Weeks*, Oliver Burkeman points to our hypercapitalist ideals as a source of both identity crisis and time sucks. We are taught from birth that our worth is linked to how much we *produce* and *consume*. The propaganda would like us to think that if we're not working or spending (either our time, money, or attention), then we are useless to the economy and are therefore worthless as a person. This leads to ridiculous, productivity-driven doctrines that we often encounter in the workspace. Sleeping is for losers. ("I'll sleep when I'm dead," these people often say. What they don't realize is that, since they're not sleeping, death will probably be knocking on their door sooner rather than later.) Naps are for the lazy. We must be the first one in and last one out every day. Success goes to those who are willing to sacrifice their time in the name of the company. Through the years, this mindset has subconsciously encouraged me to frantically switch from task to task, always producing without ever taking the time to steep myself in the moment and the work for fear of becoming a failure.

It was no wonder, then, why I found myself pondering where my precious time went each day. When I was constantly distracted, stressed out, sleepless, overworked, malnourished, bombarded with media, dealing with endless crises at work, and under immense pressure to perform, consume, and produce at all hours of the day, it was hard to create enough space in life to breathe, pay attention, and attune myself to the preciousness of the present moment. In these outrageous circumstances, it was hard to just *be* while under this pressure that had been thrust upon myself and others. The relentless, frenzied motion of society can prevent many of us from paying attention long enough to stop and wonder what it's all for. Of course, thoughts like that are dangerous to the system.

Thinking about alternatives threatens the infinite sequence of consumption, production, and growth. If we feel fully satisfied with watching the sunrise, feeling the morning dew, seeing bubbles form on a pancake, looking into our lover's eyes, or soaking in a good book on a cozy autumn evening—so much so that there is no desire to work more, make more, or buy more—then the masters of the machine don't get their precious profits. The economy would then be harmed by us not contributing to its vicious cycle because we have the audacity to feel saturated with a vibrant life without frantic, delirious consumption. In this way, slowing down could be seen as an act of treason against the state.

* * *

In an effort to reclaim our time and attention, there has been a recent upsurge to rebel against our fast-paced, tech-obsessed culture of relentless productivity. More and more people are recognizing the depressing futility of spinning our wheels endlessly and losing our appreciation of life in the process. This is evidenced by the mindfulness meditation movement, which has turned a once-fringe spiritual practice into a mainstream discipline touted by neuroscientists, psychologists, and podcasters galore. This would not be happening if, as a collective, we were not feeling the allure of just "being" instead of constantly "doing." Of course, certain corporations are using this practice to *boost* productivity and efficiency. But that misses the point. Folks are trying to produce less and be less efficient, and for good reason. Hijacking a spiritual discipline in the name of profit, while certainly on-brand for most large companies and CEOs, threatens to dilute the powerful benefits of individuals becoming more content with being in the moment, true to themselves.

Tom Hodgkinson, founder of the periodical *The Idler* and author of *How to Be Idle*, is one of the philosophical leaders of the movement to slow down, breathe deeply, and embrace doing less. His work includes teaching people how to sleep in, enjoy a good drink with friends, and recognize the importance of napping as an act of social justice. His goal is to inspire people to disconnect from technology and work in order to *reconnect* with simple, analog pleasures and meaningful moments with loved ones. Hodgkinson

The Slow Life

often rails against the hardcore hustle culture that pervades modern society in favor of a slower, simpler existence doing things that are mindful and purposeful, whether it's tending to a garden or riding a bike. Ultimately, the argument is that the best way to rebel against our fast-paced consumption culture is to do less, produce less, consume less. We need to disengage from the corporate machine as much as possible by finding pleasure in the best things life has to offer, which are often free and widely available (with regard to napping and riding a bike—probably best not to do them at the same time!). In other words: hit 'em in the wallet. The fact a periodical based on the idea of working in an amount between "less" and "as little as possible" is still growing considerably shows the hunger for rest that we are all attempting to satiate.

* * *

Although Nanny's final words reiterated the need for me to slow down, the first time my rapid pace of life caught up with me was when I received the call that my friend had committed suicide. What seemed like a perfectly normal, long-distance friendship was suddenly revealed to be a terribly sad, missed opportunity. We had barely seen each other in the two years since I moved away. Our conversations often ended with "We'll get together when we're both home" or the little lie that we'd see each other "soon." We were rarely both home at the same time, and no effort was made on either part for a visit. Why bother when "soon" was such a seductively ambiguous time frame we could both lightly commit to? Besides, we had all the time in the world. No sense in rushing or inconveniencing ourselves.

The truth is I got caught up in the rapid river of modern society and was left on the verge of drowning. Phone calls were never made. Visits never planned. Check-ins few and far between. And all for no good reason other than life was moving so fast. Up till that time I thought I was living my life and doing what was necessary to get ahead. What I failed to realize was that *life* was happening while my friend struggled in silence and Nanny sat by a silent phone. Life should have been spent with them instead of on a screen. Catching up should have been with those who actually mattered instead of the news. "Too busy" shouldn't have been a phrase I uttered in response to seeing or calling a loved one, and instead, I should have recognized it for the insult it truly was. Because what *really* was I doing that was so important? A blur of posts and work and emails and streaming?

If so, what a shallow and unfulfilling life that is.

* * *

The past decade went by in a flash for me. And that was terrifying. Whether it was my phone or overworking or doom-scrolling or brain changes, it did not matter. The reality remained the same: I did not want life to move that quickly.

The problem was clear: I was doing absolutely nothing to slow life down. In fact, my actions were making it *worse* by speeding up my perception of time. The pain I felt at the missed opportunities finally broke me free, ever so slightly, from the seductive spell of speed, efficiency, and productivity that our society promises. I saw behind the curtain and realized how empty those promises were. I came to the conclusion that a fast, efficient, and productive life was not necessarily a deep, rich, and happy life; that shallow experiences created a shallow existence; that a good life was not one crammed to the brim with activity for the sake of having something to do.

I needed to slow down. Or at least attempt to.

In the vein of Hodgkinson, I realized I needed to radically alter my perception of success in a world that defines it so poorly. I had to reorganize my priorities, my habits, my activities, and my mindset. I had to somehow become content with doing less and being more. Reluctantly, this meant a clear calendar and spending more time sitting around doing nothing in particular until something inspired me in the moment—and being okay if nothing did. To me, it felt like a radical rebellion against the societal standards that have been constructed over the past generation.

 The rewards were too great to ignore and would be well worth the effort. If I could find a way to break free from the endless rush I had been swept up in, then I would finally feel a sense of calm, rest—*peace*, even. I could become a kinder, gentler person if I wasn't so strung out for time. I could have space to call old friends and family members to see how everyone was holding up. I could rediscover the joys of random *play*: playing drums, taking photos, writing down my ideas for the sake of just recording them and *not* turning them into a side hustle or second career. I could sip tea and watch birds and be creative and drink in the marrow of life deeply, slowly, and thoughtfully. Hopefully, if all went well, I could feel like a child again, with endless wonder and plenty of time to go about experiencing it in a profound way. My brain would have more daily inputs, which would mean more memories, and time would hopefully slow down to a sustainable pace once again.

 But slowing down couldn't be the only solution to my malaise. Clearing my calendar to lay on the couch and do nothing indefinitely would also get stale after a while. Also, the pace of my life wasn't the only issue that led to my existential discontent. In addition to speed, there is another societal factor that is equally as damaging; one that makes the quick pace of life possible in the first place. It's a matter that doesn't just make life faster but easier as well. When paired with rapid speed, the result is a fleeting and distracted life that goes by in a blink without stopping to smell that many roses.

I couldn't *just* slow down. I needed to make the most of the extra time and space that comes with a slower pace of life. Not in a frantic, stressful, productivity-minded way; that would be unsustainable and just accelerate life back up again. Instead, I had to insert slow, intentional activities that fostered presence and attention. Otherwise, I'd just be slowing down only to lay around, stare at more screens, slip into a routine, and let life continue to pass by in a blur.

When we look at what it takes to actually slow down time on a cognitive level, it's those novel experiences—the new activities, the expansion of our horizons, the beautiful moments that immerse us—that stretch the timeline. And whether it's starting a garden, cooking a meal from scratch, exploring a new area, or doing things the "old-fashioned way," all these have one thing in common.

They are strenuous.

It takes a concerted effort to create new experiences that force our minds to focus on the present moment. In a world designed to get us to unconsciously slide by, slow living is incomplete without the insertion of intentional activities that require our full attention in order to be completed.

When we think of slow living, we often think of analog activities that take longer to learn and do. In addition to being slower, they also take more effort and, at their core, are more difficult. Learning to play an instrument is harder than listening to it. Cooking a large meal for friends is a greater challenge than ordering delivery. Going on an adventure takes far more effort than watching someone else's online, especially if it requires hiking up a mountain even though there's a paved road to the top. And each of these things require a level of focus that etches new memories into our brains,

The Slow Life

thus slowing our perception time while simultaneously providing the benefits of a calmer, more sustainable way of living and a more confident, competent sense of self. Analog activities require effort. Not a fast-paced, hectic, unrealistic effort but rather a slow, concerted, focused intent on the task itself.

By nature, *slow* living is inherently *strenuous*. It sounds contrary but think about it: Any mindful activity that takes time will require more effort than the quick, easy alternative.

Combining slow *and* strenuous activities could make the difference between sliding through life mindlessly and growing in a sustainable, *intentional* way. For me, that would mean doing things the "hard way" because that's what would be memorable—and to not accomplish anything, or produce more, or keep up appearances.

The things that I would do would need to be for the sake of doing them, and my own growth. It would be to honor my friend by having the strength to fulfill some of those childhood dreams we came up with. And it would honor Nanny by creating more precious moments to pay attention to, immerse myself in, and *enjoy*.

The Strenuous Life

"I wish to preach, not the doctrine of ignoble ease, but the doctrine of the strenuous life, the life of toil and effort, of labor and strife; to preach that highest form of success which comes, not to the man who desires mere easy peace, but to the man who does not shrink from danger, from hardship, or from bitter toil, and who out of these wins the splendid ultimate triumph."

—Theodore Roosevelt, *The Strenuous Life: Essays and Addresses*

My life is comfortable. Almost *too* comfortable. And while I love and appreciate the comfort and ease that our society provides nowadays, I am also keenly aware that it is becoming too much of a good thing. Despite living as a small mammal on planet Earth, it's possible for me to go for days—weeks, even—without breaking a sweat or raising my heartbeat. I wake up in a box, get into another box to propel myself at high speeds, end up in a different box where I stare at a glowing box for a few hours, then get back into my transport box so that I can sit in my main box for the rest of the night. All this happens without much physical effort, and it all takes place in the exact same temperature (roughly 72 degrees, to be exact).

When I want to eat, I don't need to burn many calories to find my next meal. I simply take my transport box to a grocery store (another box) or have the option for some other poor soul to bring my food to me, lest I put actual effort into finding my next meal. Preparing and cooking food can be outsourced to corporations who will do it for me, so why bother? And entertainment no longer needs to involve me getting up and moving about. Instead, it can all take place while I'm comfortably on a couch. All I have to do is lose my sense of reality and sell a bit of my soul to the glowing screen in front of my eyes, which promises endless amusement in exchange for just a few hours of precious, irreplaceable time. I have strayed far from my hunter-gatherer ancestors, who walked tens of thousands of steps per day and worked for every ounce of survival. Now, for the most part, I am just a tired mammal who can barely get up to change the channel without complaint.

This fear of society devolving due to a lack of friction has been around for generations. Around the turn of the 20th century, Theodore "Teddy" Roosevelt was worried that American society was becoming too "soft," especially considering the technological advances of the Industrial Revolution allowed for less toil and more leisure time. Roosevelt, for his part, was anything but a sloth. He regularly engaged in activities such as boxing, rowing, polo, hunting, canoeing, and even skinny-dipping in the Potomac River throughout the winter. In an 1899 speech known as "The Strenuous Life," Roosevelt made his case for a "hardening" of the American citizen. He argued that a meaningful life is one of challenge, strife, and the growth that comes with them. He portrayed action as a success in itself and admonished those who criticized the doers of the world as "poor and timid souls who [knew] neither victory nor defeat." In essence, Roosevelt was telling society to toughen up, challenge itself, and appreciate the sweet fruits of its labor afterward.

Like the world Roosevelt criticized, we are currently facing what journalist Michael Easter calls a "comfort crisis." While our current level of comfort is delightful and enhances our life in many ways, it is becoming far too much of a good thing. Our bodies had evolved to move across long distances, lift heavy things, carry objects, and navigate challenging terrain. We are literally born to move. Or, as my ninety-two-year-old neighbor Tom says, "Motion is lotion."

So, a lack of physical activity, naturally, results in concerning consequences. Rates of lifestyle-related diseases have been steadily increasing over the past few decades, in part because the average American currently moves less throughout the day than ever before. Currently, roughly 77% of young Americans are physically unfit to serve in the military due to obesity, drug use, or other health problems. And while we shouldn't expect everybody to be ready to serve in the military at a moment's notice, it is a good indicator to know how many among us are capable of moving our bodies through space, traveling long distances, and carrying heavy loads. This helps us understand the level of vitality (or lack thereof) in society.

Even more concerning is what a sedentary lifestyle is doing to our youth. According to the Office of Disease Prevention and Health Promotion, as of 2013, only one in four high school students meets the basic baseline for aerobic readiness. And this guideline is far from strenuous; the government report on Physical Activity Guidelines for Americans suggests only 150 minutes of physical activity *per week* as a baseline. This amounts to less than three hours a week of moving our bodies and raising our heart rates. In reality, we probably should be this active *each day* if we are able.

* * *

Our society is more comfortable than ever. And comfort is great—necessary, even. I enjoy a relaxed, cozy evening as much as anyone else. But when life brought me those challenges that tore me down to my core, I realized something important about my relationship with comfort: It's when my life gets hard that it becomes its most beautiful. It's when I face my greatest doubts that life becomes its most meaningful. And it's when I become uncomfortable that I am able to grow into a stronger, more capable version of myself.

Despite the roller coaster of emotions, the overwhelming grief, the debilitating fear, and the alarming uncertainty of it all, being pushed past my limits in those three months led to more growth than I had experienced in the entire prior decade. Once the dust settled and my breathing slowed, I felt different. I felt stronger, calmer, more capable. Nonstop action had been required of me for weeks on end. I had no choice but to take care of those who needed me; finish what needed to be done; comfort those who needed comforting; and, as quickly and effectively as possible, deal with everything life was putting on my plate. In the vein of Roosevelt, I was not shrinking from hardship.

The level of action these situations called for was not sustainable or healthy. And even though I wasn't able to focus on my own needs at any point, the experience still made me a stronger person. Once the mental and physical muscles got time to rest, they grew back with greater vitality. Little annoyances throughout the day didn't bother me as much because I had just dealt with major crises. And precisely *because* I dealt with those crises and all the unknowns, I began to feel like I could take on anything life had to throw at me. The strenuous times molded me into a more competent person with a different perspective on life, a quieter, more confident, and more present version of myself.

However, the problem was that this growth occurred as a result of an outrageous amount of high-stress situations, all happening simultaneously, which is not a recipe for becoming a well-adjusted adult. It can be likened to the "hustle culture" we see promoted online as a path to happiness through productivity—both scenarios are unhealthy and unsustainable. But I did wonder if it was possible to stimulate similar growth through smaller, more regular undertakings that pushed my comfort zone in a slower, healthier, more sustainable way. While intentionally slowing down, I would have more time and energy to fill my life with purpose. Perhaps making my activities slower *and* less convenient would actually make them more impactful. Maybe slow and strenuous didn't have to be opposites. They could coexist by creating enough time to do meaningful things in an effortful way, which could be more satisfying and memorable. Not only could I stretch time out through new experiences, but those same experiences could foster intentional growth. It could shape me into a happier, healthier, more confident version of myself long-term.

By purposefully adding more strenuosity to my life, I could break free from the comfort crisis and grow into a more capable human with a life full of rich experiences. There was nothing stopping me from actively living the life that Teddy Roosevelt felt was so necessary more than one hundred years ago. And choosing to do this, even on a personal level, would be a great act of rebellion against the false gospel of endless comfort and ease.

It is time for action.

* * *

Last night, I made the long drive back from Nanny's funeral. With Gab asleep in the passenger seat, I devised a plan.

I will spend an entire year exploring the possibility that life could get better when it slows down and becomes more strenuous. If a hurried, distracted, and frictionless routine was a consequence of speed and convenience, maybe doing the opposite would yield more positive and sustainable results. With a slowed-down lifestyle comes an appreciation for the day lived—really lived—having encounters that would stretch my limits, encourage sustainable growth, and foster mindfulness.

After we returned home, I sat down at our living room table and brainstormed different areas of life and society that I felt were too fast and too convenient for me. In addition to looking into how I got to this point, and how those factors have impacted me, I planned to create a series of activities that would push me past my comfort zone physically, mentally, and emotionally, in hopes of making space for more unique, immersive experiences.

That is how I will rebel against this malaise.

* * *

This will require much of me. It means limiting my responsibilities, cutting out scrolling on my phone, and valuing experience over convenience. The temptation to revert to my old ways will be great, but I am committed to the task of living a more satisfying and purposeful life. In honor of Nanny, of my friend, of the love of my life who is thankfully still by my side, I want to create, and be present for, a beautiful life. I want to enjoy every moment of it instead of coasting on cruise control.

And so, my journey into the slow and strenuous life is ready to begin. All I need to do is take a single leap forward into the unknown. Literally.

Jumping In

I am already shivering as I look up at the stars. In a crystal clear sky they are bright enough to reflect on the water in front of me. It is a crisp reflection on an equally crisp night. If I had been plopped here without knowing where I was, it would be impossible to know which way was up or down.

Enough stalling. The process must begin.

Off come the pants. Then the socks. And finally the shirt. Stripped down on an icy dock wondering what the hell I am doing.

A deep breath. Fears of regret. And a churning excitement deep within the pit of my stomach.

Three. Two. One . . .

* * *

It's easy to come up with a big idea and never pursue it. How many novels remain unwritten, adventures never taken, and businesses never started? Planning something excites us, gets our blood boiling, inspires dreams of a new life.

But execution? That takes effort. And it's so much easier to just *not* get started.

When beginning this year of slow and strenuous living, I knew there needed to be something that jumpstarted the experience; a challenge that could light a fire under my all-too-comfortable rear end and get me moving in the right direction instead of delaying the start indefinitely.

I've always loved the idea of rituals. Rites of passage that usher

Jumping In

us from one phase of our life into the next. They are a fantastic checkpoint from which we can mark different stages in our lives. Sure, they take some time, dedication, and discomfort. But that's what makes them meaningful.

It's so easy, especially nowadays, to just mindlessly flow from one era to the next. Oftentimes our "rites of passage" take little more than filling out a form online, like scheduling a driver's license test or completing a degree. To mark an accomplishment with a ritual, though, makes it intentional, meaningful, memorable. This is why weddings are so important: it adds gravitas to the commitment. Plus, when it comes to rites of passage, it's not a guarantee that it will actually be completed; it requires dedication, effort, and sometimes strength, making it impossible to just "slide into" a new stage of life. This makes it all the more exciting and satisfying when we *do* complete it and are able to move onto the next phase. Intentional rituals provide a healthy bit of friction that keeps us moving forward in a meaningful, fulfilling way.

Humans have been practicing rituals for as long as we've been around, whether they are religious, political, or personal. Rituals can range from a solemn vow taken in a house of worship in front of loved ones, to a Midwest man slapping his knees, standing up, and saying "Welp" when it's time for you to leave. In particular, I'm interested in these *rites of passage*: rituals specifically designed to move us from one phase of life into the next.

Typically, a rite of passage involves a person withdrawing themselves from where they currently stand in order to prepare for the next phase of life. Then there is an in-between stage where passage into the next step is not guaranteed, but the person no longer exists in that original state. Finally, the lucky person must "consummate" the rite of passage by completing the ritual exactly as specified in order to be considered successful. This can include getting a driver's license or graduating from high school. Other examples include Poy Sang Long, a rite of passage in Thailand where adolescent boys take monastic vows to earn the title of novitiate monk, or the festive *russefeiring* among students in Norway preparing to graduate from school. Most of the time there is a community aspect that monitors the process and makes sure that the requirements of the rite have been successfully met before bestowing the honor onto the participant. The most common overseer, in the US at least, being the DMV.

As I embarked on this journey of living slowly and strenuously, I wanted to start the year with *some* type of rite of passage. Something to really mark the fact that I was shifting my perspective in life and beginning anew. An action that could make it clear that, from now on, life was going to be different. I loved the idea of separating myself from my current way of living and jumping gloriously into this next phase that was sure to solve all of my problems. I was ready to strip myself away from the excessive comfort to which I've grown so accustomed and face *discomfort* head on, with courage and bravery.

So, I thought, why not strip down and jump right in?

* * *

With this in mind, call up my friend Troy, who truly is a good sport, and share my ridiculous plan. Like always, he is all in and willing to come along. Just a few hours later he, Gab, and I find ourselves on the lakeshore at the edge of town on a cold, dark, starry night. We are the only car in the parking lot at this hour. There are no lights around us. All we can see is the silhouette of the lake basking underneath the clear sky of stars above. The air is cold, and

Jumping In

I am sure the foreboding black water is frigid.

The idea is simple: instead of spending another night on the couch, I will "cleanse" myself of the past few months by dipping into the frigid lake for a cold plunge. Thus, symbolically, starting my life anew.

"You sure you wanna do this?" asks Troy, ever the pragmatist.

"No," I quip back, "but that's exactly why I should."

Gab, who is clearly the wisest of the bunch, is waiting in the car with the heat on. It is a balmy 25 degrees outside and she has no rite of passage to move through at this hour. Instead, she is taking the role of photographer from the heated passenger seat while rocking out to her music.

Troy and I walk out onto the dock and strip down into our swim trunks. The plan is for one of us to plunge into the dark, freezing lake while the other stays on the dock in case of an emergency. Then we will swap places. To determine the first victim, which neither of us wants to be, we flip a coin.

Heads.

Troy wins the esteemed honor of being miserable first.

On the long count of three, Troy reluctantly plops himself into the water and immediately becomes reborn. Or at least he is immediately frozen. He lets out a loud, primal yelp that echoes across the water into the darkness and starts laughing uncontrollably through his shivering jaw.

"You have to stay in for 10 seconds!" I yell while wrapped under my blanket on the dock, already shivering without even being plunged into icy depths. I count out loud at a quick pace to make him feel better. He makes it a few seconds past ten, which impresses me, before he attempts to hoist himself onto the dock. His limbs are moving a bit slower and less efficiently than normal, so I reach down to grab his hand and help hoist him onto the dock.

"Holy shit! That was awesome. Alright, it's your turn" he says with a smile.

At this point there are many thoughts racing around my mind:

Do I really need to do this to start off the year? Is this actually safe? Or are we going to drop dead on the way back to the car? How bad of a friend would I really be if I whimpered out now and just went home?

One of my annoying idiosyncrasies is that I put way too much thought into just about everything. I struggle to just plunge into the depths gung-ho and without remorse. It used to be the case when just hopping into my backyard pool growing up. Even though the water was the same temperature as the air, I'd stand at the edge of the deck for five, ten, sometimes *fifteen minutes* nervously anticipating the "shock" I'd feel once my body hit the water. The same tendency arose with plenty of scenarios, including asking girls out on dates (which was a rare occurrence). Even when one girl accepted my offer, I didn't believe her and immediately asked, "You know it'd be with me . . .right?" I suffer from "paralysis by analysis". And I don't want to. This, hopefully, is some type of antidote for that.

Determined as ever, I shut my brain off as best I can. It can console me after this is done. On the count of three, without thinking and with teeth chattering from the brisk air, I plunge into the frozen depths. Immediately I feel my heart jump out of my chest as the skin on my head shrinks around my skull. My fingers tighten up and quickly lose feeling after a moment of prickly pain in every digit.

I love every second of it.

I do my best to breathe deep and enjoy the sky above me. After a few moments my heart rate slows and the world opens up. Here I am, the only person in the lake at the moment, experiencing a wildly exhilarating ride that no one else, except Troy, understands.

I feel alive.

At ten seconds (it may have been twelve, I'm proud to admit), Troy helps me back up onto the dock as my limbs begin to fail. I dry off as quickly as possible and throw on my wool socks, top, and hat, which stick to the cold drops of water on my body. We begin laughing uncontrollably. What the hell are we doing out here? Sensible adults don't strip down in a public boat launch and hop into a lake at the start of winter. Maybe more of them should, though, because I feel better than I have in as long as I can remember. Thoughts of death and paperwork and stress are nowhere to be found. My mind is completely present in a moment of euphoric exhilaration. In the moment it feels like the most sensible thing I could be doing. For a moment, I feel a pang of regret for all the years I had spent as a "more sensible adult". What a waste not having fun.

When I make my glorious return to the car, Gab already has the phone out to take a video of my triumphant return. While she doesn't fully understand *why* I need this, what matters is that she *knows* I need this. She understands that I am processing everything that we have been through, and that she needs to be there for me along this bizarre form of coping. She is happy that I am happy.

Plus, she is excited about the dessert I promised her if she tagged along.

"Okay, time to go. I'm cold" she says as she puts the phone away.

"Oh yeah? *You're* cold?"

I smile as I put the car into reverse, blind the lake with my headlights, and drive off into the night as a new man.

The year is starting well.

The Changing Seasons

On a dark, gloomy weekday afternoon, I'm rapidly tapping my foot while stuck at a red light. The smell of exhaust is creeping into the car while the radio plays generic indie rock in the background. I'm looking at all of the drivers around me, silently judging both the size of their cars and how quickly they respond to traffic signals turning green. I'm feeling a bit anxious. I haven't had a single bite of food all day, and the impacts of that are becoming apparent. My mind is weary and my stomach is growling with concerning intensity. To be honest, I feel like a toddler who needs a snack. In just ninety minutes from now, I will have a huge crew of people arriving at my door that I am expected to feed and entertain. But I have no food to prepare because these clueless people in front of me aren't keeping traffic moving the way it should be. This is becoming a disaster.

And the worst part is, this entire situation is all my fault. So much for a nice, relaxing celebration.

* * *

There's a funny thing about the changing of the seasons: They don't seem to change that much when we spend our lives indoors. Which is, in my opinion, one of the reasons why time seems to move so fast.

I've always loved the little intricacies that come with each part of the year. The first plants bursting through the frosty ground. A much-needed string of bluebird days to break the stretch of gray that

The Changing Seasons

dominates the winter. A sudden burst of color in the trees that had been lifeless and dull for so long. These moments can be euphoric and all-encompassing, if we allow them to be.

I vividly remember, when I was fifteen, walking to my deceased friend's house one sunny April day. It was finally warm enough to be in just a t-shirt and shorts. As I made my way up the hill, trees began rustling from the wind coming in from the west. Instinctively, I braced myself and tensed my muscles to deal with another wintry, icy blast. What came was unexpected. Once the wind hit my back, my muscles softened and a huge grin burst onto my face. It was *warm*. Finally, it was *warm*. Long summer nights were just around the corner, I could feel it.

The opposite can be just as beautiful. One late August morning in my mid-20s, I woke up early and ventured out for a sunrise paddle board session as a way to start the day off peacefully. As I set my board into the water and pushed off from shore, there was once again an incoming breeze. I welcomed its warm embrace around my body and basked in the beauty of the late summer landscape. But this breeze was hiding something. Gently tucked underneath its warmth and comfort was a slight but noticeable chill. Invisible, almost, if I wasn't fully aware of my body and my surroundings. Fall was coming, colors and all. I could feel it.

Lately, though, the coming of the seasons have been harder to notice. Which makes sense seeing that I've been living an increasingly indoor existence.

Think of how easy the following scenario is to follow:

Wake up in a 70-degree box (aka our house/apartment). Get into a 70-degree box with wheels. Take it to our box of work, which is usually either an annoying 68 or 72 degrees. Maddening. Return to our 70-degree box with wheels and make it back to our primary

The Changing Seasons

70-degree box. Stay there until we fall asleep. Repeat until we die.

And what do I do while in these boxes? I stare at screens. Phones, computers, TVs, it doesn't matter. Whatever is on the screen becomes my reality. The only way to mark the changing of the seasons is noticing the subtle differences in the streaming lineup, whether dramas or game shows are on network TV in the evening, or keeping an eye on which sport happens to be in season. Often, the kickoff of football season or a new episode drop from my favorite show is the strongest sign of a change in the calendar.

This manicured existence means that I, and I assume many others, often only notice the *big* changes of the seasons. It's impossible to miss the explosion of color in autumn leaves, a big snowstorm, or an oppressive heat wave in summer. All that is well and good. But if we only pay attention to the natural world when we're *forced* to pay attention, there are entire universes that we miss out on experiencing.

The realization that I no longer notice the first subtle changes of the seasons hit me after my friend's death, when I thought about how much time had passed since we last got together. That observation led to a downward spiral and made me feel like I was losing my mind. It suddenly dawned on me that I couldn't exactly remember when I noticed the first leaf change in last year's fall, or the first bud of spring emerging from a delicate branch. It had been a couple years since I recognized the cool undertones in a breeze near the end of summer. Heck, the sun is constantly shifting position around the sky and yet I have a much better handle on the position of the sun in my phone wallpaper than I do the real thing outside my window. For some reason, I've become less observant of the beauty that surrounds me each moment.

This is one of the main reasons why I feel like time has been moving so quickly over the past few years. When everyday feels kind of the same, it's easier for all the days to meld into one lifeless blur. A few things of note here, a big weather event there, a seasonal festival on occasion — these checkpoints are few and far between. What happens during all the time in-between while I'm staring at my screen in my climate controlled box?

With this understanding, I decided that one of the main ways I could slow down this year would be to put a concerted effort into noticing, and recording, the changing of the seasons. If moving quickly meant allowing the year to pass me by without much notice, then moving slowly would mean being as mindful as possible of all the subtleties the world had to offer each day. This, in turn, would slow down the relentless march of Father Time — at least I hoped. With a set list of seasonal rituals, I could make sure that too much time wouldn't pass before I looked up and realized what was happening outside my window. I wanted to *feel* each part of the year, and honor it, in some way. And if it happened to be inside my box for a time, then so be it, but I'd at least attempt to make that time meaningful and seasonal.

When humans relied on noticing the changing of the seasons for survival, and responding accordingly, there was much more fanfare regarding these subtle observations. Most of the festivals we celebrate today have their roots in seasonal celebrations that our ancestors used as a way to mark the passing of time and find something to celebrate in what was a much more brutal way of life. Christmas, for example, takes many of its more modern traditions (besides the obsessive and sometimes violent consumption) from the Roman celebration of Saturnalia, which was a celebration of the winter solstice. The symbols adopted for Easter come from many springtime rituals of the Northern European pagan traditions.

Halloween, in many respects, as well. Although, in my extensive research, I've yet to find a natural connection for blowing up fireworks and downing hot dogs on the Fourth of July. Maybe something to do with the phase of the moon?

I personally love the idea of marking the changing of the seasons with a dedicated celebration, even if it is a bit contrived on my end. With something to look forward to, I become more inspired to look inward at how I am changing and outward at how the world is shifting. If I know a mid-season celebration is approaching, I will be more apt to look for signs of change. And I will appreciate these hints of beauty found in my seemingly generic suburban world.

To make this vision a reality, I committed to a year-long observance of the neopagan Wheel of the Year (in a nod to my early adolescent interest in all things Wicca and witchcraft, spells included). The Wheel of the Year was put together in the mid-20th century as a way to combine various astronomical and fire festivals that had been celebrated throughout time by various pagan groups throughout Europe. There are eight main holidays: four for each change of season (spring equinox, summer solstice, fall equinox, winter solstice) and four fire festivals that honored the midpoint of each season. The Wheel symbolizes the cycles of life, both of the sun's changing strength throughout the course of the year and the cycle followed by all life on earth: birth, growth, decay, death. In other words, it's a mindful observance of the subtle changing of the seasons meant to connect us more to the natural world through slow, intentional, observant living.

Exactly what I am after this year.

By recognizing these celebrations, it ensures that too much of the year isn't mindlessly frittered away behind drywall and in front of a screen. Instead, it will provide good reason to look closely at the world beyond my window, notice how it shifts from season to season, and to anticipate what's to come while honoring what is already here. Essentially, an acknowledgement of these daily rhythms will bring me closer into the present moment. A place that I appear to lack the ability to visit for more than a second at a time.

With a deeper understanding of the Wheel, I began planning celebrations and rituals to mark the year. Each holiday celebration/ritual needed to be intentional and fit the overarching historical theme of the day.

First up on the calendar:

Imbolc.

* * *

Imbolc, traditionally, recognizes and celebrates the halfway point of winter. Spring is in the womb, the sun is getting brighter, and we are on the downswing of the dark days. Originally recognized as an important day by ancient pagans in Ireland, Scotland, and the Isle of Man, the day became Christianized later-on as a celebration of St. Brigid, the Patroness Saint of Ireland. The importance of the date aligned with the lambing season, as this was a time in the year when food stores were running low and the coming of precious milk could be potentially life-saving (or, at the very least, provide some comfort) as winter wore to a close. I find myself fascinated by the fact that many deep celebratory roots across cultures align with moments of plenty in a scarce and uncaring natural world.

Beyond the literal need for extra food in mid-winter, Imbolc is also important for recognizing that spring is on the way. According to local naturalists, this is the time of year when certain flowers and plants begin pushing through the cold mud in England, exposing beautiful bits of color after months of gray, drab landscapes. Which must be nice, because in my part of the world there are no flowers pushing through anywhere beyond grocery store aisles for Valentine's Day. Just frozen, dormant, gray tundra devoid of any activity.

While reading about the history and significance of Imbolc on my comfy couch in a climate-controlled living room, it becomes clear that this celebration is exactly what I need. We are currently in the depths of a long winter and have gone about three weeks without seeing the sun peak through the clouds for more than a fleeting moment. January began with Nanny's funeral, and the weight of all the troubles from the end of the year has finally been settling in as we've burrowed back into our normal routines. So many ideas for adventures and beautiful experiences fill my mind, but the weather, the schedules, and the general malaise are preventing those from becoming a reality just yet. Once again much of my time is being spent watching people do beautiful things online while I gripe about how hard it is to get going when it's cold, gray, wet, and dark outside.

And so what better way to break out of that than with a celebration?

Without much thought I whip out my phone and send a text out to our closest friends, asking if they'd be willing to come over for a mid-winter celebratory feast. The response is almost immediate: everyone announces that they are clearing their schedules and agree to come. Apparently I'm not the only one who needs something to celebrate. Excited, I think about how we could celebrate the coming of spring and bring some light into these dark days. Visions of a feast come to mind, where we can share delicious dishes and desserts around a table. It will be a beautiful day that will surely bring light into this dark time.

The Changing Seasons

Then Gab, ever the pragmatist, cuts right through my fanciful vision:

"So we have a bunch of people coming over, right?" she asks with excitement.

"Yep! Wednesday night."

"Okay," she continues, "Wednesday night. After work?"

"Yeah" I respond, with slightly less enthusiasm.

"And you have an after school meeting that day, right? So you'll be getting home later than normal?"

"Uh-huh" I murmur. Her concerns are becoming more valid by the second.

"So," she begins, "what are you making for everyone to eat that can be bought and prepared in less than an hour and a half?"

I'm embarrassed to admit that...well...I didn't even consider that!

I like to think that my excitement is a positive personality trait, and that my tendency to jump into things head first without much thought or planning is a sign of vitality. However, I can see how that might be an issue when other people are counting on me to actually pull through. Thankfully Gab married me in spite of this visible flaw.

"I'll figure it out. I always do!"

* * *

It is now Wednesday morning and I have prepared absolutely nothing. But there is anticipation in the air. The pressure of putting on a celebration for our friends turns this drab, gloomy, mundane day into a spark of excitement in the middle of an otherwise forgettable week. I have just a few hours to pull everything together and make sure my friends can actually have dinner tonight.

Because putting on a full party on a moment's notice apparently is not enough of a challenge, I decide to make the day even more strenuous by fasting for 24 hours leading up to our feast. This not only serves to keep me focused on becoming a tougher person, but it also gets me thinking about food. A lot. All day I see tasty treats, smell delicious wafts of air and crave to put *some* taste in my mouth. The toughest point of the day, by far, is lunch. Walking by the lunchroom and seeing all my smiling colleagues stuffing their faces with hot, tasty meals makes me wish I could be in a food commercial and do the same, but with multiple takes to make sure I get my fill.

I escape past the lunch room and head into my classroom, where there is no food and no temptation. As my class begins filing in all I can think about is the hunger pangs encompassing my being and the delicious meal that is going to solve all of my problems. There is a key advantage to this fast, though: my cravings make it clear what I want to make for everyone. After some (tantalizing and agonizing) thought during one of my classes (when I am supposed to be teaching), I commit to lemon-garlic pasta, seared salmon, and roasted potatoes. Which, in the midst of my hunger, sounds like an unheard of ecstasy as I begin my fourth hour chewing the same stick of gum. Just thinking about it makes my eyes widen and my mouth salivate in anticipation. At least until I realize that a student has been standing in front of me, for how long I don't know, in need of help. Sorry kid — when salmon is on the mind there is nothing that breaks that train of thought.

After work brings the most challenging moment of the whole experiment: grocery shopping. The thought of being surrounded by food is overwhelming, and I'm sure that any free sample within reach will break my fast. In an effort to keep everything seasonal, even though it is the middle of winter, I plan to shop as locally as possible. Produce from the mid-week farmer's market. Fish from the

The Changing Seasons

local market that gets their supply regionally. Pasta from Milwaukee, Wisconsin sold at my nearest Wal-Mart. You know, keeping it close to home.

Our town, though, has other plans. For some reason the roads are marred by gridlock in every direction. What should be a five-minute drive from school to the grocery stores is turning into a much longer excursion; something I absolutely do not have time for. As I tap the steering wheel while feelings of anxiety start bursting from my chest up to my throat, I start to become the worst version of myself. I label everyone around me as a selfish jerk for getting in *my* way when *I* have plans to attend to — which is exactly what a selfish jerk would say. Eventually I finally get through the first of six traffic lights in a half-mile span, but my car can only travel a few feet before I have to slam on my brakes to avoid hitting the gray SUV in front of me, which stops short for no apparent reason (at least that's what I tell myself to justify my annoyance). When looking out the window, I immediately recognize where my car is: I am now idling on the exact opposite side of the road from where my car got totaled the night before our wedding.

This realization brings me back to reality. Today is supposed to be a celebration. It's supposed to mark the coming of longer days while expressing gratitude for our friendships; not throwing a temper tantrum because I missed a few lights and other people also have places to be. The absurdity and immaturity of my mood are now too obvious to ignore. Letting go of the wheel, I close my eyes for a moment and take a few slow, deep breaths. Apologizing to no-one in particular, I vow to relax and enjoy the moment, annoying as it may seem. It's just traffic, and a few months ago an accident could have prevented me from even being alive to experience sitting at this intersection. This, right here, is a miracle. *Appreciate it*, I tell myself.

The Changing Seasons

As if on cue, once my mind relaxes and my mood softens, the traffic begins to clear up. Within just a few minutes I'm walking around the local farmers' market surrounded by kind people providing nourishment for their community. The blood-pressure spike I just put my body through seems ridiculous now that I'm exactly where I planned to be, and only a few minutes later than expected.

Upon returning from the grocery shopping I feel a joy that doesn't normally hit me in the middle of a workweek. I am stoked to see my friends and to open our home. While preparing the meals, I take time to both be in the moment, reflect on the winter so far, and consider what lies ahead. At this point in the year I feel like I've disappeared to an extent. Holed up in my little nest, working on my projects, forgetting to call friends and family with my usual frequency. But this hideout has been necessary. I have been living more intentionally than I have in as long as I can remember. Most importantly, I have been enjoying a simple existence in our home in the presence of my beautiful wife. Slow and strenuous living are shining their first faint rays of light into my life.

And things, presumably, will only get better moving forward. The birds are coming back, and soon I will be woken up by the songs I desperately miss in the depths of the winter season. Days are getting noticeably longer, and the snow isn't sticking for as long. Soon it will be warm and bright enough to embark on the adventures I have planned for spring and summer, in hopes of truly living life to the fullest. Things are finally settling into an effortless balance as the Earth moves toward the same. Sure, there will still be traffic and bad drivers (myself among them). There will be gloomy days and annoyances at work. And feelings of frustration will certainly arise. The key is that I have given myself time to assess what a balanced life can look like and am working on creating it in this darkness. Like the world outside my window, this beautiful reality is slowly coming into the light, as well as the bits of peace that come with it. This meal is the first outward sign of that growth.

*   *   *

The food comes out of the oven just as the doorbell rings — perfect timing. A delicious scent wafts through our home that feels like the equivalent of a warm hug. Unlike my drive to the grocery store, now a deep sense of peace overtakes what could have been a hectic situation. The smell of fresh food permeates the entire house, the pasta tastes exactly as I'd hoped, and we are all sharing the dishes that everyone brought on their own. While Gabby tells stories to our friends in the living room, I slip away to the kitchen for a few moments to plate the food and appreciate where we are. With everything that has happened over the past few months, all the death and near-death experiences, it feels so incredibly lucky to be in this space, right here, right now.

The night wears on under candlelight with laughter echoing throughout our home. We talk about life, plans for the summer, next steps and phases, and share childhood stories. I know I could have made it easier by ordering takeout for all of us to share, which would have been just fine. But sitting around a table together with a meal I put my heart into for the people that I love just hits differently — a benefit of the slow and strenuous life. It is a reminder of what truly matters, and that whatever stressors come from work or random circumstances are fleeting. Throughout everything we went through our friends were by our side, even in the worst times. Thankfully, tonight is certainly part of the best of times. Internally, I recognize this little feast as a quiet way to thank them for the help, support, and love they provided us through our most difficult days.

The Changing Seasons

In the spirit of the celebration, I feel renewed in every sense of the word. Spring is coming with more light, color, flavors, and scents to enjoy. That will all be nice. But it is also nice to remember the joys we can create for ourselves even in the midst of the darkness.

* * *

The day after our ritualistic feast I take a stroll into our backyard and find solace under the branches of an eastern spruce, the only tree that holds its color amidst the dull landscape. Around the house I notice something I haven't heard in months: birdsong. Suddenly it seems like there are dozens of birds all chirping away above me. I imagine what they are saying. Perhaps they are wondering who I am, or maybe they are commenting on the increasing light throughout the day. Most likely, they are probably shouting out some variation of, "Hey y'all, who wants to mate with this stud in a few weeks? I'm here and ready to party!"

As I emerge from under the warm embrace of the spruce something stops me in my tracks. Outside the spruce, unnoticed until now, are roughly a hundred little green plants shooting out from the frozen leaves covering the ground. The plants are as green as springtime and I cannot believe what I am seeing. Upon further investigation with my Seek app (which magically identifies plants with just a phone camera and some radically complex coding), it turns out these plants *are* in fact evergreens imported from Japan. Presumably these little guys have been in my backyard the entire winter, doing their thing, and yet this is the first time I am actually *seeing* them. All this time I spent griping about the gray days, and yet there has been a burst of beautiful, resilient color for me to take solace in the whole time, just beneath my gaze. I take a few more minutes to stare at the little miracles before returning to the cozy

The Changing Seasons

warmth of my home.

The Wheel of the Year is spinning, ever so slowly. And I am thrilled to finally be taking the time to notice.

The Great Unplugging

I reached the secret entrance.

A bit sweaty, and with a rag-tag backpack held together with bungee cords attached to me, I checked to see if the coast was clear. If caught, I could be punished for trespassing. Worse, my secret spot would be exposed to the rest of the world and the solitude I so often sought would be shattered.

I looked up and down the street, then stealthily peeked into the windows in the surrounding homes.

No one was around to see. Perfect.

I stepped off the road and made my way down an unmarked path worn by anonymous travelers. Within a few yards I was hidden from the world by an elevated pond. No footprints left behind. Not a trace to be found. A perfect escape from society.

Wandering up the field, I passed all the classic landmarks: the connector path to my friend's house. The pavilion. The pooping spot. The creek.

Eventually I reached my destination. Slowly, I peeled off the backpack to ensure the bungee cords would stay in place. The pack was heavy, overstuffed with an unnecessary amount of food and creature comforts. Once on the ground I began the operation with surgical precision.

Out came the tent, the sleeping bag, then the yoga mat. This would be my home for the night.

When the tent was set up to satisfaction I wandered to an ancient circle of cinder blocks filled with endless stories and

The Great Unplugging

memories. I grabbed a bundle of sticks and began breaking them into small pieces, after which they were placed in the middle of the ash in a square formation. Then came the strike. A match from my back pocket was held to some tinder, the heat of which nipped my fingers. I placed the bundle into the sticks and watched the fire grow. Carefully, I added to my creation to ensure its survival. Once it was roaring at a sustainable pace I wandered over to the hillside to find the flattest log I could. After a few minutes my victim was selected and hoisted upon my shoulder. I plopped it next to the fire pit and dusted off the top.

 I sat on the log and stared at the fire in silence.

 I did not have a phone with me. Even if I did, it would have been a flip phone with no internet connection. My friends would not arrive for another four hours. All I had was the fire in front of me, the creek behind me, and the wilderness on the edges of my own little village. And hours with nothing to do but simply sit and think.

 I wandered around that tiny plot of land all afternoon, alone, solely in the company of my imagination and ideas. Why I came this early with no stimulation, I still don't know. What I found, though, was that time moved more slowly than it ever had before in my entire life. Those hours felt like days. At some points it was freeing and felt like I was on the edge of spiritual enlightenment. Then, at other moments, the boredom was excruciating and borderline unbearable. But there I sat, diligently, absorbing myself in the present moment.

 The sun moved across the sky. My mind softened. The anxiety I felt as an insecure teenage boy began to melt away and was replaced with a deep sense of calm. Without the constant stimulation I had become accustomed to, I felt like I was moving *with* the world instead of outside it. Time lost its meaning. All that existed was the everlasting present. Past and future were mere concepts that didn't jive with the wave I was riding in the moment. The peace was intense once I accepted it. I felt like maybe I could have a breakthrough, that I could truly calm down and for once . . .

Footsteps. I could hear them in the distance. I turned around nervously, not expecting another person to break me out of my trance. Heart racing, I fixed my eyes on the figure in the distance. A sigh of relief: my friend had arrived at the site. I almost didn't want to break the silence I had fostered over the previous hours. What started as unbearable became something that I didn't want to end. It had become a part of me in just a single afternoon. When my throat vibrated with a soft "Hey", it came out with serenity.

So that's what it feels like to be in a timeless world, I thought.

The evening went on as planned. More friends arrived. Stories were swapped. We laughed all night. We did stupid shit. And that sense of quiet calm remained within me throughout the night. And for many days afterward.

* * *

I am well aware that our phones get us to where we need to be, help us connect with distant family members, make shopping seamless, and provide access to information that makes our lives easier. They're an absolutely incredible tool that makes many aspects of modern life easier and better. I get it. No argument there.

What I *will* argue is that the costs of how we currently use them greatly outweigh the benefits. In other words: I think the way we are using our phones, and how they are *designed* to be used, is ruining our lives.

It's not necessarily the phones themselves; rather, it's how they're being used as a vehicle to manipulate, brainwash, distract, radicalize, stress-out, and destroy the self-esteem of entire generations. By now, about a decade-and-a-half into this civilization-sized experiment, many of us can no longer sit still for a few minutes, perhaps even seconds, without impulsively checking our email or social media accounts. We struggle to focus and our memory is getting worse by the year. We have a shorter attention span than a goldfish (the previous record-holder for world's most pathetic) and are increasingly stressed-out and anxious despite having more free time than ever and living in the safest time in human history. I know I fall squarely into that description.

Kids are impacted the most, which is doubly sad because their compulsive use is, for the most part, not even their fault. Rates of teen suicides, as well as overall instances of depression and anxiety, began increasing dramatically right at the time that social media apps became ubiquitous and the iPhone introduced a front-facing camera: the year 2012.

As a teacher, I see the effects on education in a pronounced and concerning way. My current students struggle more with memory, focus, self-regulation, self-esteem, and behavior than any previous generation. Most of them can barely go a few seconds without instinctively checking their phones, and often act out when they're denied the opportunity. They are never satisfied or content with themselves; they *must* check and compare their status against others at every second, which is exactly how the social media companies planned it (in what I imagine to be an evil lair underground while they swim in their billions of dollars at the expense of children's health and safety). The global results have included a mental health crisis amongst youth that is getting worse by the year, plummeting test scores, lower reading levels, a degradation of writing abilities, and a diluting of logical thinking. These tech-bros in Silicon Valley are trying to rob an entire generation of their ability to focus, think, and live a content life all for their own obscene profit. It's a crime.

The Great Unplugging

We should be outraged.

The dangers of how our phones are being designed have, thankfully, become more well-known in recent years. The phone itself is a tool. An amazing one. When used properly it greatly enhances our experience of life. So the technology itself isn't the issue. It's the software designed by companies to capture as much of our attention as possible so we scroll longer, see more ads, and generate more profit. *That's* where the danger lies. Our attention (and our data, for that matter) is gold. The more attention they can steal, the more ads they can sell, which means they make more money while we waste our lives mindlessly scrolling through rubbish. We know we shouldn't, but we're unable to pull away regardless. We are all victims here.

Tech-ethicist Tristan Harris, who once worked for Google and resigned over concerns regarding their unethical practices, pulled back the curtain on the inner workings of the industry. According to Harris, the primary goal of social media companies is to "hack" our psychology in order to gain as much of our attention as possible. Using gambling psychology as a guide, they use tricks like bright colors, red notifications, fanciful noises, timed notifications, likes, views, and subscribers as ways to keep us coming back for more against our better judgment. All of these prey on our brain's vulnerabilities to make the apps irresistible.

The "like" button, a seemingly innocuous feature developed at Facebook, is arguably the most problematic. According to journalist Max Fischer, once the "like" button was implemented, Facebook saw dramatic increases in site activity and retention time due to its users obsessively seeking social validation and acceptance. If our post isn't "liked", we feel a physical pain akin to being socially rejected. Our brain cannot tell the difference between in-person

The Great Unplugging

rejection and virtual. So when this happens we post more, or at least more acceptable, content, in hopes that the *next* post will validate us with the in-group. This tool is a brilliant exploitation of our innate need for social validation and inclusion. It may be the single most impactful innovation that social media companies ever created. Once Facebook started seeing the results, other apps began copying the idea with similar results in tow.

Why can the "like" button, something so simple and stupid, can hook us so easily? It taps into the core of what journalist Michael Easter refers to as "scarcity brain". The strategy works like this:

As humans, we evolved in tribes and required community in order to survive. This meant we needed to be "liked", or at least be seen as useful, to the group. Otherwise they could kick us out for being dead weight, dramatically decreasing our survival chances. As a result, we spend much of our time trying to be useful and getting others to like us. We follow trends, we say nice things when we'd rather not, and we share opinions of dominant group members, all in the name of increasing our value for the community. Which, our brain thinks, makes us safe because we are protected by friendly numbers. So, when we post on social media, the "like" button is a very public way of seeing if the community values what we are doing. Get a bunch of likes, and suddenly we get a rush of feel-good chemicals because our brain interprets it as increased odds of survival.

But what if no one likes our post?

Well, then we feel the psychological pain that comes with being ostracized. This often leads to a doubling-down of efforts to acquire more likes and boost our social standing. Typically, this may look like following a trend that's guaranteed to garner positive attention, even if it's not creative, unique, or all that impressive. At its darkest, this can lead people to turn their outrage toward another person/group to boost their own reputation at another's expense. They flip the script by raging against an "in-group", thus creating their own alternative "in-group", whose sole purpose is to point their rage and distaste toward the other. Outrage captures our attention more than anything else, which is why it's so encouraged on these platforms. This partially explains the recent increase in political polarization, and it is the primary cause of social media apps nudging us down increasingly extreme political rabbit holes. Outrage gets our attention. Our attention keeps us on the app. Time on the app leads to ad sales. And ad sales, of course, lead to necessary upgrades for the underground evil lair these companies operate out of. This is the dangerous cycle we are falling prey to. The result of these tactics is the toxic, scarcity-triggered outrage loop of mediocre content that now defines our online existence.

As you can probably tell by now, I *really* dislike the tricks Internet companies use to get us to spend more of our precious time on their platforms. I'll go as far to say I hate it and I want it all gone immediately.

And yet I can't pull myself away from these apps. *That* is what scares me so much.

I *know* all these horrible things and yet I still can't resist the pull. Even as I write this sentence I am feeling an immense urge to check if anyone liked my last Instagram post (almost certainly not) or if there's a new video on my YouTube feed that will completely improve my life (realistically it's probably something about tiny homes). These programs have cut so deep into my brain that they feel inescapable. And the results for my own life are concerning.

Life is moving faster. In my mind, the past six or seven years meld together into one amorphous blur. This is the same amount of time I have owned a smartphone. The common wisdom is that time tends to speed up as we get older. However, I suspect that the amount of time we spend online plays a large role in this sudden acceleration. The amount of times I've gone down a rabbit hole on my phone or computer and looked up to see the hours that passed is scary. My ability to focus is compromised (re: urge to watch new tiny house videos), my memory is going a bit to shit, and I generally feel like I do less in the course of a day. Plus, each day feels less memorable. Which means each week, each month, each year does, too. Hence the blur of time speeding by in my screen-doped existence.

When I shut my computer I tend to immediately reach for my phone because I don't know what to do with myself otherwise. I go from screen to screen to screen. It may just be me, but judging by how quiet restaurants are now, with most tables consisting of people sitting next to one another silently while staring into the glow of their addiction, I doubt it.

My hunch is that my tech-habit is the key factor in time moving too quickly. And in this fast-paced world of convenience, I have been looking for a slow-paced life of intentional activities. Logically, in order to slow my life down, kicking my tech habit to the curb is a necessary requirement.

But how? When the world now *necessitates* access to, and attention on, this technology, how can I navigate modern life without it?

If there's one thing I have learned at this point in my year-long experiment, it's this:

The only way to find out anything is to just do it and figure it out as you go.

* * *

For this challenge I decide to use my week off from work as a strategic tech sabbath. Without *needing* to be on the computer to check emails, join meetings, and get my work done, I can truly disconnect while at home. My hope is that an intentional "unplugging" will break the addictive loop in my brain and dilute the pressure to always be logged on. The plan is simple, but challenging:

First, I will spend 72 long, grueling hours without engaging in *any* screen-based technology whatsoever. No computer, no phone, no TV. Complete disconnect from the world I have been so wired to. A full, cold-turkey detox that is sure to leave me miserable and twitching. Even if Gab wants to show me a meme, I must resist and have her describe it to me verbally. Perhaps, if I am lucky, that will make it even more entertaining.

While the full cut-off is necessary and challenging, I understand that I can't stay away from screens forever. Like any extreme diet, it may have short-term benefits in a controlled environment. Once we return to the *real* world, though, those extreme plans fall away and often result in strong relapses. While the idea of never looking at a screen again feels oddly freeing, it is not realistic. And I need to account for that.

Therefore, the 72 hour screen fast will serve as an initial detox; a shock to the system. Once it ends, I plan on spending the rest of the week only using my devices as the tool they are meant to be and *only* when absolutely necessary. For example, I know that mid-week I need to transfer some money to pay for the mortgage (I am not about to lose the house over a simple experiment. I'm dedicated, but not stupid – and I enjoy staying married). I also need to call my parents at some point, confirm plans with friends, and use the GPS app for our travels. All that, to me, is perfectly fine. If my phone and computer help me take care of business, connect with loved ones, and get to new places, then that's all well and good. I see no need to eliminate those benefits from my life.

Instead, this rule is intended to keep me from the addictive features of my screens. This means that I can't log-on to check Instagram, scroll Reddit, obsessively update my inbox, or look for the next golden nugget on YouTube; the stuff that takes *away* from my experience of life instead of adding to it. And, of course, the stuff that is the most addictive and hardest to do without. Opening my laptop to look up directions to a new restaurant, or instructions for a home-improvement project, and resisting the alluring pull of the attention hackers feels like the biggest challenge – like entering an ice cream parlor while on a strict diet. My hope is these ten days can be just like old times, when I first started surfing the Internet without getting sucked in.

Restraint is the key to the whole plan. This experiment is meant to foster a healthier relationship with this technology, not to eliminate it. If I can't get rid of my screens entirely out of modern necessity, I need to learn to live *with* it in a meaningful way that generates growth instead of addiction. Rebellion in this day in age appears to be resisting the pull that comes with addictive social media, the fear of missing out, and the obsession with being over-informed. Resistance comes in the form of staring out the window, content with just being, wholly unproductive, and engaging in the real world. It sounds so simple, since it's what we all did not that long ago. Boy, how aggressive, encompassing, and destabilizing this long, tech-fueled, society-wide drug trip has been. We can't even remember who we were a mere fifteen years ago.

On the night before my experiment begins, I stare mindlessly at my YouTube homepage and think about what I might miss. Hoping for support, I look up from my screen to the other end of our comfy gray couch. Gab's screen is illuminating her face. Hopeful, I ask if she'd like to join me on the challenge. She laughs in my face and goes back to watching TikToks. I am on my own here.

Time to sober up.

* * *

No new emails. No new notifications. No breaking news I need to be aware of. No unread or unresponded to texts. I am all caught up.

I shut my computer with an emphatic and satisfying sound, then slide it under the table. With a bit of dread, I put my phone on Airplane Mode and lock it away in a dresser drawer.

The fast begins.

Almost immediately the reality of how hooked I am on these things becomes apparent. Knowing that I *can't* engage with my devices, I feel very anxious without them. A terrifying pull to get sucked back into the warm, comfortable vortex of an infinite scroll fills my chest; where time doesn't matter and my mind can be sedated and numbed. YouTube. Instagram. Reddit. Email. What could possibly be on there? What if I received a life-changing message about my small business? What if an outdoor company found my photography and wants to collaborate, but only gives me a 24-hour window to respond? What am I to do with myself without seeing hundreds of short videos that make no memories?

Who am I without this?

* * *

Mimetic desire occurs when we want something because other people want it, too. We all fall prey to this phenomenon. The neighbor comes home with a new car, and suddenly our perfectly fine and practical vehicle seems like an old junker that needs to be replaced. A TV at a Super Bowl party is way bigger than ours, so naturally we must go get our own big-ass TV, otherwise there's no point in watching anything. The phrase "Keeping up with the Jones's'" is real and extremely powerful.

Nowhere is the pull of mimetic desire more intoxicating than on social media. Open your feed and you will see thousands of different ways you could possibly live your life. Aesthetics, products, trips, jobs, experiences, philosophies – we get a window into what everyone else *wants* and what some of them, albeit very few, actually *have*. They tell you how great it is to run an online business and how it gives them the life they want. Suddenly, you start to consider if that's also the life that *you* want. You see a couple sipping drinks by a poolside in a country you've never heard of, and before you know it *you're* the one yearning to be there and checking flights. And boy, does that couple seem to be so happy all the time. How come they get to travel full-time and "live fully" while your daily existence consists mostly of washing, drying, and putting away the same dishes day after day? If only we had *that*, then things would be different . . .

By spending hours a day on digital media (the current running average for Americans is roughly 13 hours per day in front of a screen) we are fully immersed in a world of mimetic desire on a regular basis. We see what others want, what they have, and what they strive for. Subconsciously, we begin to want and strive for the same things.

But do we *really* want that life? Pick any one of the thousands of lifestyles we encounter online and it's easy to slide into that spiral of mimetic desire. And it's *very* difficult to recognize what is happening: that we *don't actually want* the thing we see. We only *think* we want it because others do. Such is the curse of a social species. And it's a curse that social media companies have exploited brilliantly.

With enough time and lack of discipline, too much of our personality can become what we see online. I've noticed this while listening to the vloggers my wife watches on YouTube. It seems like every third sentence is something to the effect of, "I got this because I saw it on TikTok." Oh, okay. Do you actually want it though? How does it enhance your life? Does it align with your values? Or is your entire personality just what you see on TikTok?

How often do you catch yourself saying, "People online said (insert random opinion here)"? I find myself saying this all the time in conversations, citing with certainty discussion threads I saw on Reddit. But there are problems with that: Who are these people? What are their names? Where do they live? What's their background? Why should I give a flying you-know-what about what they have to say? And are they even people? Or are they just sophisticated bots? It's almost gotten to the point where "someone online" is my most quoted friend, more so than the actual friends that I love and value in my life.

We're all susceptible to this. Which is why I feel so uneasy just hours into this experiment. Without people *telling* me what to want, what to do, what to work toward, what do I actually *want* to want? To do? To strive for? It has been so long since I had considered that for myself instead of letting others tell me hour-after-hour, day-after-day.

It's easy to be confronted with this deep, uncertain reality of being human and hide back in the glow of the screen to avoid actually answering those questions. Confronting them, working through them, and forging imperfect but meaningful answers is the hard part. But it's the key to a meaningful life of value.

The Great Unplugging

* * *

Twenty-four hours in I still feel twitchy and unsettled. Gab is prepping lunch in the kitchen while I lay on the couch with nothing in particular to do. This is normally a luxury. But without being able to waste the luxury by scrolling I feel more anxious than relaxed. In an attempt to calm down I resolve to take my first nap in as long as I can remember. After a few deep breaths, my eyes close and my mind slips out of consciousness.

Right as I am about to drift off to sleep, I snap up like father in the old *Don't Wake Daddy* board game. Gasping for air, an intrusive thought pops into my head:

"There's so much I could be *doing* right now!"

There it is, laid out right in front of me: the core of my escapist tendencies that built the foundation of my unsettled, anxious state. I am quite literally on vacation, taking a nap as the sun peeks through the window while my wife makes a delicious meal. This moment should be the epitome of relaxation. Yet I am stressed about unread emails, writing this book, editing photos, studying self-improvement topics, and watching videos on how others changed their lives with this one simple system that we all need to know about in order to be "unstoppable". Why is all that more important than simply being in this lovely moment?

We are human *beings*, not human *doings*, for a reason. As Alan Watts put it: the purpose of life is to simply be alive. Nothing more. Nothing less. We can accomplish this feat without accomplishing another single thing. And yet "just being" is incredibly difficult to, well, *do*. It feels unsettling, especially in today's day and age, to sit and just be. Rebellious, perhaps. Maybe even a bit naughty.

In *Four Thousand Weeks*, Oliver Burkeman argues that one of the primary sources of this guilt and unease surrounding being

The Great Unplugging

unproductive are the forces of intensive capitalism. Growing up in a capitalist society, we are told from birth (both explicitly and implicitly) that our value in life comes from what we *produce*. Without producing for society we cannot make money, we cannot build a stable life, we cannot survive. Therefore the more we produce, the better off we are. And if we ever stop to rest then we risk losing it all. People who choose not to produce are "drop-outs", "tramps", "lazy", "freeloaders", or "un-American". Couple that with the pressure to survive in a neoliberal capitalist society that contains a minimal social safety net with a culturally ingrained Puritan work-ethic, and it makes sense why there is such anxiety surrounding the idea of doing nothing.

And what numbs that anxiety, if only for a moment? Mindlessly scrolling through content. It keeps us from confronting the uncomfortable reality that we are who we are in this moment, and that we can be satisfied if we're willing to acknowledge that.

There is absolutely nothing I need to do right now in this sweaty, breathless moment on the couch. And if I succumb to the urge of scrolling then I won't actually be *doing* anything of worth anyway. It would be a complete waste of time, energy, and effort. *It would be a waste of this lovely moment in my life*, I think. Immediately after I process this idea, my eyes widen.

How much of my busy-ness, stress, and packed calendar is really just me indulging in the falsehood that "I have many important things I should be doing"? Am I actually that important? Or am I afraid to admit that the world can continue spinning just fine if I throw it all to the wind and stop producing anything? If I spend all day lying on a hill instead of responding to emails, posting on social media, and being a good, productive neoliberal capitalist, would my whole world collapse into anarchy because I did nothing for an

The Great Unplugging

afternoon? Of course not.

Life would go on just fine. And, I know deep down, I'd be better off for it.

Professor Cal Newport, one of the leading thinkers in the world of digital minimalism and reducing time on technology, believes that one of the biggest benefits of getting off social media is recalibrating our sense of importance in the world. When we're always on, always informed, always posting, it makes us feel that what we do and say online is quite important; that many people care deeply about our thoughts, opinions, and activities. It sounds ridiculous to say out loud, but before we post anything, subconsciously we're just *sure* that everyone in our circle has been *waiting* to see our vacation photos, to hear our thoughts on the latest political blunder, and to see what we're having for dinner. *They'll love it*, we think, *and they won't be settled until I show them.*

That is, of course, not the case. The reality is we could all stop engaging with anything online for a month and no one would notice or think twice about it. Quick: think of 5 recent posts from your friends that you've seen in the past few days. Can you even think of 5? If you are able to, congrats. Now, would your life be different if you never saw those posts? Would your day be shattered? Incomplete? For perspective, how different would your day be if you *call* your friend, right now, and ask them about their life instead of passively acknowledging it online? How would that alter the trajectory of your time, mood, and satisfaction with life?

These are the difficult questions I ask myself while remaining stiff and upright on the couch, rapidly coming to terms with my own insignificance. Yet instead of feeling crushed or depressed by this realization, I feel free. Underneath the churning desire to pull-out my computer and see if anyone misses me, I develop a subtle sense of liberation at the ability to *not* do just that. To be hidden. Unseen. To live quietly and beautifully. As Sean Penn's magnificent character said in *The Secret Life of Walter Mitty*:

"Beautiful things don't ask for attention."

* * *

A day later what initially felt like withdrawal begins trending toward abundance. Suddenly I have heaps of time to do whatever I want with. There is no feeling of being rushed or like I have to cram a bunch of activities into a small space. While it may seem inconsequential in the moment, logging on and immediately checking a few different emails, a couple social media sites, and scrolling through the news takes a toll on the brain. This practice prevents us from focusing deeply and instead results in the mind scattering in many different directions very quickly. Rather than being a relaxing way to wake up or pass some time, psychologically it's an exhausting habit. Plus, it is easy to spend far more time than anticipated just "checking in". I realize this when my mornings start to appear like a vast refuge of possibility instead of a cramped, rushed period that is desperate for more time.

The innate urge to hop on my devices still exists (I often find my hands curled in tension at the thought of grabbing my phone), however my ability to resist is slowly improving. Pathetic as it sounds, in order to retrain my brain to become human again I sit down at the coffee table, pull out my tea-stained spiral notebook, and write out a list of activities to do instead of scrolling to serve as an emergency plan when I am left with nothing to in mind. One activity that gets put on the list is stretching, and it unexpectedly becomes my go-to practice. On day two I roll out my purple yoga mat next to the couch, and end up using it so frequently that it stays there throughout the whole experiment. Multiple times per day I find myself on the mat, moving mindfully, unraveling the stress and anxiety that has been building up in my muscles for the past few years. The new habit puts me supremely in tune with my body and mind. It has been awhile since I checked in with myself like this. Spending twenty or so minutes a day feeling my muscles, being aware of my breath, and moving my body mindfully goes a long way toward feeling more centered and balanced. After a few sessions I feel loose, pliable, and relaxed, both in body and mind.

On the final day of the full tech fast I experience a profound moment. Once again in the throngs of dopamine-deprived boredom, I head down to my office after twenty minutes of aimlessly pacing upstairs. My office is simple: it includes a stool, a small table from Aldi serving as an inadequate desk, and my drum set (which I've been playing more than normal the past three days). In the corner, though, lies a dusty and forgotten piece of equipment that I haven't spent much time with in years. For some reason it catches my eye. I decided to keep it when we moved, but it wasn't used much in our last apartment and it hasn't been touched since we moved into our house. I grab the edge, which stirs up a pile of dust into my nostrils, and hoist it awkwardly onto my little table. For the first time in what feels like forever I am sitting in front of a keyboard.

In college there was a beautiful electric piano in the common room of our dorm. I never played the piano before (I'm a drummer by trade), but I found myself entranced by the keys in that room. The piano sat by a large window overlooking beautiful Lake Ontario in an unusually serene setup for a dormitory. In my free time I often found myself sitting at that piano, messing around with the sounds while nobody else was around to hear. Within a year I was spending hours per week in that spot learning songs I loved and, eventually, writing my own music. At one point I even learned how to play a song with one hand on the piano while my other limbs played on my electric drum kit to the right. I never recorded my playing or had plans to become a virtuoso. The pleasure of making beautiful sounds, simple as they were, was enough. It became an unexpected and joyful hobby that brought much meaning to my life.

Then I got a smartphone. Instead of coming back from class with nothing to do, I found myself getting sucked into the void in my dorm room. I played the piano less and less. Eventually I moved out of the dorm and continued playing on a crappy beginner's keyboard from the late 90s that I scavenged from my parents' house. It wasn't as inspiring, but it did the trick. Still, though, I was playing much less than the days when a flip phone didn't provide enough stimulation to provide amusement every second of every day.

Once I finished college and moved back home the little keyboard sat in a corner collecting dust. It came with me wherever I lived, in hopes that the spark to start playing would reignite. That spark, though, was often dampened by mindless screen time. I used to come back from class and sit by that window excited to express my emotions through song. Now, whether consciously or not, I was seeking to numb those emotions through content.

This keyboard, as I quite literally wipe the dust off, represents more than a hobby. It is a symbol of my emotional awareness and the type of person I once was. It came into my life at a time when I was someone who was willing to be bored, to try new things, to really feel and express my emotions in a meaningful way. A period when an empty swath of time was filled with wonder and pride. I miss it.

There is, of course, no guarantee that the keyboard will actually work once plugged in. But with all this free time I now have, and the realization of what this means to me, I'd be terribly disappointed if it's unusable. Nervous, I connect the wires and press as hard as possible on the power button. At first, nothing. My heart sinks. Then, suddenly, a light flickers on, as if gasping for air. After a few seconds it remains on and steady. It works! What do I play? So much time has passed. How do I reintroduce myself?

After messing around with the keys for a few minutes, I begin to wonder if I could still pull off the most difficult song I learned back in college. It is one of my favorite tunes. To learn it, though, I had to sit in my bedroom with a YouTube video of someone playing the song with the camera placed above their hands. After each note I would pause the video and write down which key they hit (I couldn't, and still can't, read sheet music). Once I cracked the code I attempted to get my fingers to move in the same pattern with embarrassing results, at least at first. After a few hours it stuck enough to sound decent. It took about a month of practicing a few days per week until the movement became fluent and it sounded just like the recording. Hours upon hours of sitting on a floor staring at a keyboard instead of a screen led to my greatest accomplishment on the instrument and something I'm still proud of. That type of focus and grit has been fleeting ever since.

Shaking off the cobwebs, I start by attempting the chords. Woefully out of the tune, it takes a few minutes of clunking around to find the right notes. Once the chords settle in, I proceed to hit a half-dozen out of tune keys in search of the main melody. It feels like I am digging deep within my psyche, pulling discarded memories out of forgotten boxes. With perseverance comes improvement. One by one, note by note, the melody starts to emerge from the dust. Once I remember most of the basic parts to the melody I put my hands in the proper position, close my eyes, and begin to play.

The Great Unplugging

Everything comes rushing back as if I've left my body. The arpeggio, the melody, the movement. Immersed in the moment my hands glide along the keys with little effort. The notes ring out with accuracy and beauty. It's back. Just like riding a bike.

Eyes closed, alone in my little office, I imagine myself back by that window in college when I thought anything was possible. For the first time in my adult years, I feel connected to that version of myself. He is still here, within me, just waiting to come back out. A huge smile breaks out on my face as I continue to play to him and no-one else. Boundless joy, in the flow, fully present. *This* is what I missed. That feeling of being truly, fully alive in an otherwise mundane moment.

And all of it in the time it normally took me to "check" my Instagram.

* * *

It's time. 72 hours. Watching the clock while sitting on my couch, my foot taps on the hardwood floor. Gabby gives me a side-eye from the other side of the couch, curious about how this is going to go. It is time to reenter the world of technology.

At this point I feel calmer and more at peace than I have in awhile. While the experiment was bumpy and uncomfortable at first, it did not take long for my brain to adjust to, and eventually enjoy, the lack of stimulation. Life feels slower. Time moves by smoothly. I am more in tune with myself physically, mentally, and emotionally. Realizing this, I tell Gab that this is the best I have felt in a long time and that, honestly, I don't want to get back onto my devices. Inside there is a strong desire to go full analog. I have no real aching to get back on social media and see what I missed.

To confirm this, though, I need to log on and face the beast. I can't remain a hermit forever; I need to develop a *healthy* relationship with this ubiquitous blessing and curse. Extremes rarely work long term.

With a sigh I pull my computer out from the drawer, plop it on my lap, take a deep breath, and open it up. The plan is simple:

First, I will check my email (all four accounts . . .which I now realize is an absurd, unnecessary number). Then Instagram. Then I'll see if anyone left comments on my YouTube channel while simultaneously looking at what the algorithm serves up for me as a way to spend my time. It sounds like a lot when it's all laid out, but before now this was a normal morning.

I move into the other room and sit down to prepare for the onslaught of information. As soon as my fingers peel the laptop open, a vortex springs out of the screen and sucks me into it. Immediately I am hit with a rush of activity in my brain. Dozens of emails greet me in my inbox, begging to be opened with their bright colors and sensual fonts. A couple of these are newsletters I enjoy reading once a week. Others are receipts for purchases over the past few days. A certain company is doing everything in its power to keep charging my credit card with a subscription regardless of how many times I attempt to cancel. A rush of anxiety flows over me as I comb through the messages. I can't decide whether to deal with the company, read the newsletters, or to sort through the banking statements. It's all too much information at once. So I do what any rational person would: all of it at the same time. As one website begins to load I pop open an article and read a few lines before shifting over to a different tab. After playing around with that for a few seconds I return to a different task, fiddle away for a moment, then switch again. My monkey-mind returns in full force, completely inept at paying attention to any one thing beyond a few mere seconds of semi-lucidity.

The Great Unplugging

When the flooded email inboxes become too stressful, I flip over to Instagram to see what I missed. My brother-in-law posted dozens of stories from his music tour in Europe. My best friend just got back from vacation and has pictures to share. A company I previously collaborated with posted new material which is just waiting to be studied. I click through it all at rapid speed, trying to catch up as quickly as possible. A rational thought does bubble up inside my head: why don't I just call everyone to see what's been going on? A nice idea, but hard to act on in the middle of a social media binge. The algorithm is pulling me back in with fury and is not about to let me go now that I am back in its grasp – that's its entire purpose. To break away is almost impossible.

YouTube, of course, does nothing to calm the rising swell of stress. A few trolling, mean, or completely ignorant comments are posted on old videos from my business channel. Sure, they are strangers who don't really matter. But the comments still hurt my feelings. It dawns on me that my feelings haven't been hurt in the past 72 hours. The strangers in line at the grocery store withheld whatever rude comments they had about my appearance, voice, or mannerisms, unlike the friendly folks on YouTube who make their opinions of me known publicly.

At this point it all becomes too much. I slam the laptop shut and notice how rapidly I'm breathing. Is this normal? Is this stress I feel always here, but numbed in the habit? I did nothing but go through my normal morning scroll (imagine how different a morning *stroll* would make me feel). Having been away for even just a few days has brought clarity to what this habit actually does to me. I am not leaving my return to the void feeling more informed, more prepared for the day, relaxed and ready to move forward. I feel anxious. Worried. On edge. Hurt.

The Great Unplugging

When on Earth did this become normal?

Unable to handle it anymore I go back into the living room, where Gab is resting on the couch.

"How'd it go?" she asks, which makes me realize I was suffering in silence on the other side of the wall.

"Awful" I say. "I don't want to be on anymore. Not now, maybe not ever. I don't know. Can we work on our wedding thank yous? I need something analog."

Gab smiles and pulls out the box of cards under the coffee table. For the next hour we work together, signing names, finding addresses, and stamping envelopes for loved ones as the morning sun peers through the living room window. Specks of dust float in the sunbeams. Gabby's face is serene. Her handwriting, as usual, is impeccable. The faces in the photos we include with each card are full of joy, laughter, and love. Sheer presence in a beautiful moment, shared together in our memories. My breathing slows, my head stops spinning. The mind returns to a more placid state, free from the rushing river that was unleashed once I broke the dam.

Once all the cards are signed and stamped I saunter over to the kitchen and start making some pancakes. As the bubbles form on each batch I stand and stare, mesmerized by the process. Outside the window, echoing from the treetops, our local songbirds sing; an early sign of spring. The scent of cinnamon and vanilla fills the kitchen as the sizzle of the griddle deafens any external noise that was still buzzing from my morning scroll. *This is how a morning should be spent*, I think. *Now that I've stepped away, I see.*

* * *

On a cool June evening in 2016 I used all of my strength to get out of bed. Just sitting up made me out of breath for a few minutes. It had been a brutal couple of weeks where I felt more miserable than ever. A dual case of mononucleosis and strep throat left me writhing in pain with every swallow and barely able to move from the bed to the bathroom. Each moment, for days on end, left me in excruciating agony. Sleep was minimal. All I could think about was how I couldn't wait for the moment of relief to come.

By that evening the intense pain from the infection had subsided, but my fatigue remained all-encompassing. Tired of lying in bed, I summoned the strength to stumble out into the kitchen, then onto the back deck, in what was my first time being vertical for more than a minute in weeks. The air wrapped around my weary body and refreshed me with a slight breeze. On the horizon, between the silhouettes of dying ash trees, a full super moon was rising in the distance. Brilliant, gigantic, and with an orange hue, the Strawberry Moon dominated the night sky as it inched upward. Propping myself up against the deck railing, I stared in awe at the silent spectacle. Minutes passed as the moon raised itself into the stars. Without warning, a thought popped into my mind:

When I'm on my deathbed, will I wish I had more nights like this? Or will I wish that I saw just a few more posts on my phone?

It was an honest question, and one I knew the answer to. I just wish I followed through.

Unfortunately, in the years since, I have missed too many "nights like this" in favor of attending to the artificial glow of a screen. While that moonrise, like my day at the campsite, appeared to take an eternity, nights online seem to rush by like a raging river. What was supposed to be a tool ended up becoming a way of life, or better yet an escape *from* life. And it isn't going away. But if I don't learn to use it as the tool it is, and soon, I'll end up regretting it on my deathbed. I know that for a fact.

The days following the full tech fast are spent doing just that:

The Great Unplugging

learning how to only log onto my devices when a specific task needs to be completed, without losing myself down various rabbit holes. My phone, for the most part, stays stowed away in my nightstand drawer. It's too addictive to entertain opening unless I hear it ringing. My computer gets opened just once or twice a day, each time with a strong will not to hover over the address bar and type in the seductive first letter of an address. With hopes of using it *just* as a tool, I fulfill the necessary obligations: I pay our mortgage, order some house necessities, and FaceTime my parents. All worthy causes. When installing our new blinds in the basement I hesitate to reach for my computer once I realize how useless the poorly animated directions that came in the box are. I know that a generous YouTube video offering detailed instructions is my only option, but I fear what might happen if I sign back on. The thought of getting sucked back into the algorithm makes me anxious, and I can literally feel my heart rate increase at the idea of all the stimulation that comes with a simple click. But it needs to be done. My goofy little experiment can't impede the installation of much needed blinds; that's where Gab's patience may run out. After a few deep breaths I open the computer and open YouTube. My feelings upon arrival surprise me.

When I look at the homepage in this state, more relaxed than my first foray back online, I am able to see what was being offered with a more critical eye. Most of the content being pushed to me is complete and utter shit. Flashy titles like "How to make MILLIONS in your 30s" (spoiler alert: already be rich and invest in real estate in a perfect market) or "You need THIS to break through a slump" (shocker: discipline) seem silly and ridiculous after not engaging with them for a time. Other videos just appear weirdly pathetic (the sad-looking guy with the title "Why I'm Single" easily wins an award in the category of "Things I Couldn't Care Less About").

The Great Unplugging

Fish don't realize that they live in water because it's everywhere. Well, when we're in the algorithm, it's pretty hard to realize we're in a bunch of trashy, mostly useless content that we are better off without and that doesn't enhance our lives. For every bit of helpful content out there, we have to sift through mounds of junk that waste our time, energy, and brainpower. When we're in it, though, that's hard to see; we're buried and miss the forest for the flashy trees. But zoom out, get some perspective, and it becomes clear how ridiculous the content we waste our time on has become.

I chuckle at this realization and enter the blinds we purchased plus "instructions" into the search bar. Like the tool it is meant to be, YouTube comes through with a solid how-to video from a dad in tube socks, a dirty baseball cap from the 80s, and a tool belt that helps me *actually* enhance my living experience. The difference, once recognized, is stark.

As the week progresses the insatiable tug of these programs starts to become less persuasive. Like not having dairy for a while then downing a huge ice cream cone, on the rare occasions that I *do* slip into a few minutes of mindless scrolling I catch myself quickly and leave feeling gross and guilty rather than numbed and satisfied. After two or three relapses, this icky feeling helps me resist completely. The desire to "check-in" fades, while the desire to "miss out" increases, as my time gets spent taking care of my body, mind, and soul. Stretching, playing piano, doing crafts with Gab, and cooking great meals all provide benefits that greatly outweigh the empty promises made by the apps on my phone and the websites beckoning to fill my time online. My initial acceptance of the algorithm after the initial full fast, after a few days, becomes an active distaste and aversion.

The spell is being broken.

The Great Unplugging

And, by the end of the ten days, I am confident in the benefits of this experiment. Relaying it to Gab one night, I explain how much calmer I feel. My mind isn't racing like normal. Life is slowing down and I'm more capable of *appreciating* the passing of time instead of constantly feeling anxious that I'm not doing something, *anything*, to fill the void. Becoming a human *being* is getting easier, and more appealing, by the day. I am more in tune with my body, my emotions, and my old hobbies. Tons of projects are now completed around the house and a sense of innate satisfaction is burgeoning within me. I feel competent and more confident. And beneath all this is a sense of, dare I say, happiness. A calm, quiet happiness that exists where there is usually a mildly churning sense of general dissatisfaction. Feelings of capability, competence, and acceptance are merging into a state of contentment. It is an alien but welcome encounter.

Our attention is our life. And we have the option to give our attention to ourselves, our loved ones, and meaningful tasks, or to willingly give it to the latest app that's full of empty promises. Too much time goes by in a blur, thanks to these little miracles in our pockets. But there is an effective antidote. Slowing down and embracing the difficult task of breaking free from our phones is a remedy for a better future. It's challenging, for sure. But it's worth every ounce of struggle in the end.

It's time to take back control of our time, attention, and ability to focus. We need to value present experience over endless amusement. We should spend our time taking care of ourselves and learning new skills instead of watching other people pine for attention. We must seek genuine human connection over the virtual approval of anonymous internet tribes. And it is essential that we remember to live while we are alive, even when life is boring or scary or uncertain – *especially* then. Because numbing ourselves in

The Great Unplugging

a sea of content is no way to live. Instead, it's an easy way to die. Just a little bit. Every single day.

    I see this clearly now.

A De-optimized Morning

On a bright Thursday morning, in the middle of an otherwise mundane week, I leave my front door in a hurry in order to get to my car so I can start another bland day of bland work. But this morning is different. While walking toward my car, the sun, peeking through the trees across the street, flashes into my eyes. For some reason, on this particular day, it stops me in my tracks. I take my hand off the door handle and look up at the trees. They are splashed in a golden light. Birds are traveling from treetop to treetop. A chipmunk sprints across my driveway, hoping I don't notice where he's going. Tiny flowers are beginning to bloom from the green stems bursting from the ground. I turn my gaze back across the street and look toward the sunrise.

Immediately, I know what needs to be done.

* * *

In our fast-paced world and optimized hustle culture, there is one casualty that seems especially peculiar:

Our mornings.

When I imagine an ideal morning a few common themes emerge. Usually I picture a beautiful sunrise and a calm, quiet start to the day. Perhaps I leisurely roll out of bed after resting under the covers for a bit, strolling into the kitchen to start a fresh pot of aromatic coffee that pairs perfectly with a delicious breakfast. Maybe I read for a bit or take time to carefully plan my day. From there I get ready and begin whatever task I need to with plenty of

A De-optimized Morning

time to spare. Heck, I'm feeling relaxed and cozy just thinking about this.

But that, of course, is almost never the case in modern life. Instead, the average morning typically consists of being jolted awake by an atrocious phone alarm and then immediately scrolling on said phone for far too long in order to "catch up" on whatever happened overnight (which is usually nothing). Once I realize how much time has been wasted, I frantically get myself ready to get out the door on time for whatever seemingly urgent obligation I need to meet. Scarf down a hefty bowl of straight sugar – I mean – breakfast cereal, chug some cheap coffee, throw on an outfit after frantically deciding what to wear, and I'm on my way.

The morning can absolutely be a time of peace, solitude, and meaningful productivity that sets us up for a great day if we develop certain routines and systems. It can also be a haphazard disaster that raises our stress levels, wastes our time, and makes us question whether we should go out for a pack of gum and never come back.

This is why, in my opinion, morning routines are such a popular topic in our productivity-obsessed society.

The idea behind a regimented morning routine is that starting the morning off well sets us up for success throughout the rest of the day. Which makes sense. I'm sure we'd all like to feel more energized and vibrant early on and have that feeling persist throughout the afternoon. It'd be great if we could use our initial daily moments to our advantage in whatever way we felt necessary. But there's a problem. The idea of the "ideal morning routine" has been completely hijacked by the hustle-culture crowd in a way that turns our earliest waking hours into another commodity that can be sold, optimized, and used for productivity.

In a world where we must produce as much as possible,

A De-optimized Morning

mornings are an excellent opportunity to squeeze more out of our time. A quick search of "morning routines" on YouTube will lead to thousands of videos of well-meaning folks explaining how you can hack, optimize, and *win* your mornings in order to create the ideal version of yourself. These videos have varying degrees of intensiveness and difficulty. Almost all of them share the common theme of waking up earlier than you do now so that you can do more than you currently are. The most absurd routine that I have found requires waking at 4:00am every day, meditating, writing in a gratitude journal, doing a full workout, going for a walk outside, reading at least ten pages of a nonfiction book, working on your side hustle for about an hour, drinking a $100-per-container supplement, taking a cold shower, performing a full skincare routine, and *then* heading out to work knowing that you've fully accomplished the goal of being an asshole before everyone else wakes up. In addition to these YouTube videos, there are now literal courses that allegedly teach us how to "win the morning" so that we can achieve our dreams and become the greatest version of ourselves. A big promise to fulfill by 8am.

According to these gurus, no longer should we slowly wake up and get ourselves together while savoring the early morning solitude. Nor should we emerge from bed without a detailed plan and schedule. Instead, we should rise and grind, stick to our routine, and produce as much as we possibly can before the sun skirts above the horizon. If you're not in the early morning club, then you're missing out.

And if you are? Well, my friend, you are getting *ahead*.

Ahead of what? Or of whom? I'm not sure. But you'll be ahead, alright. Because life, and mornings, are a competition now.

* * *

A De-optimized Morning

When did gradually shaking ourselves out of unconsciousness become such a "thing"? Like many areas of our culture, the fast-paced, tech-centered, rise-and-grind nature of society often creates more problems than it solves here. Imagine the anxiety that comes with having this long list of "to-dos" before the sun even rises, the benefits of which we're not quite sure of. Or consider missing out on some of these checkboxes one day and feeling like we *lost* the morning. If we don't achieve perfection, then we've lost, and that's a pretty awful way to start a day. Plus, these standards are outrageously unrealistic. Maybe if you're a single dude with few obligations and a need to get some discipline in your life, these ideas can help. But if I were to try these tasks each day, the sheer noise created would annoy Gab to the point of stumbling out and dragging me back to bed. For the average person working a regular job and managing a family, the most intense of these routines are simply unachievable. Are they now losers because they are not kicking ass each dawn?

Of course not. But it sure can feel that way when we see thousands of people online doing what we aren't, or maybe aren't even capable of, and bragging about it. Never mind that the vast majority of these people are flat-out lying about their routine. They create the *illusion* that these routines are necessary, achievable, and repeatable. Even if they claim to be up at 4:30am when it's bright outside in their video, or their clock in the background says 11:30 as they allegedly make breakfast at 6am.

That's not to say we *shouldn't* be mindful about how we start our days. Certainly, living intentionally in all phases of the day is something we can strive for, as it provides a more meaningful, fulfilling life. This includes how we spend our time in the moments after we wake up, scratch ourselves, and stumble out of the bedroom.

A De-optimized Morning

If we are intentional and mindful about our actions then we can feel more relaxed, more purposeful, and more focused heading into the day ahead. Naturally, there's a balance that can be struck between having a productive morning and giving ourselves time and space to relax and ease into the day. But balance is often hard to find.

* * *

It was 4:50 am on a freezing Tuesday morning in upstate New York. Outside snow was falling gently on the street, illuminated by soft golden streetlights. It was so frigid that each snowflake immediately turned to ice on contact with the tundra. Beyond my bedroom window it was silent because normal people don't wake up at 4:50 am when there are less degrees on the thermometer than there are fingers on my right hand. Groaning, I rolled over and shut off my awful alarm, which was blaring "Hells Bells" by AC/DC into the darkness of my bedroom.

Groggily I stumbled out of bed and into the living room. Keeping the lights off, so as not to wake up the rest of my family, I opened the front door and felt the blast of cold air rush into the house. On the doorstep was a gift that no twelve year old would have wanted:

A stack of newspapers, just waiting to be delivered.

As I leaned over the hoist up the pile, I cursed Wayne with all my might. This was *his* fault, anyway. Without him I could still be sleeping like a normal middle schooler. Instead, I had become the victim of a con-man.

A few months prior I came home from school to find that some guy with leathered skin and a white goatee had appeared in my kitchen. I had never seen this man before in my life, but he was schmoozing my dad into allowing pre-Industrial child labor to make its way back into the local economy.

A De-optimized Morning

It was Wayne.

In front of our 80s-style oven he and my dad discussed a job opportunity for me. I still have no idea how this arrangement came about, or how my dad met this guy, but by the end of that conversation I had been volunteered by the council of elders to serve as tribute for a neighborhood paper route. And thus my fate was sealed.

As possibly the last traditional paperboy in America, while every other kid was getting a developmentally appropriate amount of sleep, I was forced to wake up at 4:50am every day in order to saunter through the darkness and drop newspapers in doorways and on porches. (That is not entirely accurate. On weekends I got to sleep in until 5:50am). For three long years, every school day, every holiday, every blizzard, every rain storm, began with me hazily packing papers and heading out the door where the often brutal weather would sober me up throughout the course of the walk. While my fellow classmates were sleeping in until nine or ten in the morning, I watched every sunrise for three years in exchange for $2.50 an hour. I began that paper route as a boy and left as a man, mainly due to the impacts of sleep deprivation.

As evidenced by my dad's enthusiasm about my early morning shift, I wasn't raised in a household of balanced morning routines. When it came to early mornings my parents exemplified the two extreme ends of the spectrum.

Growing up, my father was the epitome of a productive morning person. Motivated by an Army commercial he saw as a kid, his favorite motto was, "We do more before 7am than most people do in a day." This often resulted in his footsteps loudly pounding the floor well before sunrise (which prevented me and my sister from sleeping in even if we wanted to), slamming kitchen drawers,

A De-optimized Morning

running power equipment, and, most famously, shocking my sister awake with the sound of a power washer blasting her window at seven in the morning. That, of course, was my personal favorite. He was, and still is, the epitome of an early-morning productivity guru before that was even considered to be a part of our culture.

Delicate and slow, he was not.

Enduring all of this with the spirit of a hardened soldier was my mother. I have vivid memories of my mom struggling through the mornings amidst the overwhelming energy of my dad swirling through the house in the early hours. Each day I'd come out of my room to see her curled up on the big brown couch, her face occasionally peeking out of her thickest and most comfortable blanket only for a delightful sip of her precious coffee. Stunned and barely functional, she'd slowly come back to consciousness over the course of an hour or two, in just enough time to make the dreary drive over the hill to work each day. Productivity was the last thing on her mind in the morning. Instead, she was purely focused on survival (especially on Mondays or right after a vacation). The idea of a productive morning routine to her would be sacrilege.

Thanks in large part to that paper route, which hacked my brain at such a vulnerable age, I take more after my dad. The paper route routine made me a morning person by nature, and that schedule has stuck ever since. Couple that with my long-standing perfectionism and interest in self-improvement, and I was fertile soil for the ideas of the win-the-morning crowd. Nowadays I don't need to begrudgingly deliver the local news to the neighbors, but that vacuum of responsibility has led to me trying every routine under the sun with the goal of experiencing the promise of the "perfect morning" and all the serenity, strength, and focus that would come with it. I have woken up at 4:00am to hit the gym, drank a variety of

A De-optimized Morning

disgusting green drinks, journaled about everything I'm grateful for, meditated, done breath work, and managed various side hustles, all by 7am.

None of those routines, though, ever lasted more than a week or two. Because they were unrealistic. Borderline impossible to maintain. Internet puffery. Appeals for attention. And, at their core, fake.

There's a phenomenon I notice with my high school students: when an assignment is too difficult, or they feel they have fallen too far behind in class, their default response is to give up. Rather than continue trying to reach a goal, they see the opportunity as too far out of their reach. So why bother?

This is reality for most people. It's why most diets fail. Why most of us can't stick to a fitness routine long-term. And it's certainly why we all forget about our New Year's Resolutions by February. When we bite off more than we can chew, and the dream seems impossible, the easy thing to do is to simply stop trying. Why waste the energy on something we are not going to attain anyway?

The same rings true of these morning routines. The suggestions online are so cumbersome and overstuffed that most people cannot possibly stick to them. Which, often, results in a wild pendulum swing to the other end of the spectrum. Instead of being ultra-productive, many of us spend our mornings sleeping in, hitting the snooze button, scrolling on our phones, and not doing anything worthwhile. While focusing too much on productivity can be unhelpful, absolving ourselves of *any* productivity and responsibility can be equally damaging.

A typical morning that involves waking up late and scrolling through social media is a one-way ticket toward a stressful day. When we check our phones at the moment we open our eyes, our

A De-optimized Morning

still-tired brains are suddenly flooded with the ideas, perspectives, and experiences of hundreds of people. Imagine if a hundred strangers marched into your room the second you woke up to shout at you about what they just did. Naturally, your response would be to call the police and get these weirdos out of your house! Or, at the very least, guard your privacy a bit better so that your bedroom becomes more of a sanctuary. And yet this is exactly what we do when we open our phones and check email, social media, or the news first thing in the morning; our brains struggle to tell the difference between real and imagined intrusion.

While being ultra-productive isn't the answer to a great start to the day, neither is throwing it all to the wind and becoming a slug. Like with any routine or lifestyle change, we need to strike a balance. The extreme wake-up times and endless morning checklists are ridiculous and unsustainable. But the solution is not to do nothing but lay around and scroll before haphazardly throwing together an outfit and scarfing down a breakfast before rushing out the door. There is always a middle way. Even if I never had an example of one in my home.

I'm considering all of this after a particularly stressful week. Work is insanely busy and is pushing me to my limits of screen time and interacting with other humans. Our week was also filled with a variety of pricey but necessary house projects that were anything but relaxing to complete. By three o'clock each day I've been feeling physically exhausted, mentally drained, and emotionally unavailable. It's one of those periods in life where it feels like I do a million things throughout the day, but nothing of value is actually accomplished.

My theory is, if I can start my days more intentionally, then the good vibes and energy would flow through the rest of my waking

A De-optimized Morning

hours, stressful as they may be. I'm just coming off another productivity-bout and want nothing to do with a detailed morning routine. But my current habit of checking YouTube comments, scrolling through multiple inboxes, and browsing the latest NFL news on Reddit is wasting time and making me feel anxious by the time I leave for work. How can I strike a healthy balance between my tendency to optimize and my habit of slugging around online?

That's why that sudden glare of sun in my eyes on this Thursday morning sparks an epiphany:

When was the last time I watched a sunrise?

Sure, I notice that the sun rises each day. We all do. I'll put Captain Obvious to rest now.

But when was the last time I actually dedicated time to sit and do nothing but watch it happen? I think back to a few hikes I have done over the past year where the sun rose while I was on the trail. But never on a normal workday do I make a point of mindfully observing the daily spectacle. Does such beauty need to be contained solely to moments on a trail? Is my suburban neighborhood not inspiring enough to enjoy the start of the day?

Maybe, if I start my day by simply watching the sunrise, then life will slow down a bit. Feel less hectic. Massage my brain and leave me more nimble to complete my long to-do list. Perhaps starting the day with *beauty* instead of productivity or laziness could make me a better person. A natural start as a small act of rebellion against a tech-obsessed world.

As I step into my car and turn the key, I feel inspired to find out.

* * *

So many days pass by without noticing the constant changes in nature. The clouds floating overhead, the leaves dancing in the

A De-optimized Morning

breeze, the light shifting as the day progresses. Instead of appreciating this cosmic show, I often am buried in a glowing screen compulsively checking email inside a dimly lit shelter. It's one of the main reasons I challenged myself to celebrate the Wheel of the Year, and it is a big motivation behind the resolve to watch the sunrise every day.

Technically I never know when my last sunset, or sunrise, will be. It could be today for all I know. A lot of that depends on how focused the drivers are between my home and school. And yet most days, this beautiful scene plays out right in my front yard and I don't even bother to notice because I'm too busy on "more important matters". If today were to be my last day on Earth, and I knew that was the case, the most important thing to me would be to watch that beautiful scene one more time. Not to check social media, or email, or to cross another thing off my to-do list. No. It'd be to sit, be, and enjoy the solace as my final sunrise emerged dramatically in the distance.

The sunrise is the perfect time to do nothing but be alive in a fleeting moment. It's the best reminder that life is short, unexpected, and that we're guaranteed nothing. That "more important matters" can wait. Because if the sun doesn't rise or set, then none of those things will matter anyway. So I might as well watch and appreciate the event that makes it all happen to begin with. Right?

Which is why I am committing to a "de-optimization" plan. Instead of doing as much as possible each morning, I plan to "do nothing" but one simple act: watch the sunrise. For these 20 or so minutes, each day, my only routine will be to wake up, grab my glasses, make a cup of coffee, and walk onto my deck. From there I plan to stand underneath the trees and watch the sun go through its daily, thankless performance of illuminating the neighborhood and

A De-optimized Morning

signaling the coming of another precious day. No email, no social media, no journaling, no exercising. Just standing, staring, and enjoying the moment. The goal being to feel relaxed, focused, and ready to fully experience a beautiful day.

As I go to bed the night before my experiment begins I feel weirdly excited. What wonders will I see that typically go unnoticed? How relaxed and calm will I feel going into work? Maybe *this* is the anecdote to my stressful mornings.

* * *

This morning sucks already.

Instead of emerging from my house into a sparkling, colorful world of birdsong and bunny rabbits, instead I step out onto a soaking wet deck while getting rained on. Being drenched in my pajamas isn't exactly how I envisioned this beginning. It takes every ounce of mental discipline to remind myself that every day can still be beautiful even if it doesn't create a spectacular painting in the sky. It's just a lot harder when you are damp and sticky first thing in the morning.

I bring my coffee mug to my lips and step back under the awning over the deck door to escape the rain. This backyard is still new to me. We have only lived in this house for a couple of months and I still don't feel fully connected to the land. Back home I spent most of my days rambling around my back woods, getting to know each nook and crevice while becoming a dedicated protector of that land against future development. *That* is my home, thanks to almost thirty years of daily play in that space. What I am looking at now, technically, is my home too. But it doesn't feel that way. It feels like an arranged marriage and this is the first meeting between me and my future spouse. Sure it's nice, and pretty, but there's no connection (and certainly no love) yet. *Maybe after this challenge*

A De-optimized Morning

there will be a spark, I think. I miss the forest of my youth, and hope that, maybe someday, I can feel the same affection for this little plot of land.

For his book *Local*, adventurer Alastair Humphreys spent an entire year exploring a single map of his home area. He also felt a bit out of place where he lived and wanted to learn to love his boring, uninspiring area. Through a year of exploration he found an entire universe existing in the drab, over-industrialized London suburb which he called home. There were plants he had never seen, animals he never witnessed, and the realization that thousands of complex human lives were taking place all around him, each with an experience as intricate and magnificent as his own. A single map, he concluded, could be enough for an entire lifetime of exploration. In the end (spoiler alert) he grew a much greater appreciation and, dare I say, love for an area that he initially wanted nothing to do with.

While I certainly don't hate where we live now (we did *choose* to buy the house, you know) I still don't feel any deep connection or emotion toward it. We moved to this house in a season of death. Our closing was in mid-December, meaning that, up to this point, our entire time on this little plot of land has been surrounded by snow, sticks, and gloom. Now we are *finally* entering the season of rebirth, and little signs of Earth's fertility are popping up around the yard. Maybe when I see this land in its full glory it will imprint itself on me.

Looking out, there is a small patch of micro-forest; a collection of maples, oaks, eastern white pines, and a thick underbelly of leaves. The ground is covered with sandy soil and moss. While most suburban homes consist of barren, over-watered turf soaked in dangerous chemicals, the previous owners of our home apparently let nature take its course. Maybe they saw the value in allowing

A De-optimized Morning

natural life to flourish, even if it was just on a small plot of land. Maybe they were too busy to care about yard work. Or, as was probably the case, they were too old to do anything about it. Either way, I am grateful for their (lack of) service.

Each of the trees are dramatically competing for limited sunlight. Some are leaning so far over the house it makes me wonder how they haven't fallen in all these years. At the apex of the leaning trees are branches turned directly skyward, desperately looking to outwit their brothers in competition for the same sun. A strong south wind begins to blow, the culprit of the warm and tropical air, which makes each of these giants sway aggressively in the breeze, creaking and crackling with each dramatic movement. Spurts of rain seem to shoot out of the air right in front of me and dampen my morning hoodie. While not quite comfortable, I definitely feel *alive*.

And that is certainly a foreign experience for an early Monday morning.

* * *

Without a dedicated morning routine, I tend to fall into the trap of checking to see what everyone else in the world is up to. Knowing this is an issue, I decide one day to dramatically limit the scope of my "checking in". On this day, I shrink my field of attention by deliberately paying attention to, and checking-in on, the locals only.

I emerge onto the deck feeling more curious than annoyed. My neighbors woke me up well before my alarm by being outrageously loud. The noise was incessant and blared right through our bedroom windows, making it impossible to sleep in on this delightful Saturday morning. At first, of course, I feel like a victim of their careless selfishness. *How could they be so loud so early? Don't they care that everyone else is asleep?* But then I figure I should see what all the commotion was about. Who knows? Maybe it is something

A De-optimized Morning

worth waking up for.

The Earth is still damp from the southern storm that rolled through earlier in the week. Cumulus clouds, remnants of the lingering humidity, crawl over the house. The scent of warm mud brings back a flash of memories and a sense of comfort. Spring is here. *That* is the cause of the commotion.

The locals are a motley crew: robins, cardinals, tufted titmice, chickadees, and bluebirds. And boy are they all incredibly stoked to finally get some warm air and a bit of sun. After a long, hard winter (or migration) they are celebrating the beautiful morning, bountiful worms, and perfect weather for mating. No wonder they are so loud. I wouldn't be able to contain my excitement for those things either (as long as we replace worms with fresh-baked bread).

The robins are by far the loudest, singing in a massive united chorus that echoes across the neighborhood all the way to the pond on the other side of the block. They are still in the trees, probably getting ready for the day's hunt, as I notice plenty of worms have been washed up from all the rain. It is a free buffet and the robins are getting themselves pumped up to truly have "all you could eat".

I close my eyes and begin to breathe slowly. The chorus of birdsong sweeps around my body and creates a bridge between myself and my sky-dwelling neighbors. On a normal morning I probably would have ignored their cackling. But I am glad to be taking part as an audience member in the micro-forest. If we are going to be living together, we might as well be comfortable with each others' presence.

Then, suddenly, drama.

Two bluebirds swoop down from the canopy on an aggressive attack of another lone bluebird hanging out below. They squeal and squabble as the rustle of feathers pounds the airwaves of the forest

A De-optimized Morning

floor. In the commotion the three of them, almost as if one being, continue fighting while flying back up into the trees. Maybe it is because the caffeine hasn't latched onto my brain yet, but the tussle surprises and exhilarates me. The spectacle is far more entertaining than any comment thread I would have read otherwise. *I wonder which bluebird is at fault. Maybe the two are bullies. Or maybe that one is a jerk and deserves it.*

The floor of the micro-forest begins to morph from a fuzzy, lightless gray to a deep shade of amber and burnt-orange. As the sun emerges, life on the floor will soon awaken and catch-up to the commotion in the canopy. Like our time zones, light stirs energy in those it hits first. Looking around, I am the only human out catching the light; the sun's energy is kept all to myself. I soak it in, awakening with a sense of power and peace.

The bluebirds stop their battle. The robins quiet down and make their way to the buffet beneath me. I take one last breath, say goodbye to my neighbors, and wish them well as I retreat back into my home.

* * *

More days of rain have come and gone, preventing the soaked Earth from ever fully drying out. Today, finally, is forecast to be sunny.

I am almost two weeks into the experiment and this is the first morning without a single cloud in the sky. A few stars, and Venus, still linger in the predawn canvas as I step out into air that is a bit chillier after the fronts passed through. Today I am wrapped in a thick hoodie and my hiking pants, although I keep my bare feet out in the crisp air.

The trees are desperately waiting for a few days of sun so they can fully pop into their most colorful outfits. The ends of each oak

A De-optimized Morning

branch are adorned with tiny crimson buds that look like thousands of lollipops pressed against the sky. With just a few nice days, they will soon burst into leaves and begin feeding on desperately needed sunlight.

Finally, their first break comes.

Rays of sunlight begin gracing the tippy-tops of the trees, basking them in a golden hue. Slowly the light works its way down, gradually bathing each of the trees inch-by-inch in its life-giving glow. Wanting some for myself, I back up to the edge of the deck and prop myself up on the railing. I am still too short. The trees and their genetic height advantage get to feel the sun's glory long before I can. Jealous, I return to the middle of the deck and wait for the sun to grace my skin.

Daylight is something absolutely critical to our well-being, and something we do not get nearly enough of.

Our bodies run on a circadian rhythm, which regulates our levels of wakefulness based on the amount of light that we are experiencing. In a more natural setting we would typically rise with the sun and fall asleep soon after darkness settled, with the amount of sleep adjusting along with the amount of daylight throughout the year. Generally, we would sleep more in the winter (due to the extended darkness) and be more active in the long days of summertime.

Technology, though, has changed that. And much to our detriment.

Thanks to the miracle of electric lighting, we no longer have to shuffle to bed once the sun goes down. We can illuminate dozens of mini-suns in our homes to keep the party going long into the evening. When camping I am usually fast asleep within an hour or two after sunset, in part because it's pitch black and there is nothing else to

A De-optimized Morning

do. At home, though, I can easily be kept awake by our living room lamp and the bright glow of the TV playing reruns of *South Park* until well past midnight. Outside the home, street lights blaring blue LEDs into our windows at all hours of the evening, regardless of activity level, can make the night feel obsolete. This shortsighted strategy prevents darkness from ever falling in some areas. The excess of light at night, both indoors and outdoors, has disastrous effects on our sleep, circadian rhythm, and, therefore, our health.

The same goes for the morning, but in the opposite direction. Whereas our bodies crave natural sunlight once we wake up, it is all too easy to remain in artificial *darkness* in spite of the morning sun. Our homes are far darker than the world outside in the morning, as I can attest to by my eyes needing to readjust each time I go back inside after the sunrise. A typical morning of staying inside a room with the shades drawn while looking at a screen starves our brain of the light it needs to get moving and let the body know it's time to begin the day. Even if a light is on in the room, it's not enough to fully stir our body awake.

Our light is too bright for us to sleep at night, but too dim to wake us up in the morning. The worst of both worlds.

As soon as the sun splashes on my backyard the world erupts into energy. The animals are privy to this power of light.

When our eyes come into bright, natural sunlight in the morning, hormones are released that effectively regulate our circadian rhythm and energy levels. We get more energy during the day and fall asleep easier at night if we are exposed to the natural rhythms of light that the Earth has to offer. Sunlight reaching our eyes, especially in the morning, helps us feel more energized, focused, and happy throughout the course of the day. Sunlight reaching our skin not only increases levels of Vitamin D but also,

A De-optimized Morning

interestingly enough, increases libido in both men and women. If that's not enough to get you into a morning routine of watching the sunrise, I don't know what is.

While I am not measuring the amount of hormones being released into my body, I certainly feel a difference on these early mornings. By the end of my time outside each day I feel significantly more energized, focused, and calmer than if I had stayed inside and remained in a stunned state of drowsiness on the couch. It is the difference between feeling frazzled and sluggish versus feeling fresh, clean, and alive. As time goes on, I even begin to ditch my coffee and tea because the caffeine is no longer necessary to keep me going.

Like the trees, all I need is the sun.

Eventually the sun is high enough to angle its light onto me, having already fed the trees their initial rations. I close my eyes as the warmth hits my skin. Feelings of peace wash over my body while energy begins bubbling from below. It is a perfect combination of motivation and relaxation. I am ready to tackle my to-do list stress-free and with an energized confidence.

And the only cost of getting this energy was standing outside and closing my eyes.

* * *

There is nothing worse than being alone. Or, for that matter, left out.

As a social species, connection with others is absolutely critical to our survival. Connection ensures that we have a support system, a safety net, a sense of purpose, and agency. It shows not only that others matter to us, but that we matter to them. Describing the human condition without meaningful connection is simply impossible. It's one of the reasons why we are so glued to new information. To be "disconnected" is to appear aloof, out of touch, uncaring about your fellow humans and their condition. In a hyper-connected world, to be disconnected can be seen as doing a disservice to humanity.

But being *overly* connected isn't good for us, either. If we can't tear away from the constant happenings around the globe then we prevent ourselves from deeply connecting with our *own* life experience. Our mind wanders elsewhere while our life continues *here*, right in front of us. We should absolutely be connected to society and what is happening around the world so that we can be informed citizens. We just don't need to be steeped in that every day, all the time. At a certain point there are diminishing returns.

So often we prize connecting with others online and in far-reaching places over a deep sense of connection with ourselves, the people in our lives, and the places where we live. We worry about the misdoings of governments on separate continents while children in our own towns rely on donated food distributed at schools in order to eat on weekends (food stores that are increasingly bare as community connections and a sense of local responsibility dwindles). We obsess over an environmental injustice in a place we will never know while local governments collude with toxic waste dumps to open facilities bordering public water supplies. We dream of far-off excursions that will inspire and excite us while a beautiful landscape lies unnoticed just outside our doorstep.

If we are going to connect, our strongest ties should be with people, places, and causes we can meaningfully impact with our efforts. Because when we try too hard to connect with *everything* going on, what we actually end up connecting with are vague ideas and concepts instead of concrete realities. A beautiful landscape I see on Instagram exists as an imagined reality. The bursting of life

A De-optimized Morning

in every corner of my field of vision in the morning is an intense experience of life as it is. Right here, right now.

As the month wears on, *everything* slows down thanks to this little sunrise routine. My mind becomes less frantic in the morning and transforms, through diligence, into a softer, calmer, and more focused version of itself. My breathing slows to a point where I wonder how rapidly I must actually breathe on a normal, hectic morning. The drive to do more and check-off as many boxes as I can dissolves into a calm desire to stretch, gaze, and appreciate what I already have in front of me. Most importantly, I develop a *deeper* sense of connection. The compulsive urge to learn about everything that happened while I slept fades away. Instead, I am more interested in catching up on the happenings of my little micro-park. If I skip my sunrise routine now, then I miss out on what my favorite birds are up to, how the tree buds are progressing, and if the gray squirrel remembers where he buried his acorn. I can't possibly start the day by neglecting my new friends.

Our time is fleeting. We never know which sunrise will be our last. With each passing day, whether we enjoy it or not, we have one less sunrise that we get to experience. The clock is ticking, always. And we can choose to stretch time out as much as possible by noticing, appreciating, and being present with the magnificent world that exists right outside our doorstep. Or, we can speed it up by accomplishing tasks at a frantic pace while constantly worrying about the *next* thing that "needs to be done". My month of sunrises has felt like the longest month of the year, but in the best way possible. I feel a love and connection with my home that didn't exist before this experience. I've learned so much more about the life in my backyard and how precious it really is. And I coast about my day with a sense of calm and wonder that matriculates into other areas of

A De-optimized Morning

my life. I am a better human for having fostered a true sense of connection in my life.

* * *

The sunrise routine continues for a few days after the month ends, but a series of gloomy mornings toward the end of the week breaks the streak. During the challenge I would have ventured outside regardless to watch the more subtle changes in the Earth that occur on a gray morning. But, without the "challenge" hanging over my head, on those days I stay inside and reconnect with my laptop.

It only took two days of starting my day with an artificial glow to become agitated. Sitting in my comfy little office chair at school, desktop at eye level, I fidget. I tap my toes, shake my knees, and look out the window every thirty seconds. It is as if I had three shots of espresso and can't contain my energy with such a low caffeine tolerance. I am bottled up, caged, *domesticated*. Something, it appears, is wrong.

The next morning I decide to go right back outside the second I wake up. Still feeling a bit angsty as I lean on my deck railing, the early sun graces the back of my neck and gives me a warm welcome back. A robin fat enough to be mistaken as a pumpkin rests on a branch and stares at me; he has clearly eaten well while I was gone. The world springs to life once again, like it always has. Even with a strong cup of coffee in hand, my twitching stops. My angst evaporates. My mood softens. Such is the power of the morning sun.

I can no longer imagine starting my morning any other way.

Eating Dandelions

It is 7:30 on a sunny Tuesday morning and I am frantically trying to find a pair of clean underwear in a massive pile of laundry.

I am, naturally, annoyed at myself. In spite of how hard I've been working to be a perfectly peaceful, serene, put-together individual, my morning has not gone according to plan. And, as a result, I am now rushing to get ready and arrive at work on time. For no other reason than, well, *I'm always on time.*

* * *

When did I become "important"?

As adults, it's easy to develop an outsized sense of importance – that others hang on our presence, our words, and our ideas. If we don't show up somewhere, we will be missed. We *must* be at work, even if we're sick. We must perform at all times and all hours of the day. Any action to the contrary is evidence of laziness and, deep down, perhaps a sense of worthlessness.

For me, this manifests in my obsession with punctuality. Ever since I was a kid it has been drilled into me that, if I'm not ten minutes early, then I'm late. Which, honestly, is great advice. Time is the most valuable thing we have in life, which means I should respect mine and others' by being *where* I should be, *when* I should be. On my paper route as a kid I was never late once in three years. One night, at twelve years old, an overnight hospital stay was required after my arm snapped in half during a football game (life tip: when you haven't hit puberty, don't try to tackle someone who already has). That night I awoke from my anesthesia-induced haze feeling anxious and mumbled, "Mom, how am I going to deliver the papers?" In her audition for Mom of the Year, she left the hospital and delivered the papers to keep my streak alive.

I (really, we) never faltered once. And I take pride in that.

In spite of my dedication to punctuality, I never really stressed too much about it. I just showed up where I was needed when I was needed without much thought – it became second-nature. The same could be said about my dedication to my studies and my work ethic. I've always been a hard worker. In school I did my best, and was rewarded for the effort, but never lost sleep over it. These mindsets were deeply ingrained parts of my personality that seemed to flow without much thought or effort most of the time.

All of that changed when I started working.

Suddenly, when I had a shirt, tie, salary, and a pension, I became somebody else. I was now a "professional", responsible for the education of hundreds of kids. Being young and untenured, there was a deep urge to prove myself to anyone and everyone. If I faltered, I could be seen as unreliable and incompetent. Suddenly the stakes were higher. Losing a $2/hour paper route meant nothing. Losing a salary that Gab and I relied on, and tarnishing a reputation that could keep me from further employment, meant everything.

Plus, a funny thing happens when we become professional adults. Things that were easy and just flowed as kids, for some reason, become laborious. Activities that enriched our souls become laughable wastes of time. The childlike urge to play and explore gets choked in the collar that we tighten each morning. Suddenly, life seems in many ways to be less wondrous and, ultimately, less fun.

In childhood most things in life aren't seen as a big deal. We are resilient and roll with the punches, scrapes, and bruises.

Deadlines are optional, inconveniences aren't worth ruining a day over, and playing outside with friends is time well spent. As adults most things in life *still* aren't a big deal, but the difference is that I often make them out to be. Little inconveniences can ruin my whole day. My endless to-do lists hold my dreams and hobbies hostage. Running through a field, laying in the grass to watch clouds, staring at the stars, all of these once daily rituals of childhood have become rare opportunities for myself and many adults. And, when I am fortunate enough to engage with them, there is an urge to track time, optimize performance, or work toward an end *goal* instead of just doing them for their own sake. Of course I have more responsibilities than when I was young. I have higher stakes. My list of obligations is objectively longer. But just because I have more on my plate does not mean I need to ignore the more beautiful, playful aspects of life. It is not a requirement.

At some point the world shifts from a landscape to be explored in awe to a list of things to do, a set of data to analyze, a stockpile of milestones to accomplish. Check this box. Then another. Then another. It's all so productive.

But where, then, is the magic?

* * *

My hectic morning takes place on Beltane, better known as May Day. The Celts used Beltane to mark the beginning of summer, as May brought warm weather and the dramatic blooming of flowers and leaves across the landscape. Traditionally, Beltane (like many other festivals along the present Wheel of the Year) was celebrated with bonfires in the hopes that the fire would bring protection and good fortune throughout the rest of the year. Other rituals focused on renewal and fertility, in line with the stunning life that bursts forth in early May. One particular ritual involved washing one's face with the morning dew, in hopes that it would bring youth and energy throughout the year. Each ritual related to Beltane has common themes: life, beauty, energy, and connecting with nature as deeply as possible. A common misnomer is that this was also the time when love-making hit its peak. But, alas, that would occur later in the year, during the warm summer months, when it was easier to stay out in the darkness and there were more bushes to hide behind.

I used to connect with nature far more often than I do now. Growing up I would mourn a fallen tree, meditate on boulders, swim in the creek and lose myself for a while. Most nights were spent outside, under the stars, contemplating the enormity of it all. Mornings were often passed romping through the woods in my backyard as I noticed the light changing with the rising of the sun.

Adulthood changed much of that. Now, I move so fast and care so much about trivial matters that nature can often feel like a separate entity; something that's *out there*. I'm a professional now: I need to feel, and appear to be, important. To whom? Or for what? The answers to those questions are murky. But deep down there is a drive to be seen, respected, acknowledged for my hard work. And over time that leads to me thinking more about my inbox than the beauty that surrounds me at all times. Stars don't matter. Spreadsheets do.

* * *

This morning, though, I peek through the cracks in that facade. Having found the right pair of underwear, I leave the house with just enough time to arrive at work with my usual punctuality. My boring, obsessive, unnecessary punctuality. As I walk out the door, though, something is different. I remember that it is Beltane. And that, although I do have a fire planned for the evening to celebrate, it would be rude to ignore the beauty all day just for the one scheduled ritual later on. Instead of hustling to my car, I decide to pause and take in my surroundings. It's a perfect morning. Rays of golden sunlight peer through the houses across the street. I follow their paths into my lawn and onto the tops of my feet. My bag drops to the ground. I breathe a deep, satisfying, almost freeing breath.

Without much thought, almost as if moved by the invisible influence of my ancestors (or subconscious, or God, whatever you want to call it), I move forward into the grass and crouch down. From there, I wipe my hands all over the lawn, collecting as much morning dew as possible into my palms. With another deep breath I exhale and cover my face in the dew, making sure each and every part gets washed with precision. "Eternal youth, here I come" I think as the dew tingles my skin. Maybe it's all in my mind, but I feel exceptionally energized and refreshed. Or, maybe, there's something to this ritual. There must be a reason so many people did this for so long.

Before standing back up, my eyes meet one of America's greatest villains:

The dandelion.

There is hardly a more hated plant in the United States than the dandelion. Referred to as a "weed", "pest", "problem", and "propagator", these innocent plants are obsessively exterminated throughout the country for very little reason.

A simple Google search on dandelions results mostly in thousands of articles about how to kill them. Not that they are edible, or that they help pollinators, or that they are pretty to look at. Instead, those looking to learn about dandelions learn only about methods for their global annihilation. Dangerous chemicals that are most certainly harmful to human and animal health spread across lawns where we walk, lay, and play in order to kill a plant deemed a "weed" by . . .well . . .everyone. But who was first? Who convinced us all that this simple flower was worth bathing our properties in murderous substances?

I have let my yard grow a bit natural, so mine is filled with tiny specks of gold. To me the dandelion is beautiful. It provides intrigue and joy in a landscape. They remind me of simpler times when I'd lay in the grass and blow their seeds into the wind to see how far they could carry. They serve as a symbol of the weightlessness that exists within all of us if we could simply drop our baggage for a moment.

Dandelions are miraculous. With the right wind, their seeds can travel over 100 kilometers to explore and lay roots in completely foreign lands. They are an essential food source for pollinators in early Spring which, given the teetering state of pollinator populations, should be enough to justify the flower's survival. Beyond the necessity for our ecosystem and their wondrous wandering abilities, they are downright beautiful. The pops of yellow that occur above fields of green in early Spring can seem like a miracle after months of cold, gray, and ice.

And yet we kill them relentlessly because that is the responsible, adult, suburban thing to do. Is there a better symbol for the loss of childlike innocence and wonder?

Staring at this particular dandelion on my front steps, I remember that it is beautiful. That nature is beautiful. I think of how important it is for nature to be a part of my life, not something separate. It becomes apparent that my job often consumes my state of mind, even when I spent the first moments of the day peacefully watching the sunrise as part of my regular routine. But work, while an important thing, is not *the* only, or most, important thing. Being silly and childlike and whimsical can still be a part of my identity, even as a professional adult trying to "make it" in the world. In fact, "making it" should refer to a life well lived, not a title on a work ID. There is no need to destroy or ignore beauty in the name of success.

Seeking connection, I crouch down and pop the dandelion off its stem. Playing with it in my hands, I look deeply into the complex web of structure that makes up the delicate flower. I remember that all parts of a dandelion are edible, from the leaves to the stem to the flower. Without a second thought, I pop the dandelion into my mouth and begin to chew.

It is now a part of me. Literally.

As I taste the not-quite-bitter yet not-quite-sweet flavor profile, I start laughing. What on Earth am I doing? A grown man doesn't stop in the morning to wash his face with dew and munch on dandelions in the front yard. What if my boss is waiting at the door and asks why I'm late? How would he react to my response: "Sorry, sir. I was eating dandelions"? This is ridiculous!

And that's exactly why it's important.

That first bite of dandelion unlocks a wave of nostalgia in my brain. I remember how it felt to be a goofy little kid, to not care so much about responsibility and mature matters, to live in the moment and act with presence of mind. The crispness of this flower wakes me up more than any alarm or cup of coffee ever could. It's an elixir that puts me into a different and healthier state of mind. Whereas others try their best to destroy the beauty of dandelions because that is simply what adults must do, I chose to rebel and instead made the dandelion a part of me. "Take that, society! I eat your enemy for breakfast. And I love it!"

I finish chewing with a grand smile on my face, then continue on to my car. Driving to work feels different. Lighter. Less of a hassle. More of an activity of choice than a lifestyle of obligation.

I arrived at work two minutes late. The exact amount of time it

Eating Dandelions

took to stare at, and eat, the dandelion. I could not care less.

Now, whenever I am feeling crushed under the weight of adult responsibility, I remind myself to go outside and eat a dandelion. Doing so reconnects me with my inner child, calms me down, and lifts that weight off of my shoulders. It allows me to see the beauty that is around us at all times and to slow down enough to reconnect with it, to make it a part of my experience. And if that makes me late, or irresponsible, then so be it. I am living my life, which is *the* highest priority.

Because when I stand in a field and chew this precious little flower, I am reminded that there are far more important things in life than being important.

Facing My Fears

Looking down, it is clear that a fall from this height will kill me.

I never thought that I would be in this position: suspended on a cliff, my life clinging to a knot of my own making, each digit on my body forcefully pushing on tiny features in the rock face in order to keep me in place. One wrong move and I will slip, my bodyweight pulling full force on the rope, the knot I tied a few minutes before the only thing keeping me from plunging to an untimely, messy, tragic death. My fear of heights is intensifying, and leaves me shaking in a precarious position where shaking is the last thing I need to be doing.

The sun blares on the left side of my body as the waterfall roars in the background, the most immersive song in the soundtrack of the forest. The only other noise in the landscape is my labored breathing, captured solely by my own ears, as all other life in the vicinity is either on the ground far below or gracefully circling in the clear blue sky above, waiting for my demise. A spacious chasm exists between my body and all others. In this vertical space my only company is the ancient, slippery rock that I cling to.

Halfway up the cliff, I am stumped; there is no visible path up the wall from where I am. My left hand pushes down on a tiny ledge the width of my pinky. My right fingers are crunching into a small hole that had formed in the limestone through millions of years of erosion. Below, a little bulge in the wall supports the weight of my right calf, straining with all its might to stay in place. Above my head

Facing My Fears

there is a potential hold for my left hand, one that would ensure a smooth and safe movement to the next phase of the climb. The problem is I can't figure out where to put my left foot. The entire wall in that area is smooth and devoid of any hold that would allow a confident thrust toward the sky. Without securing my left foot, there is no way up.

My heart races, pumping through my ribcage. Sweat pours down my face, fingers shake, muscles ache, the combination of physical exertion and mental panic becomes exhausting. Turkey vultures start to circle above, their silhouettes periodically blocking the sun, their shadows swooping across the cliff and serving as an ominous prediction of what could happen over the next few moments.

After a few minutes of frantically looking around for the next move, the unfortunate reality of the situation is made clear by my friend below, who shouts up his advice on how I can continue forward:

"Trust your left toe. Put all your weight on it and move up. If you do that you can reach the hold with your left hand. Then you're good. Just trust the toe."

Trust it all to my left toe. Sure. Why not?

A deep breath in. A long sigh out. Shift the weight. Move my left knee over the foot. Keep the pressure in my fingers. Rotate my right heel toward the wall. Push down as hard as I can on my left big toe. Create the friction. Stick to the wall. Flex every muscle. Breathe in. Three. Two. One . . .

* * *

At some point we must all face our fears. While our current state of society makes it easy to run, hide, and avoid the less-appealing aspects of life, we do so at our own peril. The strenuous life is one of putting ourselves out there, fighting valiantly, and being someone who is, according to Theodore Roosevelt, "actually doing the deeds". The pride comes from the attempt, not the result. Run and hide from our fears and we become "poor and timid souls", as Roosevelt describes. Face them head on, with our "face marred with blood and sweat and dust", and we become valiant warriors worthy of self-satisfaction. Which is, of course, easier said than done. But doing things the hard way, the slow way, the *strenuous* way, is often more satisfying than the easy, fast, and convenient alternatives.

With that in mind, I must admit:

I am terribly afraid of heights. Always have been. No matter how hard I try, I can't seem to shake it.

Whenever I come up to a ledge, be it in a building or on a mountain, my stomach sinks, my head starts spinning, I gasp, and immediately need to take a few steps backward. In those moments all that pops into my head is how easy it would be to fall and what that experience may feel like.

Falling isn't actually what I fear. Rather, it is the fact that it's so easy to just hop over the rail and fall to my death, leaving everything behind. Honestly there's a small part of me that would find a sense of relief from all the stress and pressure of life. But, thankfully, there's a much larger part that would feel immense sorrow and grief that I'd no longer get to experience all the beauty that life has to offer. Up to this point, the latter part of me has won out every time. And I intend to keep it that way.

Yet the fear of falling remains in spite of all the logical reasons why it shouldn't. I've tried more times than I can count to overcome this fear by facing it head on. I've traversed sketchy bridges, ziplined over mountains and waterfalls, hiked trails where one gross misstep would result in a death-confirming free fall. Heck, I even make sure

Facing My Fears

to look out the window every time I fly. I'm serious about overcoming this.

So far, though, it's all been in vain.

The activity that has gotten me the closest to overcoming this fear is rock climbing. In part because it has helped me work through, and overcome, other fears in my life.

* * *

Back in college I wasn't the social type. I never drank, and I found going out to parties to be both woefully boring and an experience that gripped me with intense anxiety. A typical Friday night usually involved me getting a takeout burrito and cozying up in my apartment (where I lived alone) to start a *Modern Family* marathon before bed (which, I am aware, was also woefully boring). It was not uncommon for me to get home from class on a Friday evening, close my door, and not speak a word out loud until I was back in class on Monday morning. I'm still working out if it that's a badass example of complete self-reliance, or a concerning cry for help that I ignored for years.

Much of that changed one Friday afternoon when my friend Hannah invited me to go climbing at a new spot that had just opened up in town. Going out on a Friday night? I wasn't sure. But the setting of climbing appealed to me more than clubs. "It's super casual," she said, "and it seems more like your vibe." My social anxiety was still sending me signals to go back to my house and enjoy a tasty burrito in the darkness, but I went along anyway and embraced the discomfort.

I arrived a few minutes early to what looked like an abandoned warehouse that hung a homemade sign displaying *THE WALL* above the door. I wasn't sure if this was in the right place. A sketchy warehouse by the river usually isn't the setting for a pleasant and uneventful evening. Maybe this was all a plot to murder me – or worse – to join a cult. Hannah and her group, allegedly, were already inside. Putting my concerns aside, I walked up to the door and opened it, not realizing that my life was about to change with those first steps through the foyer.

As soon as I walked into the building I felt a sense of calm and peace. A feeling that screamed, "Oh yeah . . .*this* is where I belong."

A song from one of my favorite bands, *Sigur Ros*, played as I entered. I gazed up at the climbing wall, then looked around to see nothing but happy, smiling people sitting in thrifted furniture chatting, laughing, and cheering each other on. Homemade granola was being sold for a buck on the counter, and there were a couple dogs hanging out with their owners throughout the place. This was the most comfortable I had ever felt since leaving home, and it happened in an instant.

Within ten minutes I already made new friends and found an activity that would bring me peace and much needed socialization. Climbing, and its people, would help me work through my social anxieties while keeping the TV off and burritos un-purchased on Friday evenings. It became a refuge. An activity I enjoyed, and one I got pretty decent at. The climbing style there was called bouldering. Instead of suspending high-up from a rope, the wall was only a max of ten feet high with a ground covered in thick mats and cushions. So even a gnarly fall from the top would result in laughter, not death. Besides, at this point, talking to people was scarier than heights, anyway.

I formed great relationships with some of the folks there over the following months. Nothing too intimate, but it was a relief seeing more people around campus that I knew and could confidently chat with. Even today, ten years later, I'm still in touch with some of

Facing My Fears

those original folks from The Wall. Silly as it may seem, that first night was a major turning point in my life that I look back on very fondly. I wish I could experience that initial feeling again.

The Wall closed down at the start of my senior year. Not enough memberships were sold. It was a crushing blow, but one that only affected a couple months of my time there.

When I shipped out to New Zealand for the spring semester to student-teach, I found a climbing gym that claimed to have the tallest wall in the country. I made sure to get there. Far away from home, an ocean away from being a continent away, I once again found peace up on a wall where no one could reach me. It was akin to wandering alone in the woods without my phone. I've always loved being unreachable. Even if just for a moment.

Back home there were no climbing gyms, and I wasn't confident enough (and didn't have any partners) to climb outside. This is where the tension existed in my affinity for the activity: I loved climbing and what it did for me, but I was still afraid of heights. This is why I always relied on gyms.

In a climbing gym it's almost zero-risk. There are waivers, safety checks, and corporate responsibility to make sure everything is in safe working order. You're attached to expensive equipment that is completely fail-safe and checked repeatedly for its functionality. If anything appears slightly off, the whole place closes and the equipment gets replaced. In all reality, there is no need to be nervous. I'd get a little skeeved out going really high on indoor walls, but then I'd remember that the gym wouldn't be open if there were any safety hazards. It helped to see dozens of others doing the same thing at the same time, blissfully accepting the guaranteed safety of it all, many of whom were part of birthday celebrations and bachelor parties.

Now contrast that with the thought of climbing outside. Unless I went on a guided trip, all the responsibility for safety would be squarely on the shoulders of me and my partner. No waiver. No team of experts. No frequent safety-checks. Just me, a friend, and our ability to competently provide enough rope for one another and to tie the right knots, in the right way, to prevent us from falling to our death. As someone who struggles with confidence and competence, *that* wasn't solace. That was sheer terror. Hanging from a wall on a knot of my own doing seemed like a reckless amount of confidence for someone who could barely keep my shoes tied throughout the day.

Not climbing outside, though, made me feel like an imposter. Like so many other times in my life, I prevented myself from doing the really hard things for fear of failure. I claimed to climb and enjoy it as a hobby, and yet it was only in manicured settings rather than the "real deal" in the rugged wilderness. I felt like a naive enthusiast as opposed to a competent and confident expert due to my fear of looking incompetent (and in this case, failure resulting in severe injury or possible death). In other words, I felt like a fraud. Or worse: a *poser*.

So when my best friend Troy had learned how to safely and effectively climb outside over the past year, under the guidance of a very experienced group of friends, I wasn't shocked when we were hanging out and he dropped this on me:

"Dude, you should come outdoor climbing with me. I can teach you everything you need to know."

The thought filled me with dread. Troy was arguably the smartest person I knew, but did I still trust that we could escape that perilous situation safely? Sure, he had done it dozens of times before and was perfectly fine. But he's also a biomedical engineer and good with physical directions, puzzles, and Legos. I am none of those things. Would I be able to manage hanging halfway up a giant cliff, knowing that the knot I tied was the only thing between me and an untimely death, devastated wife, and closed-off future, without panicking and making the situation more dangerous? Was I actually capable of learning something I sucked at to the point of risking my life on it? Or was this fear rooted less in the actual climbing, and more in my fear that I *was* a poser, incapable of actually being the person I wanted to be? There was only one way to find out.

"Let's do it. This spring. Teach me everything you know."

* * *

On an icy weekday evening in February I meet Troy at our local climbing gym. As I walk through the door and stare up at the towering walls with people dangling from them in precarious positions, my feelings entering the facility are different than ever before.

When I moved to the area a couple years ago I was both stoked to see there was such a great gym in town and eager to rekindle the sense of comfort that The Wall fostered a decade prior. Gym climbing never worries me. I know it's safe and regulated, so I can focus purely on the climb. It's a freeing feeling to be halfway up a wall knowing that no one can reach me even if they wanted to. Up there, I can't be bothered. It's a feeling that is increasingly difficult to come by these days now that a phone is always in my pocket. Taking a call on a wall, though, is nearly impossible.

"Sorry, can't talk. I'm 30 feet in the air and trying to figure out where to place my big toe." It's the perfect excuse to ignore the outside noise. And in this safe world of corporate-sponsored gym climbing, it's a refuge.

Climbing in this way puts me in a state of flow. First coined by psychologist Mihaly Csikszentmihalyi in the 1970s, *flow* describes a mental state of complete presence and focus where time seems to melt away; a state that could ultimately be a key to long-term happiness. Unlocking this power within our minds can be very impactful. Being in a flow state has been shown in studies to reduce levels of stress and anxiety while increasing feelings of competence, resilience, and (as hard as it may be to describe) overall happiness. Given the power of this state of mind, much writing and research has been completed on the topic over the past generation, including how to create the experience virtually on demand.

According to the research, in order to achieve a flow state, a delicate balance has to be struck in our minds. We must be fully engaged in an intrinsically meaningful task that is at the frontier of our already high abilities in that activity. In other words, when we are engrossed in a challenge that's at the edge of our abilities in an activity that we're already pretty good at, we can achieve this elusive flow state and experience all its powerful benefits. The opportunities here are endless. An activity that generates flow state could be anything from playing a difficult song on the drums, to making defenders miss on the football field, to making the perfect cut in a woodworking project, and (for me) moving your body in the precise manner necessary to move up a climbing wall. These actions, without even realizing it, can put our minds into a state of presence, peace, and happiness. It's one of the reasons why The Wall helped ease my social anxiety: it put me into a state of flow.

Why is that?

Cognitively, flow state is achieved because our brain has labeled a task as meaningful to our well-being, but it is *almost* sure we can complete it. This means that the brain basically tells itself, "Okay, if I can be fully focused on this thing that's really important, then I can probably do it and achieve the positive outcomes that will help my survival." Once that survival mechanism kicks in trivial matters like the weather, that text we just received, or what we're having for dinner don't matter. In order to complete the activity, we must be completely focused on what we're doing and how we're doing it. There's no time or space for our mind to wander aimlessly or to question our methods. We become so consumed by our actions that the rest of the world melts away and the only thing that matters to our brain is the moment. Thus we are put in a state of presence and immersion that doesn't give negative emotions like anxiety or self-doubt space to exist. In a way, it almost sounds like a fleeting state of enlightenment: completely present and mindful without the constant internal monologue disrupting our experience of life as it is.

If a task is too easy then we won't achieve flow; our brain can accomplish it without needing to be fully focused. For example, I can easily flip pancakes while holding a conversation because my brain doesn't see the task as overly challenging. We also will fail to reach a flow state if the task we're engaged in isn't intrinsically motivating or meaningful. A necessary task at work might be difficult and at the edge of our abilities, but if we don't actually care about what we're doing (on, say, a sunny Friday afternoon) then the brain has no incentive to fully focus on it.

Flow also hinges on us already being competent in the activity we're involved in. Playing quarterback is extremely difficult. So, naturally, we can achieve flow state by playing it, right? Not necessarily. If I've never actually played quarterback in a football game, when the time comes to perform I'll have to overthink and analyze every single move and decision that needs to be made because I'm not confident or skilled in my abilities. That's *not* flow.

Our competence has to be at a level where we can perform the motions fluidly without thought *in addition* to the action being difficult. It's not enough for us to do something challenging. We must also know what to do, and how to do it, subconsciously, thanks to hours of practice and internalization. For example, a quarterback doesn't drop back for a pass in the Super Bowl and think, "Okay, I need to shuffle three steps to my left, point my left toe at a 45-degree angle, make sure my left elbow drives back into my hip, and get my follow-through closer to the right side of my body in order to avoid getting hit by the helmet of the defender just to my left so that the ball can drop exactly on the outside shoulder of my receiver forty-yards downfield." Instead, they just *do it*. All of those actions happen without a thought because they can already do those movements naturally. The response is automatic and unanalyzed.

(That description, by the way, refers to a pass completed by New York Giants quarterback Eli Manning in Super Bowl 46, widely considered to be the greatest pure throw in the history of the National Football League. When asked how he pulled it off, Manning said that in those moments you just rely on your training and trust your body. There's no time to think, you just do the thing. The ultimate description of flow and its amazing outcomes).

In modern life it can be hard to reach a state of flow. Our world has become so convenient and frictionless that it's incredibly easy to glide through each day without needing to challenge ourselves or explore the limits of our abilities. We can coast through just fine, and live comfortably, without ever knowing what we're fully capable of. It's easy to go *with* the flow, but that can often prevent us from *experiencing* flow. Instead, we exist in a world where we live cautiously and carefully, afraid to go outside or cross the street. As a result, we submit to a dull existence of couch-sitting and doom scrolling that softens ambition, risk, and resilience – a time speeds by because of it.

One of the reasons I'm so drawn to climbing is because it's one of the quickest ways to put me in a relaxed state of flow. When on the wall, I need to be fully conscious of every movement my body makes, from my left pointer finger all the way down to my right big toe. There's no time to think about anything other than the present moment. And when the flow state really hits mentally I begin to flow physically, too. Up the wall, fluidly, in a way that feels like it's the most natural thing in the world. It's addicting. It wasn't just the comforting social atmosphere that drew me to The Wall all those years ago; it was the realization that, for however long I was on the wall, all of those things in life I was afraid of didn't matter. My internal monologue shut up for once. For a few fleeting moments I wasn't the socially anxious kid with low self-esteem; I was my most authentic self, like a kid who received a makeover in a movie montage.

The same cannot be said about what I am getting myself into. I know nothing about lead belaying on my own (without the warm blanket of a competent employee), so this process most certainly will not put me into a state of flow. Instead, this is a challenging task that exists way beyond my competency and that also risks my survival, which according to Csikszentmihalyi will put me in a state of, literally, "anxiety".

Great.

Instead of confidently going through the motions, I *know* I'll need to overanalyze every step of the process, every movement, every routine. Rather than supporting Troy on his journey up the wall effortlessly, my mind is going to be racing over what to do, when to do it, and how to make it happen in the easiest possible way

Facing My Fears

(and, preferably, without killing my friend). The normal relaxation I feel when safely moving up a wall on a corporate-approved safety device won't be found in this experience. I will have to embrace my insecurities and work through the discomfort until my skills are at a level that makes flow possible. Because an anxious person in charge of a serious task is not the best situation for anyone. Just ask a driver's ed instructor.

Even when my abilities *are* at the level where flow is possible, eventually, will I be able to achieve a flow state when fear is brought into the mix?

At what point does fear overtake presence and confidence? And how will that impact my actions in the moment? Even with all my attempts to quell it, my fear of heights is still very real. I imagine being halfway up the cliff outside, moving through a flow state, when suddenly the fear surges through my body. Can I remain relaxed, focused, and at the edge of my abilities if my flight or fight reflex is pumping through my veins? In reality I *need* to achieve a flow state in both belaying and climbing for this challenge to work out safely; anxiety and fear could lead to devastating mistakes. The only solution, then, must be to embrace the insecurity and discomfort and move through it anyway. I need to expand my comfort-zone mentally and physically to the point where belaying and climbing are no longer terrifying. Through practice and visualization the mechanics will need to become natural so that my focus can be solely on the next move of my body, not the fact that I (or Troy, for that matter) am suspended from a cliff relying on my own competence to get me home for dinner.

* * *

Troy and I stand on the thin carpet in a secluded part of the building beneath a massive wall covered in hand holds. As soon as

Facing My Fears

Troy pulls out his rope to begin my first lesson, my heart drops. In this scenario I won't be able to focus on the mechanics of climbing. Instead, I have to remember, and perform with confidence and fluidity, a laundry list of maneuvers that will be the difference between Troy successfully scaling an impressive cliff and him falling to a horrific injury entirely at my hands. He makes sure to remind me of this reality multiple times.

Our plan is for Troy to lead climb up the cliff, leaving me to belay in order to keep him safe. Lead climbing involves a climber moving up the wall and clipping their rope into carabiners that are placed along the route. If a climber were to fall, assuming their belayer (e.g. me) is competent (a large and ill-advised assumption), they would fall the distance to the last carabiner they clipped into below. Sometimes this is just a few feet. In other cases it can be up to twenty. Regardless, falls can be dangerous if they're not properly belayed or proper technique isn't applied by the climber who is falling. My task will be to give Troy the exact amount of rope he needs for his ascent up the wall, and to be ready to catch him if he falls by pulling the rope in a specific manner while simultaneously jumping forward and running up the wall myself. My plan is, naturally, for Troy to not fall so that I won't need to test my abilities in this area.

Once he reaches the top, he will secure the rope through a series of chains bolted into the cliff face, which then allows me to "top rope" climb; a method of climbing that doesn't involve falls, feels more secure, and is the type I am used to from climbing at the gym. This method of climbing is still dependent on Troy's management of the rope at the top of the cliff and the knot I tie into my harness; another fact that fills me with dread. I am willing to learn how to belay Troy while he lead climbs, but I'm not willing to lead climb myself knowing that a fall could end with me swinging into the wall violently and smashing my face. With a public facing career, and Christmas card photos to take as a newly married couple, I can't risk destroying the money-maker.

"Alright," Troy starts, "so the first thing you need to learn how to do is flake the rope. Which basically means you get it organized and straight so that there are no knots while you are belaying."

I am already lost.

When it comes to kinetic activities, I'm a slow learner. Ask me to memorize something or learn some complex concept and I can figure it out pretty quickly. I'd be happy to tell you all fifty states and their capitals in under sixty seconds or explain to you the complex reasons why societies either thrive or descend into chaos depending on a specific set of factors. But when it comes to manipulating objects, like tying ropes, building something, or wrapping presents, I am admittedly pathetic and useless. Growing up I could never put Legos together. I'd always mess up the directions, get frustrated, and smash them across the table and call it abstract art. If you look closely at any of the IKEA furniture in our home, you'll notice that bookshelf backings are put on backward, shoe racks are precariously balanced in an effort to make up for an early mistake in the directions, and there are always extra screws lying around. When working at a gift shop in college I'd sometimes be asked by customers if I could wrap their purchases. My response was always the same:

"Can I? Yes. Do you want me to? Absolutely not."

Feeling focused and determined, I mimic Troy's motions with empty hands. Troy then hands me the rope to try. Time to shine. I flake the rope with a nervous sense of confidence, and ultimately it turns out okay. I breathe a sigh of relief. Maybe this isn't going to be so bad.

"Alright, that's step one. Now we need to tie off the end of the rope so it doesn't slide through the equipment."

Crap. I guess that was the easy part.

Troy walks me through a series of seemingly innocuous knots that have extreme purposes.

"This knot makes sure, if I fall, that the rope doesn't slide out from you and result in me falling to my death."

"This knot makes sure that I don't lose the harness and free-fall without any protection, probably to my death."

"This one makes sure the rope stays put at the top of the cliff so it doesn't slip and fall while you're climbing up, because then you'd fall to your death."

One-by-one I practice with full attention while masking a deep sense of unease simmering within me. My confidence shakes when I finish a knot and feel proud, but Troy says, "Yeah that's fine . . .for now." Which essentially translates to: *I don't want to discourage you on our first lesson, but if you do that when the time comes our families may want to start brainstorming our obituaries.*

* * *

Once the knots are all tied it's time to practice the actual climbing. Troy hooks himself up to an auto-belay system that allows him to climb safely up the wall without any of my input. If he slips and falls, the auto-belay will catch him and gently guide him down to the gym floor. This gives me an opportunity to practice giving him enough rope, getting my body in the right positions, and catching falls (albeit in slow motion) without any actual danger.

As time goes on I feel more confident in my ability to do the actual belay. I've been giving Troy enough rope, and he is maneuvering up the wall comfortably. When it comes down to the

Facing My Fears

actual climbing, I do pretty darn well. Then, Troy utters the words I was dreading:

"Alright, let's practice a fall."

Troy walks me through the mechanics of what to do if he slips and falls on the wall with the patience of a saint. Now, keep in mind, this could all happen in a split second without any notice whatsoever. So I need to have this maneuver down so comfortably that I can perform it in an instant without having to think about it. Taking too long to process what to do can result in Troy falling a dangerous distance before I catch him.

If you're ever in the position of lead-belaying a friend, here's what catching a fall requires:

First, you need to be focused on the climber. No checking Instagram to see if anyone liked your post about climbing outside, no letting your mind wander about what's for lunch or how long the cliff has been there. Complete focus is paramount.

As soon as you sense that the climber is falling, you need to actually *jump up and into the wall* so the weight on the pulley system catches them before too long. And, while you're jumping, you also need to pull down on the rope as hard as you can with your left hand while simultaneously pulling out and slightly (but not all the way) down with your right hand. In just a split second, if all goes well, you'll end up suspended a few feet in the air, feet on the wall, arms pulling the rope taught. And, presumably, breathing heavy sighs of anxiety about what the hell just went down with some moist pants to boot.

(If you are reading this and happen to be an accomplished lead-belayer, feel free to chuckle with concern at how poorly I described that process. Also, please send your thoughts and prayers).

We practice this over and over on the auto-belay, and each time he ends up stopping above the ground. Crisis averted. Still, though, this is a process that allows me to move slowly, mindfully, and with plenty of time to think about what I am doing. Time that I won't have in a real scenario.

At the end of the session Troy informs me that I have done well. I pass . . .for now. He is also the most blunt of all my friends, so I take this as a sincere compliment. Next, he says, we will continue practicing until I feel confident enough to get lead-belay certified by the staff at the gym. From there, we can practice indoors for real until the time comes to go outside in just a few months.

As I leave the gym I feel a mix of emotions that are foreign to me. To be honest, I am completely out of my comfort zone. Most of my body is warm with feelings of being an imposter, of not actually being competent enough to do this. The consequences of a mistake are not lost on me. On my walk across the deserted parking lot to my car, I deeply question if I am actually an "adventurer", and if I can actually do things this hard. Or if I am just a sheltered and weak man who likes to *think* about doing big, adventurous things, but proves to be too cowardly and incapable when the time to perform arrives. This thought leaves me terribly sad. Is being the person I want to be out of reach? Will I have to accept my role as an adventure-appreciator, never one to accomplish these triumphs on my own? Can I ever be "the man in the arena", as Teddy Roosevelt once put it? Or will I remain, as he described, "a poor and timid soul who knows neither victory nor defeat?" All of this clouds my thinking as I turn the key in the cold ignition.

At the same time, though, I feel a sense of pride and excitement. In spite of all of these doubts, I am doing the thing anyway. Just a few minutes ago I tied the knots even though I was uncertain. I practiced the falls even though I was afraid. I committed to becoming certified even though I was sure I'd be humiliated and told-off by the staff that this was for "real climbers", not weekend warriors who bit off more than they could chew.

I am *in the arena*.

More than anything, though, I feel uncertainty. Actually being able to lead-belay Troy up a cliff is not guaranteed. There will be a point where I have to make a calculated decision on whether or not to move forward with this based on my abilities and confidence level. And it is not 100% assured that I will. Really, it's more like 50-50. And that excites me. It makes me feel alive. It reminds me that life begins at the *end* of my comfort zone, not well within it.

All in all, as I pull onto the main road and make my way home, I feel excited, happy, proud, scared, uncertain, incompetent, foolish, anxious, determined, a bit badass, and a bit wet in the nether regions.

Exactly how I want to feel this year.

* * *

Over the next few weeks Troy and I continue to meet at the gym for practice. And each time my incompetence at remembering physical tasks becomes alarmingly apparent.

The routine goes like this: When starting out, without fail, I forget how to tie a simple knot at the end of the rope. Then my brain freezes when setting up the belay device. My hands consistently find themselves on the wrong ends of the rope. I frequently forget the motion to give Troy the slack he needs, and take out the slack he doesn't. Time after time I become flustered and feel like I am in way over my head. Once we get through the initial jitters I can actually perform fairly well. My belaying improves steadily with each session. We agree that I need a little more practice, head home, and a few days later come back just so I can forget everything I learned the previous session and start all over. Progress is minimal, but it *is*

Facing My Fears

there.

After a month Troy decides I am ready to test for lead-belay certification. Upon hearing this, my palms sweat like a con-man eyeing an undercover officer. This test involves a staff member from the gym analyzing my every move as I work through the entire process of belaying. Everything from flaking the rope to tying the end knot to how much slack Troy has at each stage of the climb will be noted and assessed. The exam ends with a climactic fall from Troy, where it is my job to catch him and prevent his fall from continuing down to the gym floor below, where his previously signed waiver will appear almost immediately after his body makes contact as a reminder from the staff that their hands are clean. To say I am feeling Csikszentmihalyi's diagnosis of "anxious" is an understatement.

On a fateful evening we call over one of the staff members and begin the exam. His presence, while calm, intimidates me. Walking up to the rope that lies along that damned thin foam floor, my mind blanks. For the life of me my brain can't figure out which way the belay device went and how to feed the rope through it. It's a maneuver I have done hundreds of times at this point, and yet my flummoxed mind can't handle this simple task. The evaluator laughs and tells me to just relax. "Get your head on straight, you're fine dude." A nice sentiment. And also easy to say with confidence when you're not the one worried about the livelihood of your friend. I take a moment to look at the chalky plastic holds in front of me, breath, relax, and clip in. It's time to go.

As Troy begins to work his way up the wall by grasping the variety of colorful features, all I can think about is the upcoming fall. Am I prepared to catch him? How is it going to feel on my end to be vaulted up the wall by his momentum? These thoughts swirl through my mind as I crane my neck upward toward the fluorescent lights in the ceiling and do my best to feed him just the right amount of slack. I am anything but relaxed and present throughout the exam. My mind is consumed with the fall, the fall, *the fall*. My slack-giving becomes imperfect as my hands start shaking with nerves. Not exactly a vote of confidence for my abilities.

Before I know it Troy looks down and yells that he is ready for the moment of truth. This is where I have put most of my practice and energy into. I've rehearsed it a thousand times at home in my mind and in my kitchen (much to the amusement of any neighbors peering through our open window). As soon as Troy falls I need to pull down with my left hand, pull out and down with my right, and leap off my left leg up and into the wall to make sure he doesn't swing too fast and slam his feet. I have more faith in this little feat of athleticism than I do with tying knots; leaping is something I can do without much thought.

Looking up at Troy, I tighten my grip on the rope to the point of slight pain along the harsh, neon red fabric. On the count of three, Troy lets go. As he plummets through the air I leap with all my might and pull down on the rope with every ounce of strength I have. My harness shoots up toward the ceiling, pulling me with it part way up the wall in a moment of zero gravity. My feet plant firmly against the vertical surface, with my toes crammed inside my shoes. In less than a second all is still, and I have no idea how it went. I am hoisted against the wall. My pants are dry. Looking up, I can see that Troy is dangling above me. He is alive.

"How'd it feel?" I yelled at him.

"Pretty good! Soft. Nice job." Knowing Troy, he wouldn't lie in this situation. His words of support give me confidence. As far as I can tell, I am going to pass the exam!

I lower myself, then Troy, back to the ground. My hands are still shaking a little bit, and my heart is racing fast. But I did it. Still too pumped with adrenaline to feel any sort of pride, I step back from the wall and adjust my harness to remove the forceful wedgie in my pants. As we begin undoing the rope, I look over at the evaluator to get my feedback.

"Really nice job" he says, smiling. "Good catch on the fall and your technique's alright. You did well. But there are a few things you need to work on and that I'd need to see before I can give you the certification."

My heart sinks. I failed.

Realistically, woe to me for thinking I could pass something so difficult on the first try. Such arrogance I came in with. But in reality this is the greatest blessing I could have received at this time. Failure exposes me. As I feel pangs of embarrassment and shame while scraping the shoes off my feet, I realize that *most* of my life at this point has been set up for me to succeed and that I have been comfortably sheltered from the discomfort of true failure. I am in a healthy relationship. I picked a safe career that I'm good at. I often do workouts I know I can finish. Over the past few years I have kept myself from going on adventures where completion and accomplishment aren't certain. As time goes on, due to my own insecurities and fear of failure, I have essentially created a "failure-proof" bubble around my life. Sure, I always achieve the goals I set. But that's because the goals themselves have a low bar and include little to no risk. It's why failing this exam stings so hard. My heart dips into my chest and I begin to feel horrible about myself. *This* is why I avoid failure: it exposes my deep lack of confidence and self-esteem. It attacks a vision I have of myself as being this confident, competent man with a bit of *savoir-faire* in him. Which is, of course, a facade supported by years of flaky accomplishments that never truly tested me.

While hurtful, this failure is exactly what I need. The truth is this setback doesn't *attack* the vision I have about myself; rather, it *exposes* how flimsy and fake it really is. It brings to light how little I have challenged myself through the years and how my life has become a bubble of carefully curated successes designed to fuel my increasingly fragile ego. This is why I avoid hard projects and strenuous living: I don't *really* want to fail. And now here I am, the first major project that makes me feel like a fish out of water that I have attempted in as long as I could remember, and I am flopping around the floor, suffocating with incompetence. The exam has burst that bubble I blew for myself. There I am, on the gym floor, publicly exposed for the first time. I feel vulnerable, weak, and a bit ashamed. But I also feel free. As if I can see clearly who I am, where I am, and what I need to do to get somewhere new. The chains of my self-constructed prison are shattered.

When jumping into cold water, the anticipation is often the worst part. We fret and fear about how it's going to feel and how uncomfortable it may be. This fear of what *might* happen paralyzes us and keeps us on the deck, high and dry. Once we commit to taking the leap, though, everything changes. We realize that the water isn't that bad. In fact, it's quite invigorating. We feel alive. We laugh and hyperventilate as our body warms up to its new environment. A sense of accomplishment washes over us and we begin to invite others into the water with us. Suddenly, we are experts.

Fear of failure has kept me on the deck of life for far too long. I have accomplished quite a bit in my life, but just about all of it has been safe and almost assured. Taking a leap like this is rarified air. I am now exposed, in the pool, free from my previous inhibitions that kept me from jumping before. Once the initial sense of shame runs its course I actually start to feel a bit giddy. For the first time in years I am truly a novice. I'm not good at this thing. I kind of *suck*, actually. And someone who *is* really good at it just told me that I'm good *enough*. Harsh to hear when you've made a life that reinforces how good you think you are all the time. Which is why it is such a powerful message.

The evaluator gives me a few tips for my next attempt. I'm not far off, he says. I just need more confidence and fluency. It's the same message I receive from another evaluator in my second attempt at certification a couple weeks later. Which, by the way, is another failure.

"Close" he said, "but too rigid. You gotta be fluid, man. Like a dance. Here, let me show you."

In other words: I need *flow*.

I exist as a blank slate. An open-minded student. As the evaluator dances fluently around the belaying area, a true master of his craft, my body mimics what he teaches me and I practice with renewed vigor. Shame evolves into excitement. To think of all the activities I have kept myself from trying, just because they seemed too hard and I was afraid to fail. Heck, even buying potting soil for plants in the house was a struggle because of my worry that I'd do it wrong and kill them off. And here I am *actively failing* for all to see; a public display of embarrassing humility. Instead of crumpling into a ball of self-loathing, my head remains high as I practice the movements with the teacher by my side, albeit far more awkwardly. Suddenly, all of those activities I put off trying seem more enticing – the rationale behind the delays are absurd. I feel like a new man, in a new world, free from inhibitions. I am failing, *sucking*, publicly and visibly. And I love it.

"You got it man! Exactly! You got the movements down. Next time, you're gonna nail it. I gotta teach a class so I can't retest tonight, but find me next time you come in and we'll get you certified. I can sense it."

The confidence from a master is reassuring. The only problem is that Troy and I already scheduled our climb for 48 hours from now, and there is no backing out now. Too much delay and complacency may take over. At this point the climb must be completed *without* official certification or the confirmation from trained experts that I am fully ready to do this.

"You feel okay going outside?" Troy asks as we pack up. I keep my gaze on my handmade backpack that's covered in chalk, unable to look him in the eye.

"Yeah, I feel alright. I got this." I think about asking if *he* is okay climbing outside with me as his belayer. But I hold back. Troy is an honest man, and I'm too afraid to hear what the truth might be.

The resolve is firm: I must go prove myself outside. And I am going to succeed after weeks of failure. No matter what. Troy needs to sense this confidence so he can feel reassured, too.

The commitment stokes feelings of energy and life that have been missing for quite awhile. A fire burns within, churning through my belly. A rebirth is waiting on the bottom of a cliff out there somewhere.

* * *

An intrusive alarm rips me out of my shallow unconsciousness after a pitiful attempt at sleep. All night my dreams focused around one theme: falling and dying. Each psychedelic haze of a scene was more dramatic and disturbing than the last. Upon waking, as if I actually fell asleep, the muscle I pulled in my shoulder the day before begins to ache. The mobility in my arm is incredibly limited, perfectly timed.

Maybe these are signs that I shouldn't go.

But it's too late. In just ninety minutes Troy will be waiting for me at the bottom of a limestone cliff, eager to make his way up. After all the work, the practice, the expanding of my comfort zone, backing out now would be a humongous mark of cowardice. It has to happen.

A bowl of hastily eaten cold oatmeal would be an unsatisfying final meal, which serves as another reason to survive the day's activity. Gab, who is already wary of this entire experience, expresses a comforting calm as I hoist my backpack over my shoulders and grab my car keys. She seems more confident than I am. Maybe she's hiding something because she knows how fragile my ego is at the moment.

"Have fun! You're going to do great. Just let me know how it goes so I know you're okay." Simple words that create a deep sense of assurance. She trusts me. Not just to succeed, but to come home and continue our amazing life together. It isn't just faith in her voice – it's a declaration of necessity on her part. I can't let her down.

My arrival at the trailhead comes a few minutes before Troy's – enough time to sit and soak in the reality of what I'm about to do. Feelings of nerves switch over to excitement on this picturesque spring day in upstate New York. It's a brisk morning, with light fog lifting to reveal a bright, sunny sky above. Clouds of breath are visible in the slightly humid air, as the sun starts piercing its way around the cliffs in the distance. The sky develops into a deep blue with the retreat of the fog, tiny buds appear on every branch in all directions, and the cacophony of birdsong is sublime. Parked on top of the cliffs we'll be climbing, the view in the distance is stunning. An expansive rural valley sweeps across the landscape, punctuated by the small city skyline in the distance and tiny hamlets scattered across the natural playground. It's one of those views that makes you feel infinitely big and microscopically small at the same time – a connection that binds you to the grand scope of life while also reminding you of your insignificance within it.

The silence breaks with the sound of rubber crunching on loose stone. Within a few seconds Troy climbs into my passenger seat and together we eat bagel sandwiches I picked up along the way. Lox on a whole-wheat bagel seemed to be a more satisfying last meal than the bland oatmeal I scarfed down an hour prior.

Our plan is to hike down to the bottom of the cliff, practice on a "warm up" route, and then get to the "real" climbing – routes that will challenge our physical prowess and mental fortitude. Once we reach the climbing area there lies a clear trail to the bottom of the first cliff. We stop and drop our gear in the dirt. I am underprepared, to say the least, carrying a small, overstuffed backpack that holds my climbing shoes, chalk bag, harness, and a day's worth of dried mangoes, cookies, and a few pears. Compared to Troy's haul it is quaint. His pack holds seventy meters worth of rope, dozens of clips and carabiners, a tarp, and a large pole with no discernible purpose. Real equipment for real climbers. If someone came upon the two of us it would be obvious who is more likely to end up on the evening news.

Too nervous to exist in the moment as it is, I numb myself by scrolling through my phone while Troy does the dirty work of setting up. Distraction is what I need in order to keep myself from becoming overwhelmed.

"Alright, it's time." I look up to see Troy holding out the belay device. He's ready to climb, and, like it or not, I have to be ready to help him up there. No turning back now.

Facing My Fears

Centering myself, I begin to take a few slow, deep breaths to calm my mind and remind myself that there is no evaluator here watching me. It's just me and my friend playing in the woods like we have our entire lives. The only difference now is that I need to move some rope in a few different ways. Other than that, everything is the same as it has always been. My feet crunch on the fallen leaves below as Troy walks over confidently with his equipment. This is what true friendship requires: trust for each other's lives.

After inserting the rope into the belay device and pulling out some slack, Troy rechecks my work as well as my harness and body position at the base of the wall.

"All set," he says with confidence, "so once I get up there I'll hook into the pig-tails (hooks attached to the end of chains that were bolted into the top of the wall) then you can belay me down. From there you'll tie in and then it'll be top-rope. Just like the gym."

This, clearly, is *not* just like the gym. The stakes are higher, the wall taller, the routes more difficult, the consequences more grotesque. But that isn't the entire picture. It's also far more beautiful and peaceful on this little plot of land tucked away in a forgotten corner of the world. There is no music blaring here, no waiting to get to a route, no shirtless dudes loudly showing off to the crowds below. Here lies a serenity that cannot be replicated inside a warehouse. Instead, the rock in my vision, and the landscape as a whole, took millions of years to slowly develop the majesty it emits. And here we are, ready to move with the landscape that was so carefully carved out, taking what it gives us and understanding with humility when our agency as humans will be no match for the natural landscape. In this spot we are not tourists or observers. We are *part* of the environment, inextricably one with all around us.

This recognition keeps me calm, focused, and confident. I am in my element, in *the* elements, and there is no reason to be afraid. It's time to play.

Troy's first few moves up the wall are complimented by my smooth movements on the belay below. While not perfect, it's my best performance up to that point. For the first three clips I provide the right amount of rope, not too much or not too little. Toward the top, though, things become complicated. The rope somehow tangles around my feet for a moment as a result of focusing too much on my hand movements. Swiftly I sidestep the pile while Troy tries to get the rope into the final clip. This mistake leaves him a bit short on rope, a definite annoyance for the climber, but not a grave mistake. Poor timing on the part of a rookie, something to be expected in this environment. When Troy hooks the rope through the pigtails and tells me to "take" (meaning to take all the slack out of the rope so he can safely repel) I breathe a sigh of relief. He has made it up the wall, alive and well. I didn't kill my friend. Maybe I am alright at this thing after all.

Troy unhooks from his rope, undoes the knot, and hands me the flaccid end:

"Alright . . .your turn."

Slowly I gather myself, breathing deep, doing my best to remain present. Remembering my training, I carefully tie the knot through my harness and tighten it as much as possible. Troy looks on as the inspector. After fumbling around with shaky hands, the knot is ready for inspection.

"How's this?" I ask.

"It's fine," he says.

That's not good enough.

"I don't want fine," I explain, "I need perfect for this."

Together we retie the knot as Troy directs my every move from

Facing My Fears

over my shoulder. Twist the rope twice. Take the end and feed it through the loop. Now feed it through both hooks on my belay. Follow it around the first knot, weaving it through, keeping it tight and to the outside. Pull it taught. Now add another brake knot on top of extra security. Tighten and sit back.

"There you go," says Troy. "Your best one yet."

I stare down at my creation. *Does my life really depend on this thing? Can I really trust it?*

Troy works himself onto belay and gives me the go ahead to begin. My hands and feet caress tiny features on the wall in order to propel my body skyward—all it takes is a moment of courage to begin the movements. The rock is cold, still shaded from the low angle of the early morning sun. My breath condenses quickly on its surface, providing moisture on an otherwise dry slab of Earth. After a few feet up, where a fall would only hurt my pride, I sit back and let go of the rock in order to test the rope. While leaning into my harness and swinging away the rope pulls tighter and tries to unravel, but the knot remains unmoved. There isn't a single sign of frailty or failure.

If it can hold my weight eighteen inches off the ground, it will hold it with fifty feet of air beneath me. There is no difference.

The little experiment boosts my confidence enough to continue working my way up with a bit of gusto. Technically it's an easy climb, hence the name "Warm Up", with many large hand holds and full ledges to place my feet. The route requires working my way up a crack feature on the left side, standing on a large ledge, and then maneuvering my way back to the right for the final few moves in order to officially finish the route. I make it up to the ledge with ease and take a moment to catch my breath. My body trembles with nerves and adrenaline. Looking up at the wall, it's unclear how to maneuver in order to reach the top. From this point there are no good, solid holds – just little bumps and cracks that can barely be held. The trembling increases as my awareness vignettes into a tunnel. This is the *real* test, with a real chance at falling and testing the knot in a less controlled manner. I am high off the ground, too high to be honest. My heart races. Troy attempts to give me advice from below, but when the brain is being captained by the amygdala technical advice does not translate. One sentence from Troy, though, makes it through the internal screaming:

"You just gotta trust your feet."

Looking up, I grab a protruding rock on the left side of the ledge. Then my left knee comes all the way up to my armpit, resting on the one decent spot to place a couple of toes. From there my body propels itself upward, hoping to find something, *anything*, on the right side that can keep it stable. Luckily there is a knob that holds three of my right fingers and, in desperation, I smash my right foot against the wall thinking that the friction will keep it in place. A primal yell powers through my lungs as I make the move, echoing down the cavernous mountains to the river valley below. My fingers stay in place, as do my feet. I have reached the top. It's done.

"Great!" I can sense Troy's excitement at my finishing. "Just lean back and I'll let you down."

Panting (from nerves, not exhaustion), I let go and am gracefully lowered back down to Earth. Almost like returning to the start of an amusement park ride, it's a calming descent after an exhilarating moment. Still shaking, a sense of freedom washes over me. Scared, proud, relieved, and electrically charged, I am *alive*.

"How do you feel?" Troy asks once my feet hit the dirt.

"A lot of things," I respond, "but overall good. I feel like the seal has been broken; like the mental block no longer exists."

Facing My Fears

Troy responds with a monotone bluntness:

"That's good. Because now we can start the *real* stuff."

We pack up our gear and head further into the forest on a narrow trail anchored on one side by the cliffs and the other by a sheer drop into the valley. A simple misstep would send small rocks plummeting into the bowl below, a not-so-gentle reminder to stay steady and to be mindful of each movement. Upon reaching the next wall I recognize what Troy meant about the "real stuff". This cliff, compared to the "Warmup", is taller, grittier, and flatter. There are barely any holds I can make out no matter how much I squint. To my untrained eyes it just looks like a sheer, flat wall of limestone that is near impossible to traverse up. Not only is the wall itself intimidating, but the climbing area is tiny. At the base of where we begin are some mangled trees and, of course, the drop-off into the abyss below. Plenty of chances to fall, smack the head, crack the spine, and become the latest prey to this looming, intimidating, brutal feature that does not care whether we live or die.

Once again, Troy needs to lead his way up the wall first in order to set up the top rope that I'll be climbing on. Unlike the "Warmup", which he breezed up without any issue, this route is a puzzle. Oddly enough, belaying him does not spark any jitters. A serene confidence takes hold as I anticipate each of his moves and dance on the dirt below, just like my instructor taught me. As someone in need of constant validation, I wish the instructor was here to see my progress and hype me up during Troy's long, difficult climb, and to assure me that I am in fact doing well. But that's impossible. I'll have to settle for just the two of us existing quietly in this primal space.

At one point Troy needs a break – this has never happened before. When he sits back into his harness and separates his tight grip from the wall, a wrong move on my end could send him hurtling downward and smashing into the overhanging rocks that litter the route. In order to keep him in place I move back as far as I can, my heels gracing the edge of the trail and the drop-off below, and sit back into my harness while pulling down as hard as possible on the rope. This counterweight keeps Troy in place, hovering thirty feet above me. I begin to chuckle. There are good reasons to be scared and worried, sure. In this moment, though, those feelings are carried away by a flash flood of serenity. Here we are, in the woods, Troy literally dangling like a toy on the end of a string. The waterfall continues to roar in the background as more birds stir and add their symphony to the soundscape. Ravens and turkey vultures compete for coveted territory in the air above, while a spunky red squirrel rummages for forgotten acorns on the Earth below. *This* is a peace that can only be found at the edge of my comfort zone.

Troy eventually makes it to the top of the wall, but he faces a tricky repel down. I have to lower him as slowly as possible in order for him to avoid all the obstacles in our area. Thankfully the repel is a success, and Troy returns to the ground with all bones, joints, and limbs in place. Once again it's my turn to climb, but this time on a more serious route. There is a high chance that, at some point, I could slip and aggressively force all my weight onto my knot. There's an even *higher* chance that I won't actually be able to finish the route. And, if I'm lucky enough to make it above the tree line like the route requires, there is almost a guarantee that my fear of heights will kick-in and I'll need to gather myself on the wall.

This is the true test.

I'm just playing, I remind myself. *Just playing . . .*

The climb is difficult. While there *are* places to grip and maneuver myself on, they are microscopic. Looking down at my feet

I don't think they are actually ever *on* a hold. Instead they are smeared against the wall, relying on friction to stay in place. The tiniest little bumps in the cliff hold the pressure of my big toe and my thumb. I splay my upper body out wide, keeping my chest and elbows pinned to the rock face in order to garner some sense of support and stability. Each movement is a calculated endeavor.

About a third of the way up the pressure in my toe gives way. My left toe slips off the wall and dangles in the ether below. Luckily my hands are in secure positions and hold in place despite the slip, preventing both a full fall and swinging like a trapeze artist above the trees. I gasp, then begin hyperventilating for a moment. With great care I place my toe back where it was before, but in a slightly different position to provide more stability.

And then it hits me.

I just came face-to-face with my greatest fear: slipping and falling off the cliff. I felt the intoxicating surge of adrenaline that assaulted my entire being in less than a second when that toe momentarily lost its place. My fears of falling and dying rushed through my mind at hyper-speed and stopped abruptly by the time of my next inhale. And, in spite all of that, there is a truth that can't be ignored:

I am okay.

Suddenly, my fear of falling vaporizes. No longer am I at the edge of my comfort zone. Instead, I have burst right through it and am now exploring a new frontier of possibility. The limits I placed on myself for so long are now shattered, with the rare opportunity to place new ones further out into the experience of life.

Before moving again I take a few deep breaths to let the adrenaline waft away like candle smoke. After the hormonal shower passes, feelings of presence begin bubbling up. Feeling calmer than anticipated, I do the one thing I said I wouldn't: look back and down at the world around me. Turning my head, I see my entire home area encased by various mountain ranges. And here I am clinging to a wall, hidden in the landscape that I call home. There is no longer any separation between the landscape and body. We are one. Thoughts slip away with each passing moment that the vast landscape meets my gaze. Egotistical worries about how I look or whether I am competent are nowhere to be found. Fears, so paralyzing for so long, shatter.

I enter *flow*.

From that spot I maneuver up the wall with effort and mindfulness. There is no more thinking or worrying about the possibilities – just pure, human movement from here on out. Raise the right hand, shift the angle of my left thumb, raise the leg up to my elbow, turn the foot 90 degrees, shift the weight, and push. Grab with the right hand. Smooth, steady, thoughtless. But wholly mindful.

At the top of the route there is a large ledge that provides plenty of standing space. I hoist myself up, get my bearings, and raise my arms in triumph. A warm sunbeam meets my ear-to-ear smile which leaves me tingling with the buzz that comes from drinking the sweet nectar of life. From below, I hear Troy yell his request which echoed its way up to me:

"Ready to come down?"

"Not yet!" I shout back. "I'm going to reward myself for a second."

Endorphins pour over me on top of the ledge as my eyes bulge at the enormity of it all. Peace swells within amidst an acceptance of the sights and sounds beyond. Not a thought enters my mind for a few moments in a rare experience of immersive presence. I am on

Facing My Fears

top of the world, in some senses literally, which fills me with pride. The heights we can reach when we're willing to expand the frontiers of our comfort zone are intoxicating.

Eventually I agree to be lowered down. While making my descent, I stare intently at the knot tied in front of me and smile.

My best one yet.

* * *

I came into this experience to face a complex web of fears that weaved together personal insecurities and external anxieties. To come face-to-face with inner demons and notions of incompetence. To feel fully alive in spite of how dreadfully uncomfortable that can be physically, mentally, and emotionally. To do something incredibly difficult that I didn't think I was capable of doing, something that *needed* to be a complete success or it would not have happened at all.

At the end of the day the activity itself was meaningless. I climbed up some rocks with my friend. I didn't help someone in an emergency, change someone's life, or make the world any better for having done it. I was, as French climbing legend Lionel Terray would say, a "conqueror of the useless". But that doesn't mean the experience wasn't worthwhile.

Like many things in life I could have kept this easy and comfortable. I could have just stuck to the gym, climbing progressively harder routes, but never really shattering the frontier of my comfort zone. It would have been easy to say, "Outdoor climbing sounds fun, but *I'll* never be able to do that." It would have been convenient to go on a guided trip where I didn't have to develop any skills or do any of the work myself. It would have been frictionless to sit at home and wonder "what if" while strengthening a sense of mediocrity.

Facing My Fears

Each of those actions would have led to a more hollow, less fulfilling existence. With any activity we strive to do, whether it's climbing, hiking, writing, painting, or playing an instrument, being a "poser" is a very real and devastating reality. But it becomes worse when we don't do anything about it. That identity is planted when we say we'd like to do something but never actually do it. It grows when we eschew opportunities to just give the thing, whatever it is, a try. It's watered every time we say, "That's too hard", or "I'm too tired", or "I'll wait for the right opportunity". And it flowers when we lose the resolve to ever bother trying after so many years of growing comfortable with our inaction. So much of our life is wasted wishing we could do something or be somebody when the opportunity to begin is always available to us, right now, if we are willing to take that courageous first step.

Instead of resting in my comfortable, frictionless incompetence, I did the hard thing. I pushed my comfort zone mentally, physically, and emotionally while taking the route of greatest friction. And in the heat it generated I lost myself: my sense of self-importance, a bit of my ego, and the feelings of shame that came with failing over and over. On top of that mountain I can honestly say I was fully, ecstatically *alive*; charged with the immense energy and joy that is available to us in any moment we'd like to tap into it. All we have to do is venture to, and through, our edge.

Fear and insecurity still persists within me, of course. Feelings of confidence and competence are fleeting. But now I have a different point of reference to think back to when those feelings of insecurity, anxiety, and ego arise. No longer do I just look back on that first evening at The Wall when I cautiously ventured through the doors to a new life and sense of self. Now I can look back in my mind's eye on that stunning view, kept to myself, heightened by my exhaustion and adrenaline and pride, coupled with a healthy bit of heavy breathing and an immersive state of flow. And in that memory I find confidence, I find peace, I find a deeper belief in what I'm capable of. It's a reminder that my limits have shifted outward, and that they can continue as long as I'm willing to take the more difficult road less traveled.

We need more challenges like this. We need to confront our fears instead of hiding from them. We live in a world where we can essentially go our whole lives without putting ourselves in these types of challenging situations that force confrontation with the raw reality of our state of being. We can appear super confident on social media without actually knowing what we're doing. We can hide behind a screen and text messages instead of being vulnerable face-to-face with another human. We can take the path of least resistance and never know "what could have been" because we were too afraid to bet on ourselves or our idea. We can settle, rather comfortably, and live out our lives as what Teddy Roosevelt described as a "timid soul who knows neither victory nor defeat".

Whether it's as simple as asking for a promotion or as intense as facing those situations that make us freeze, hold our breath, and paralyze us with intense dread, in order to live fully we must find the edge of our bubble in an experience that demands an appreciation of its beauty, and get to the other side. No matter what.

Lest we forget, life takes place *in* the arena.

Off the Wagon

We are currently in the middle of another uncharacteristic heat wave. Our temperatures have been the warmest on record just about every day, and I'm baking in the humid morning air as the sun beats down on my back as if I'm lying on a bed of coals. Standing in a little path I raked out in my backyard, I stare up at the fractals of leaves scattered above me from the dozens of oak and maple trees that line my property. They are dark green, illuminated in the warm glow of the first sunrise of summer.

The past month since my climbing experience has not been my best in terms of slow and strenuous living. While my climbing adventure was a huge win, I have lost focus since then. Sometimes the circumstances of being a married man with a full-time job and family obligations overtook my planned strenuous experiences. Other times it was the weather that foiled my ideas. More than anything, this past month it has been my own laziness that has gotten me off track.

Whereas the first part of the year I was on a roll with my slow and strenuous experiment, May into June has been a different story. Mindless scrolling pulled me back in like the lure of a sketchy used car salesman with cheap cologne. My sunrise routine has ended for the time being in favor of more frantic mornings. I ate all the dandelions in my yard. Ideas I developed to push my boundaries have been put off and delayed again and again, often with some pretty lame excuses, leading to a weaker body and softer mind. My hopes were to have a cookout and bonfire tonight to celebrate the solstice. But work "got in the way" again and now my only plan is to sit out here and feel the sun on my back. I haven't been living out Nanny's wisdom lately. And I'm feeling it.

The difference in my mental disposition is marked. In the Spring, committed to this new lifestyle, I felt like I had discovered the buried treasure of good living. My mind was more focused. My emotions were calmer. My body was stronger. Overall, even in those few short months, the best version of myself was being forged out of the stone.

Now, though, these past few weeks have taken their toll. My laziness in terms of routines, challenges, and rituals has led to a noticeable difference in my disposition. I am more anxious again. My mind is harder to tame. I have been seeing my friends less often and feel less connected to the world outside my inbox. The past six weeks have flown by quicker than the start of the year, which terrifies me. This is discouraging, since I made so much progress early on. But it is also a powerful realization.

In just a few short months of slow and strenuous living I can already feel dramatic, positive changes taking shape within me. When I *was* on track, time slowed down. Hours stretched into days as the little nuances of the natural world around me became more apparent. Weeknights were filled with warm memories of friends around a fire or dinner table. Previously normal workweeks became memorable instead of blending together. Little inconveniences did not matter as much. Long lines, traffic, and being put on hold with a bank for forty minutes were no longer big deals. I found joy in the little things, constantly mindful of my experience. Presence, a fickle state I could never quite court, was coming around more and more frequently without even noticing.

The difference between those first few months and the

previous six weeks is dramatic, and gets me thinking: *This really works.* Slowing down, disconnecting, and engaging in immersive activities really has changed me for the better. And in a comparatively short time. That is, when I do it.

It hasn't been easy to maintain, hence my slide back into laziness, but it also isn't impossible. It just takes a concerted effort to keep up with the rituals, routines, and experiments, *especially* when all I want to do is plop on the couch and zone out for hours at a time. Maybe the past few weeks haven't been a wasted opportunity. Perhaps having life speed up again due to my lack of discipline is the exact thing that needed to happen. Would this change be noticed without the contrast?

As I breathe deeply, in and out, I remember that this is the longest day of the year. The day when the sun is strongest and light makes its final triumph over the dark. It certainly hasn't seemed like it, but every single day for the past six months has gotten a little bit lighter. Now, bit by bit, we will slowly descend back into the darkness. Every year this makes me sad, even with a full summer ahead. The end is in sight. Even though there is a summer of long nights, lake days, bonfires, and grilling ahead of me, the crushing reality that it will be cold and dark and gloomy again is disturbing. All the more reason to double down and appreciate the state of the world right now.

On this, the brightest day, I should be determined to shine my brightest. In the Spring the seeds of my best self were planted into fertile soil. And buds have certainly bloomed. Now, with the long days and powerful sun, I should be like the Earth around me and use this beautiful time of year to my advantage. Like the tiger lilies at my feet, I need to soak in as much natural energy as possible to burst into the fullest expression of myself. *This* is the time to grow, from here on out, so I can enter the next dark period with as much internal light as possible.

My eyes close. The sun continues to creep over the house and warm my bare skin. Its power, its presence, is felt. Silently, I thank it for its return and the effort it took to get back to this point in the sky, so high above. I understand that, at its peak, it will need to coast through the rest of the year. Its energy is here for me, for all of life, right now. It is doing its part. Now it's up to me to do mine.

* * *

Twenty-four hours later I am sitting on my deck in the darkness, the only light coming from the twinkling stars above and the orchestra of fireflies dancing in the yard. The Earth is alive and exploding with energy. Between the stars and the fireflies there is no need for manmade light to appreciate the warm, serene evening. Nature, thankfully, has taken the reins.

Under this Strawberry Moon I mindfully savor a large, juicy strawberry to celebrate. Given the darkness and stillness this evening, I'm inspired to really focus on one particular strawberry. It is ruby red and explodes with sweet juice the second my teeth bite into it. But not too sweet – the perfect balance of flavor and sugar and the sweet nostalgia of summer nights. It may in fact be the most delicious, incredible strawberry I have ever eaten. Or, it may just be the first one I have paid attention to in a long time. So much of what I eat gets inhaled while holding a conversation or watching TV. This little strawberry helps me realize how little I actually pay detailed attention to my food. Food, despite its importance, is an afterthought. Usually, I have no clue where the nourishment I receive comes from, who grew it, what its journey was between planting and my palette. I do know where this berry came from: the market down the road, whose farm is just a few miles to the west. Months ago I planted my own strawberries in hopes of enjoying them this evening, but they unfortunately succumbed to some type of fungus and died unceremoniously. If only I knew where all my food came from and could shake the hands that feed me. What a powerful experience that would be.

The enjoyment of this precious moment comes from the months of discipline I have built to this point. Having let things slide for a time, I now recognize the beauty and importance of these often overlooked opportunities in our lives. I have a front seat to a cosmic orchestra. A stunning display of life and energy – an ephemeral moment that is a great fortune to see, process, and be present for. How many similar moments have I missed in my life because I wasn't paying attention? Those moments will never return. But there will be more. How many? I can never know.

This is all happening on the second shortest night of the year, which makes its fleeting nature all the more prevalent. The beauty of the moment, without warning, teleports me to the memory of Nanny's last words. Suddenly I am back in my apartment, tears welling, Gab by my side. Nanny is on the screen in front of me, fading in and out of consciousness. Even with what little she has left, she still appears to be making the most of the life within her. She flashes that smile that always brought a sense of comfort and a knowing that I was loved.

"You have such a beautiful life. Enjoy every moment."

I am enjoying this moment, Nanny. I am loving every second of it. And I am here for it. All of it. Every star and firefly and tree and blade of grass and breath of fresh, warm summer air that fills my body with a buzzing energy that reminds me of how alive I am. It is beautiful, Nanny, and I promise I am enjoying it.

As my throat catches the emotions rising up through my body, what I must do to make the most of the time I have left this year becomes clear. I must enjoy every moment of precious sunshine that exists now and that I yearned for just a few months ago. I need to shatter my comfort zone and break out of my mental rut with an experience that may not be wise, but that could certainly be one I remember forever. I need to break out of the comfortable malaise I slipped into with work as an excuse; to commit to something brutal. Something that will require all the energy and vitality that has been building inside me. A challenge that will allow me to shine brightly. One that puts me in the arena, living the strenuous life.

Without a second thought I pull out my phone and call Troy.

"Troy, it's time. This weekend. I'm tired of putting it off. Let's send it."

A Little Farther

It doesn't matter how beautiful the scenery is around me. The reality is that I am scared, in over my head, and want to quit.

Looking up I see that the sun is slowly fading behind increasing, ominous-looking clouds. I am drenched in sweat, my teal sun hoodie soaking with the effects of my effort. My blue Yosemite hat is covered in white patches of bug spray, but provides me no defense against the black flies constantly swirling around my body and nipping at my ears like flying razor blades. Every part of me hurts and wants just one simple thing: to stop moving. All of my toes are in pain, in particular the right big toe after two miles of jamming into the front of my shoe while sliding down slippery rocks. The outside of my right knee is flaring up again, making the most natural human movement of walking feel like torture. My shoulders ache from carrying my pack, which feels like it is being filled with rocks with each passing step. My face is so sweaty that my "no slide" sunglasses keep sliding off in spite of the company's guarantee to the contrary. Maybe there's a return policy.

Surrounded by pine trees wafting the comforting scent of Christmas toward me, I stop. The mountain's enormity begins to overwhelm me. Here I am, this infinitely small speck plopped on the side of an ancient mountain that, millions of years ago, was as tall as the Himalayas. This thing has existed long before I was born and will continue to persevere long after I am gone. In the timescale of this mountain, I am nothing. Barely a blink. I am just a tiny, quivering mammal who is hungry, thirsty, in pain, and completely

A Little Farther

lacking control in this situation.

I stop and try to gather myself. The wind begins to howl, almost blowing the hat right off my head and over the ledge that leads into the abyss. Troy is about two minutes behind me, meaning I have just enough time to calm down and hide my serious doubts about what we are doing. Tears begin to well. I realize that the section we just went through on this hike would be *really* sketchy to try and retrace if we wanted to bail. The rock is too steep and too slippery. The clouds thicken and the wind strengthens, as if to remind me once more of how little control I have in this situation. I am miles from civilization and cell service. We haven't seen anyone else on this isolated trail. We are alone. I have just enough food to last an expedition that goes perfectly, but nothing more for a worst-case scenario. Same goes for the water that sits in my overheated rubber bladder with a chewed up, moldy hose to drink through. I hang my head with the realization that there is no other option:

We must continue forward, because there is no way out.

All I can hope is that, like every other time in my life, my dad is right. Somehow he always is, and I am fully banking on that trend continuing today. Because it is his fault that I am here, and it will hopefully be his wisdom that guides me through to the promised fulfillment ahead.

* * *

Chances are, you are reading this while sitting on some type of comfortable cushion. I am willing to bet that your lower back muscles or hamstrings are not engaged in order to keep you upright and that your breathing is currently shallow and haphazard. Your shoulders are probably slumping forward (although now you may have just rolled them back) and you are, presumably, protected from the elements inside a comfortable, temperature-controlled building.

You may even have a crisp, refreshing drink by your side to sip on while you contemplate these words.

Our society is an absolute marvel of convenience and luxury. And that is becoming a big problem.

Humans in industrial societies are now able to get far more with far less effort than ever before. The world has turned into a bastion of convenience in every possible way, allowing us to live fruitful and fulfilling lives without needing to exert much effort. From remote controls to smartphones to car-centric town design, it is entirely possible to wake up, go to work, come home, eat thousands of calories, and go to sleep without so much as raising our heart rate or breaking a sweat.

In the moment this type of convenience feels great. I personally love the fact that I can watch endless shows on my TV without having to get up and move. Or that I can make a comfortable living by sitting throughout most of the day. I don't think we should reject all of these modern marvels and go back to the Stone Age. But the merchants behind these products and programs that keep us sedentary love that we love them – it's what keeps them in business. So, the less we move and the more we consume, the better off they are. Which is why they are designed to allow us to easily slip into these comfortable routines of lazy consumption. They have become a trap that we are all susceptible to.

While the powers that be may be better off financially with our *Wall-E*-like presence, we are far *worse* off because of it. Convenience in everyday life is helpful and, in many ways, enhances our experience. But too much of it and we start to wither away physically and mentally. When the balance swings too far in the other direction we become weak, soft, and unable to muster up the gumption to challenge ourselves in any meaningful way. Our lack of physical exertion, and the mental fortitude that develops, is resulting in harmful consequences for individuals and society alike. A life that is too convenient results in some inconvenient realities.

This reliance on ease and comfort explains, in part at least, why obesity rates are skyrocketing in the West as activity rates plummet. The average hunter-gatherer averages close to 20,000 steps per day. The average American achieves a whopping 4,000, or roughly a quarter of that, all while eating an unbelievable 3,500 calories per day. Maybe if we were getting those steps in, or running marathons, then such a high calorie count would make sense. But activity is hard and takes away from Netflix's view time, so we are aggressively encouraged to stay on the couch, inside, and consume instead of getting the free exercise. This results in those excess calories being converted to fat which, in a pernicious feedback loop, makes it harder to get up and get active. Resulting in a downward spiral that is very difficult to break free from.

This makes sense. Evolutionarily our bodies do their best to conserve energy whenever possible. Needlessly wasting energy could have disastrous consequences when food is scarce. But food is no longer scarce (in the sense of having to forage or hunt for our next meal). And the opportunities to get energy are abundant. Therefore, if anything, we should be more active and fit than ever before given that we have greater access to replenish those lost calories. Fighting evolutionary psychology, though, proves to be difficult enough on its own. Factor in the social structures we have created, which require (or at least strongly encourage) us to sit in front of screens for most of our waking hours, and the task can seem almost impossible without concerted, conscious effort.

The issue is that this slip into comfortable complacency makes us both unfit and unwell. It's no surprise that preventable diseases of abundance, like Type 2 diabetes, are skyrocketing at the same time that our activity levels are dropping. We are in an evolutionary mismatch: our bodies are made to move, eat real food, and experience environmental stressors that make us tougher and more resilient. All but eliminating those needs, while adding their polar opposites in abundance, is a recipe for the health disaster we are seeing. When an increased heart rate becomes an inconvenience, when activity falls by the wayside because we don't want to sweat, our bodies suffer immensely. And it goes a long way toward explaining what my CrossFit coach describes as the "embarrassing state of the American body."

The physical fragility developed by our frictionless existence creates mental fragility as well. When we are *always* comfortable, we are far more likely to be *uncomfortable* whenever environmental factors move outside our preferred settings. Take the temperature of our environment, for example. It is very possible to go through a whole day in the dead of winter completely in a temperature zone of sixty-eight to seventy degrees. This is unnatural, of course, but when we merely go from house to car to work to car to store to car to house, it's the most likely scenario for many Americans. When we get *too* comfortable with these temperatures, we begin to expect them at all times. So, sure, we are comfortable throughout the day in our manicured, artificial environment. But what happens when we step outside and feel the fierce, cold, biting winter wind? We tense up, shiver, and realize we are woefully unprepared for the reality of life on Earth. We can't deal with such a wild swing outside of our temperature zone, and so we further resolve to never interact with the environment as long as we can help it. We are only comfortable in an unrealistically narrow range of existence, and haven't built up the resilience to not be bothered by any experience outside that zone.

We are more uncomfortable than if we built up the resilience to deal with different temperatures; every fluctuation becomes an irritation.

At that point the discomfort is entirely mental. Our body is capable of so many incredible things and adapts to a wide range of environments. To think a human body that evolved to run for miles in the tropical heat and hunt down large prey suddenly, in an evolutionary blink of an eye, couldn't possibly walk a mile or two to the convenience store is absurd. We have the physical capability. It is the *mental* toughness, grit, resilience, that is the barrier. A weak body supports a weak mind, and vice versa.

It's not like we have to *love* being uncomfortable or finding ourselves in less-than-ideal environments. It's that we have to just *deal with it* when we do find ourselves there. I've always loved being outdoors, but Gab struggles mightily dealing with the bugs at certain times of year (to the point where she'd rather stay inside than go out at all). At one point she asked me why I like being out with bugs so much. My answer was that, no, I don't like bugs. They suck. I wish they'd all go away and never come back, ecology be damned. But after dealing with them so much throughout my entire life they just don't bother me much anymore. And certainly not enough to prevent me from doing the things I love outside. After a while, we build a mental armor to deal with the nuisances, the inconveniences, the little pains of life. We notice them, sure, but they don't pull us off track. So even if it's hot, cold, buggy, or muggy, we can enjoy ourselves and continue to have a good time. We don't crumble at the first sign of discomfort. Which means we can have more interesting and fulfilling experiences.

The more we expose ourselves to being uncomfortable, the more comfortable we become.

I have noticed this lack of grit and resilience becoming more prevalent online, too. Log onto Facebook for just a moment and you'll be flooded with examples of folks with nothing better to do but complain about the most asinine things imaginable. Rather than taking these little inconveniences in stride as someone with a deliberately developed mental toughness would do, the average user is so *incensed* by whatever misfortune has been bestowed upon them that they must alert the masses to the injustice. The world *must know* that the waiter wasn't exceptionally polite, or that the person at the intersection didn't follow the rules of a four-way stop, or that a doctor's office should never be running even a moment late. Because *they* are important and should never be slighted or inconvenienced. When our whole day is catered to *our* needs, *our* preferences, *our* experience, it is easy to forget that we are just a small part in, as Carl Sagan described it, "a vast, cosmic arena." Our sense of self inflates as we get used to getting what we want. And, when we don't, we become so frustrated and distraught that the world apparently needs to know about it. In the end, it is all a desperate call for validation of victimhood in order to sustain a fragile and false sense of self-righteousness brought on by an excessively convenient and comfortable existence that breeds entitlement.

As a history teacher, one of my favorite sayings is: "While it may be bad right now, it was *always* worse before." In other words, people were much tougher in previous generations than we are today. I love learning about the incredible feats of physical and mental toughness that those who came before exhibited in the harshest of circumstances. When students or non-history teachers complain about minor discomforts and situations I am quick to remind them that their grandfather, or perhaps great-grandfather, almost certainly fought in a war. The Greatest Generation is named as such for a reason: they managed some of the greatest challenges humanity has ever faced and helped create a strong, stable society out of the depths of those crises. Many of them experienced unimaginable horrors, tragedies, and circumstances that required every ounce of strength and human spirit to navigate through. From the heroes of D-Day to the deepest fortitude of Holocaust survivors like Victor Frankl to the average families who packed everything they owned onto rust-bucket cars and traversed deserts in search of a better life out west, the citizens of the Great Generation without a doubt earned their title. Their grit and resilience remains something to be marveled at.

Ours? Not so much.

* * *

At sixteen, as a coddled, entitled, mentally weak victim of our culture of convenience, I had the great fortune to come face-to-face with just how comfortable my life was in comparison to those who came before. I was an exchange student in France and had the remarkable opportunity to visit some of the beaches at Normandy. It felt like a perfect summer day, even though it was mid-April. A clear blue sky was above my body as a warm breeze came from the sea and pushed past me. While wandering through one of the American cemeteries, to my left I saw thousands of grave markers in a perfectly mowed lawn, the scent of which reminded me of long summer days back home. Each marker was pristine and pearl white, with the names and ages of the deceased etched in with great care and precision. To my right, below the cliff, were the sounds of a small beach town full of carefree, happy people relaxing on a beautiful day by the sea. I sauntered through the cemetery in silence, internally marking the ages of the young men etched into the crosses. I thought about how confident, tough, and brave each of these men were. And how they were probably scared out of their minds and wanted to go

A Little Farther

home to their parents. But they didn't. They continued forward knowing that their actions could lead to a better world. A world like the one that existed on the beach below me.

Looking up from a gravestone, I saw an old man with a cane slowly making his way toward me. He wasn't pensively wandering like I was – he was on a mission. And I was his endpoint. I felt a lump in my throat. *Am I in trouble?,* I thought. *Did I accidentally do something wrong?*

To show my politeness and deference to age I spoke up first: "Hello sir, how are you?"

The man continued toward me, his plaid golf cap and sweater vest approaching my personal bubble. He hid behind a pair of Ray-Bans, his right hand resting on the glimmering top of a solid black cane. Finally, a little too close for comfort, he stopped and looked me in the eyes.

"Are you American?" he asked with a thick French accent. He must have heard me speaking to a friend before I went off on my own.

"Yes sir, I am." I replied, unsure where this interaction was going.

He looked at me for a moment, then lowered his sunglasses with the cool confidence of a man full of wisdom.

"Thank you, son. Because of your people, my people are free. I grew up in freedom, with a good life. And it is all because of you Americans. So thank you, son."

I stood there, dumbstruck. Never before had I been thanked for the actions of others. My own incompetence and lack of contribution to the world suddenly became embarrassingly apparent. The comfort and convenience in which I was brought up was held to the light against this man who had it far, far worse when he was my age.

A Little Farther

Unsure of how to respond, I thought about letting this man know what I *really* thought about his compliment:

Sir, you should not be thanking me. I have done nothing with my life. I am a moron, a mooch, a parasite, sir. Do you know what I do with my time? I wake up in a nice house and go get a free, world-class education that I whine and moan about every single day. Then I go home, sit on the couch, and drink an obscene amount of soda in order to destroy my one precious body so I can focus on sitting on a comfortable couch playing video games all afternoon before having a nice meal served to me on a porcelain platter. I have contributed nothing to society, sir. So please do not thank me.

These thoughts remained locked up behind my closed lips. Eventually I let out a weak "thank you" before the old man nodded and continued along his way. That was the first time in my life I considered a cause greater than myself. My tiny little bubble that I lived so comfortably in was shattered. Here I was, surrounded by bodies of men much tougher and braver and more significant than I, with nothing to show for it but a sense of entitlement and lackadaisical ambition. The confidence and competence exhibited by the people around me, beneath the ground, helped create the deeply comfortable world I had taken advantage of. But it would have been a shame for them to know just how little I had given back in return.

I never saw that man again, but I think about him often. He stands firm as a symbol of a world that is bigger and more important than my daily inconveniences and quibbles. He reminds me that I need to toughen up, be grateful for what I have, and to fulfill my potential – and not to whine about trivial inconveniences online. I try my best each day to be more like the version of me that the man saw beneath my soft hands and unweathered skin on that beautiful

A Little Farther

April afternoon.

*   *   *

The reality is, when we are *too* coddled, *too* comfortable, *too* soft, when we don't do hard things, everything else *seems* hard even if it's not. The problem is that doing hard things is, well, *hard*. It's so much easier, especially with all of the engrossing amusements available at our fingertips, to simply slip into the easy, comfortable route and go on without trying to toughen up. Doing hard things toughens our resolve, increases our confidence, and develops a greater competence that allows us to navigate the world with less worry about things going awry. Why worry when we have evidence from the past to prove that we can handle a tough situation?

Humans need to feel useful, valued, and important. It's why many of us are so eager to please and why we feel a sense of pride when we do something helpful for others. Agency, or the belief that we can positively affect an outcome, is developed through both the ability to overcome a wide variety of challenges and the eventual belief that we are capable of handling whatever life throws at us, using those previous challenges we have overcome as evidence to support that belief. Whether it's dealing with a major issue like the death of a loved one or a daily challenge like taking a cold shower, agency can only develop when we push our comfort zone ever so slightly outward, which gives us a greater breadth of experience to draw on when life's inevitable challenges come our way. Therefore, when a car crashes or the weather turns or we are more tired than expected, we can have the competence to manage the situation and the confidence that we will come out the other side okay. It is agency, forged in fire, that creates a cool, calm confidence in us.

Without this evidence, though, we don't feel like we can positively manage the situations life throws at us. And so we tend to whine and moan about pointless little things that don't actually matter, when in reality we should be getting out from behind the screen and pushing ourselves in the elements to develop some fortitude. The people I see complaining online are facing a lack of agency, otherwise they would not feel the need to gain external validation for their issues and instead would deal with them on their own. In these cases, the challenge they face is the opportunity to grow. They, we, *I*, need to see challenges as opportunities if we are ever to become the greatest version of ourselves.

How, though, can I feel strong, accomplished, confident, and competent if I never really *have* to be in situations that require me to be those things? If full days, and sometimes months, can pass by without a bead of sweat, an extra beat of the heart, or a moment of feeling out of my element, how can I develop my own "greatest" version of myself?

Thankfully, I do not have to charge up the cliffs of Normandy in the face of heavy gunfire in order to end one of history's greatest evils to do so. Our comparatively safe and comfortable world is a blessing that I am grateful for every day. I don't need to completely toss away my technology, conveniences, or creature comforts in favor of sleeping on rocks or putting myself into imminent danger. This is the external world that, albeit imperfect, is what great people struggled to create.

It is *how* I navigate this world of comfort that determines how far I come as an individual. Laying around in a nice temperature all day while watching content may seem nice at first. But it gives me no purpose in life. No ability to do hard things. No sense of agency. No toughness. And, therefore, no certainty that I am able to capably handle whatever life throws at me. Instead, I need to do more than what is expected, push harder than I need to, and make life a bit less

A Little Farther

convenient.

Or, if you ask my father, I just need to go a bit farther, a bit earlier, than others are willing to.

* * *

On a cold December morning I stumbled out of my front door for another round of that damned paper route. This morning had a different feel to it, though. The world was quieter, more serene. Orion and Sirius twinkled in the sky above me, dominating the view of the heavens. Most homes had their lights off, the residents remaining asleep in their caves, protected from the brisk winter air. The usual cars and trucks that occasionally passed by on the state highway in the distance were nonexistent. It was Christmas morning, and the world had yet to awake to the annual, ephemeral magic.

I was the only one outside at 4:50am that day. I had, out of a sense of duty, gotten up earlier than everyone else. It was one of the first moments that my dad's advice really struck a chord within me, and is a moment that brings me peace even when I think about it now.

At some point in my childhood, I don't remember exactly when, my dad said without thinking much of it:

"If you are willing to get up a little earlier, walk a little farther, venture out when it's a little hotter or a little colder, then you'll have the whole world to yourself. And a much better experience."

His point was that most of us succumb to limiting our life experience to the comfortable mean. If it's a bit too hot or cold outside, we stay indoors. If waking up at the crack of dawn promises a faster, traffic-free journey, we sleep in and deal with the traffic instead of forcing ourselves out of bed. And if a trail offers a longer, more strenuous option, we ignore it in order to stay on the main path with multitudes of other people. It explains why I'm always alone while walking on cold winter nights or when I'm out for a morning stroll before the sun rises. It's not comfortable, but in the end the solace and unique experiences make it worthwhile. Sure, we can stay with everyone else and have a fine time. But if we are willing to move a bit more, arrive a bit earlier, or walk a little farther, chances are we will have a quieter, more relaxing, more meaningful experience of whatever it is we are doing.

That serene Christmas morning has always stood out to me as proof of concept. I watched as lights slowly flickered on inside certain homes, aware of the magic that the residents were about to experience. I breathed in the cold air, unshared by anyone else, and felt the magic of the holiday in a different way. Upon delivering the last paper, instead of rushing home to see what was in my stocking or under the tree, I returned at a casual pace. I didn't know when I would have the whole world to myself like this again, appreciating what was to come before anyone else was up and aware. The gift of solace was enough to engender patience.

The key to living more strenuously isn't complicated. We just need to recognize where our comfort zone is and devise ways to expand it outward. Then (and this is the hard part), we must get out of bed earlier than we'd like, venture to the edge of that comfort zone, and push through it to a new frontier. It'll be a little farther, a little less comfortable. But when we're done we can look back at that new horizon with pride, agency, and confidence.

* * *

When I started planning strenuous challenges for the year, my mind naturally drifted toward outdoor adventure. While the slower and more cerebral challenges were necessary and inspiring, the thought of a brutal physical experience stood out in my mind as more appealing. I tend to be the most agitated when I am stuck indoors, unable to move or get my energy out. Which, unfortunately, happens a lot more frequently now that I'm settled down with an adult job and adult responsibilities. In theory, setting out on a massive adventure that would shred my physical limits could provide a mental reset of sorts. I could do something so difficult that I would have no choice but to physically endure the discomfort to the point of being brought back to my core, where little worries and anxieties would be meaningless in the face of the task at hand. Doing the hard thing could humble me, calm me down, and help me become a better, more level-headed person. It could put life back into perspective, making the tiny inconveniences of daily life less annoying and easier to manage. Experiencing something brutally difficult could, at least for a while, make traffic or a long checkout line seem like the insignificant situations that they are. At its core, an adventure like this would require me to put my dad's advice to the ultimate test. I'd have to go much further than most in order to experience the benefits I hoped for.

    The idea for the exact adventure came as I was flipping through a little guidebook detailing the most worthwhile hikes in the Adirondack mountains. Near the back of the guidebook was a hike with a difficulty rating labeled as "Only If You Can". Intrigued, I stopped turning the pages and began to read about the potential adventure.

    The author labeled this as one of the most difficult, grueling hikes in the entire Adirondack Park. It would require *starting* by climbing two challenging High Peaks (mountains with an elevation over 4,000 feet, of which there are 46 in the Adirondacks). Once those mountains were climbed, however, the journey was just beginning. Instead of turning around and heading back to the start, the trail required eight more miles of relentless elevation change through rocky trails, bald peaks, and bug-filled forests. It would be challenging and relentless, the author noted multiple times throughout the write-up, but if one was willing to endure the suffering they would be rewarded with one of the most spectacular hikes in all the Adirondacks. In other words, to venture a little farther beyond where even only a few people go would guarantee a solace and majesty unmatched anywhere else.

I was sold.

Immediately I began planning out the route. This would be, without a doubt, the most strenuous hike I had ever done. The distance combined with over 9,400 feet of total elevation change would be enough on its own to make me nervous. To make matters more uncertain, however, was the fact that I would have to complete it within a day. Given my schedule (and not wanting Gab to deal with a night alone while I emergency sheltered on some mountain where she couldn't reach me) this hike would have to be endured in a single go. No stopping. No camping. No calling for a ride. Just endless, determined forward motion.

Telling myself that I should wait until I had more time would have just been an excuse to avoid the challenge. I needed to commit to the adventure when it was possible, even if that meant making it even more difficult. Waiting for ideal circumstances becomes an excuse for long-term inaction. And so I checked the weather forecast, circled a date on the calendar, and committed to completing the trek through hell, high water, or bugs. It had to be done.

I was ready to destroy my comfort zone in the name of the strenuous life.

* * *

It is a muggy but cool morning in one of the most beautiful parts of the country. Surrounded by rocky peaks and a pristine lake,

A Little Farther

Troy and I hoist up our bags and begin the journey. He is here because I sold him on the majesty of the hike and the life-affirming benefits of enduring a major challenge. I also gaslit his concerns about covering the distance with his bum ankle. But he's here. Sometimes the ends justify the means.

I am equal parts excited and nervous. My muscles are limber and strong; my stomach filled with cold oatmeal and peanut butter. Beginning the hike, we are immediately met with the harsh reality that lies ahead. The trail, if it can be called one, is just a pile of rocks puked out by an old glacier going straight up the side of the mountain. Each step is a lunge that engages all the muscles in my lower body, a move that will have to be repeated thousands of times over the next twelve to fourteen hours. Within five minutes my heart is pumping and I'm breaking out in a sweat. I planned this adventure to challenge myself, but didn't expect to be wiped in less than half-a-mile. This does not bode well for the rest of the day, but I have to remain mentally strong if this is ever going to be completed.

Before we began, I knew that the most challenging part of the hike would not be the physical torment. Instead, it would be dealing with my own head. There are no bears, mountain lions, or (presumably) serial killers on this trail. There are no avalanches or wildfires or murder hornets to contend with. If we just keep walking forward, all day, eventually we will make it to the other side in one piece and return home to a nice, warm bed. The greatest threat lies between my ears. It is the raw experience of my sense of self in a state of suffering, and the emotions that will consume me. It is reckoning with the reality that *I* am the only thing that stands between me and the experience I'm dreaming of. I am the gatekeeper to a better version of myself; the scariest realization of all.

After the initial climb up the trail, which I assume the mountain put in place to weed out the most casual adventurers, we come to a delightful flat area of the trail that overlooks the valley and lake below. It is a cool, breezy outcrop that dries my sweat and refreshes my spirit. I put my uncertainties aside for a moment and remember that *I love this*. Being outside, immersed in nature, away from the stresses and screens of daily life. This is peak existence.

At a certain point the trail reaches above the tree line and becomes a four-limbed scramble up an almost vertical rock face. Small blue rectangles are painted on the ground to remind us that we are in fact going . . .somewhere. If this were wet it would be an extremely sketchy stretch of trail that would bring up serious conversations about if we should continue. Thankfully, though, this side of the mountain is bone dry and the grip on the rock is fantastic. I catch my second wind, and the physical training that I put myself through with this hike in mind is starting to pay off. Now that my body has accepted what it needs to do, it calms down and provides the energy I need to move forward gracefully. My mind, frazzled by the initial difficulty, also rests into a steady equilibrium. My mental state becomes meditative, my breathing coordinating with the locomotion. The world slows down. I turn around to soak in the majestic view behind me, a reminder of both how I am infinitely small in the grand scheme of things, as well as infinitely large and connected to all life that exists. And to think just minutes before I was completely unbalanced both physically and mentally.

When we begin something that shocks the system, be it mental or physical, our bodies and brains immediately rise up in a tizzy like a wasp nest that has been stoked from below. Thoughts, feelings, blood, all swirling frantically trying to figure out the best course of action. An initial reaction to this involuntary response is to stop whatever it is that's causing the frenzy – to stop thinking about that difficult situation, to stop moving, and to avoid this internal discomfort brought on by the novel situation. Maybe we stop moving and lie down. Or we plop back onto the couch. Perhaps we begin scrolling mindlessly or turn on a show. All of these have the same motivation: to avoid the situation at hand. If we stick with it, just for a moment, the world tends to find a way of slowing down. Our mind and body realize that we are in fact okay, and that danger is not imminent. The swirling slows to a churning, then a ripple, and finally the peace we all seek in daily life. Acceptance breeds contentment. And, now accepting of this new situation, our minds and bodies can move forward in a calm, ready state. Our fitness improves. Our minds become resilient. The thing that was so scary a minute ago can now be dealt with with confidence. It always could have been, of course, but often we need a moment to work through the fear and realize that truth. This is when, and how, we grow. We just need to stick it out through the initial storm. And all will be okay.

The top of the first mountain is a view I had dreamed of seeing. This peak in particular was always on "my list", and to be here is an accomplishment worthy of trekking back down and heading home. I could spend all day up here, soaking in the purple mountain majesty. Time, though, is ticking. Daylight is burning. I stand on the edge and gaze at the endless valley beneath me, the cavernous space that I wish I could fly around freely. Within a minute or two the breeze stops and the bugs begin to swarm. The mountain knows: we need to keep moving.

From this point we need to go down most of the mountain before turning our ankles back upward to ascend the next High Peak. The descent is far gnarlier than the smooth, thin lines in the guidebook. Much of the trail, like the way up, is just sheer rock face sloping down at a concerning angle. This side of the mountain,

A Little Farther

though, is soaking wet. With each step my feet slip out from under me, my toes jamming into the front of my shoes so hard that the top of my left trail runner actually starts to rip apart. Most of the descent consists of me sitting my rear end on the soaked rocks and sliding down gingerly, being careful to avoid somersaulting over my feet and down the mountain. At one point I fall at an awkward angle and catch myself from sliding down the granite slope with my left wrist. The joint stings and I know immediately that I have at least a bad strain, perhaps a sprain. It stiffens and swells a little bit, adding another nagging pain to manage with each step. The outside of my right knee is tight and begins to ache with each motion forward. Sweat pours. Bugs accumulate. And we are only about a quarter of the way through the journey.

This sucks.

* * *

Companionship is essential when times get tough. Having a tribe, even of just two, allows us to manage our emotions and push much farther than we ever would on our own. Troy was absolutely essential in getting me to confront my fear of heights and go rock climbing. Now, knowing that he's just as excited about this experience as I am, he'll be the one to keep me moving forward. Although it's unspoken, neither of us want to be the one that calls it quits. Beforehand we both agreed that, if one of us couldn't continue, we would immediately make our escape plans. No hard feelings, no ragging on each other. Now that we are here the feelings are different. We are both willing to endure far more than we would on our own due to fear of letting down a friend. Neither of us wants to be the one who cannot endure.

After another grueling ascent up the soaked rocks on the side of the second High Peak, we *finally* reach a stretch of flatter trail. I hit a good pace and end up a couple minutes ahead of Troy. Eventually I reach an outcrop that exposes a sweeping view and precarious drop to the bottom. In this little opening the wind picks up and almost blows the bug-spray soaked hat off my head. My sun hoodie, drenched in sweat, starts flapping aggressively in the breeze. I take a few steps away from the edge and use the massive presence of the mountain to feel a little safer. This mountain is gigantic, and on it I am worthless and invisible. No different than a flea on a Great Dane. It doesn't care if I live or die. The wind that's whipping through my clothes has traveled hundreds of miles and covers a vast expanse that my mind cannot even comprehend. Ancient trees that will be here long after I am gone surround me. Each one is an ecosystem, home to countless lifeforms that require it for survival. And there are more than I could ever possibly count in a lifetime. I realize how far from home I am. How, in this expansive view, I don't see a single sign of human civilization. I have not heard a car or plane since we embarked on the trail. My phone has no service. If we wanted to turn around, it would be a categorically unwise decision given the conditions of the trail we just descended. It would take at least as long as completing the trail we are currently on, with a known risk of injury. But the trail ahead could potentially be just as treacherous. And what if it is? What if we get hurt? What happens if we have to hunker down and shelter for the night, a night with forecasted thunderstorms, with no service and Gab worrying alone in a bed that we are supposed to lie in together?

I crack.

My heart races and my shoulders quiver. I feel completely overwhelmed and alone. The grandiosity of it all is too much for my mind to handle. I try to catch my breath as it leaps around; it needs to slow down and become controlled. I remember how gassed I felt at the beginning of the trail and that, once my body settled into the challenge, it became easier. Now I must do the same with my mind – a much more difficult task.

Instead of feeling intimidated by the wind, I try my best to be with it. It is strong, biting, irregular, irrational. It keeps the bugs away, which is polite of it. In a way, it's more refreshing than scary. I realize it is not out to get me, and that it would be whipping across this mountainside regardless of my presence. The wind becomes the wind. Nothing more, nothing less.

Grounded, the view remains expansive but becomes more friendly. Like the wind and the trees, this landscape exists as it is. There is no need for me to label it as scary or overwhelming. It is all okay.

While calmer, I still feel a deep sense of uncertainty about what is to come. We have one more push to the summit before beginning the "true" trail that we came here for. This trail consists of three more summits, each slightly lower than the previous, with more unforgiving uphill and downhill. It might be dry and easy to traverse. Or it could be steep, soaking wet, and sketchier than where we just were. The only way to find out is to be there.

Troy approaches from behind and takes a rest. He is sweating and downs big gulps of red Gatorade. I pull out a protein bar and begin munching, struggling to find the energy to break apart the chocolate chips with my jaw. Unaware of everything I just experienced, Troy sighs and looks up.

"You good?" he asks.

"Yeah. You?"

Troy finishes another gulp of his Gatorade.

"Yeah, I think. This is hard."

"I know," I say, looking down the trail, "and we haven't even

A Little Farther

hit the main part yet."

A moment of silent recognition, followed by packs being hoisted onto our backs and continuing forward. A friendship forged in suffering.

* * *

We reach the summit of the second peak after another grueling uphill section consisting of nothing but more rocks left by those damn glaciers that exited this area without cleaning up their mess. At the top we take a well earned rest, and the rocks I lay down on feel more comfortable than any bed I've ever owned. In between strong gusts of wind the sun peeks through the clouds and provides essential warmth. After dozing off for a moment, Troy pulls out his peanut butter and jelly sandwich for lunch. I realize that I have not packed nearly enough and would quite literally kill for the satisfaction of a juicy orange or a chocolate milkshake. Instead, with no opportunities around, I munch on my homemade mix of almonds, blueberries, and dark chocolate. The sugar hits like a drug.

I look out to the Great Range of the Adirondacks, a view that rivals any of the National Parks that I have been to. Looking to the left I see the gradual descent of the mountains into the Champlain Valley, with Lake Champlain beckoning in the distance. *What I would give to just jump in the lake and float right now*, I think. My gaze lowers from the lake to the trail that stands between us. A rollercoaster of brutal geological forces with a path so overgrown that it is clear not many people, if anyone, has been on it for quite some time.

Discouraged, I think about my dad's advice. If conditions were better and this was the goal of the day, we could turn around and check two High Peaks off the list. There are some people who do just this. Our mindset would be completely different if this were the case. We would sit here for a long while, enjoy our food, rest up, then head back the way we came (mostly descending) knowing that we were halfway done already. This would be done, preferably, in drier conditions in order to decrease the risk on the way back. In that case it would be a tough but very manageable day.

Where we sit now, though, we are roughly one-third of the way through our journey. And the rest is completely unknown and impossible to plan for. There is far more elevation change than if we simply turn around. It is farther than most ever go, evidenced by the thick overgrowth on the trail.

In this sense, we will quite literally be going farther, and longer, than most. We will see more than others and are sure to have a unique experience that only we can understand. Up to this point my dad's theory is holding true – there is no one else here and the journey has been incredible. I have to trust that it will continue to be if I am going to get the gumption to actually finish this thing.

After some brief stretching and heavy sighs about what is to come, we swing our sweaty, dirt-covered bags (which somehow get heavier each time) back onto our sweatier but less dirt-covered backs and continue forward. In spite of the uncertainty, the crushing realization of how far we have to go, and the pain in parts of my body I haven't felt in years, we push forward. The curiosity about what lies ahead and the adventurous spirit that lies deep within us overtakes the worries, even though those worries and fears still swirl inside our minds. I don't know if those ever truly go away, no matter how hard we try. Yet I am developing a certainty, as we take the first steps on the trail toward the unknown, that pushing forward anyway leads to a better, more fulfilling, experience of life.

The trail begins its gradual descent in a non-linear fashion: up, then down, then back up, and back down. We are above the tree line here, and the area is a barren alpine landscape full of tossed rocks and forgotten lichens. The wind continues to howl but now pushes us from behind in a show of support. Looking forward, it appears that the Earth may be calming down a bit. We push forward, mindlessly chatting about the view at the summit and what the strategy should be for our food and water supplies, given how much we have already consumed and how long we still have to go. Then, after a quarter mile of a rocky rollercoaster of a trail, something magical happens.

Without even realizing how we got here, we are suddenly surrounded by an expansive, lush, green landscape. We blinked and opened our eyes to a completely new paradise that plopped itself on this mountainside in that brief moment of darkness behind our eyelids. The sun breaks through the clouds and shines on vibrant green bushes, low grass, and small pine trees that stretch as far as our vision can muster. The rocky peak behind us blocks the wind, allowing for a deafening silence that allows us to actually hear our breath and take in the beauty without being thrashed around by the elements. Birds provide the soundtrack for the landscape as dozens of butterflies float about from flower to flower. Colors pop like a poorly edited Instagram photo with the saturation pushed all the way up – except this image is the real deal. A warmth radiates from the clear blue sky above, lessening the chill that seeped into us on the summit. And we are totally, completely, absolutely alone and away from all human activity. Despite the vast landscape not a single road or highway is in view. No planes circle overhead. Our feet are the only ones marking the trail. The loneliness on the other side of the mountain created a tornado of anxiety and insignificance. This, however, is not loneliness. Rather, for some reason I can't quite explain, it is solitude. Knowing how isolated we are in *this* spot, unlike just an hour earlier, fills me with a deep sense of presence and unexpected joy. My joint pains are anesthetized as I follow the paths of the butterflies and grin at the beauty being injected into my soul. I have never been in a landscape this lush, this vast, this wickedly beautiful.

Troy and I begin to laugh. He lets out a guttural yell that echoes into the vast expanse of ancient landscape that encases us. I begin looking around for a hidden home made out of stone and covered in moss, where I am certain that a forest sprite who has the secrets to life and enlightenment lives and is waiting for us. In a daily life of emails and bills and stale air, the idea of magical spirits seems silly, naive even (never mind how we talk about our increasingly sentient AI assistants). In this landscape, though, *not* believing in these whimsical forest spirits would be the naive choice. I see how the legends of the past were formed. I understand the belief, the real, raw certainty, that other beings in different planes of reality live with us and have the potential to influence our lives. Out here, at the will of the elements and feeling safe and comfortable beneath an ominous and howling behemoth to our backs, I can sense their presence. We are not alone. The spirit of life and love and the universe is with us, embodied in each breath we take and every form of life that meets our field of vision. And I am not *un*certain that a gnome isn't crawling into my backpack to provide me protection and guidance throughout the rest of the journey. I choose not to check and take comfort in my belief that he's in there, somewhere. Out here, a life of magic and mystery is preferable to the cold logic of life back home.

Further down the descent we reach a rocky outpost that jets out from the lushness and overlooks the valley below. I work my way out to the edge and, once I plant my feet, take a deep breath. My heart fills with joy. To my right is the Great Range, those epic and foreboding mountains that simultaneously beckon the curious adventurer and warn them to stay away. On the left is the remaining landscape we must traverse, filtering out slowly and gradually into the Champlain Valley. And in the middle of all this, tucked away on a mountainside that almost nobody travels, is what Troy and I dub the Garden of Eden. For it has given us new life, new perspective, and a new appreciation for what we are doing here.

Staring into the vastness, I think about my dad's advice. To this point, we have gone *much* farther and *much* longer than most people ever will. And even with that, we still have a significant distance to cover. Going the extra mile (or nine) is not easy. At its most extreme, it may take you to far and dangerous places with no guarantee of survival. Sometimes it leaves you panicking on a mountainside contemplating your own powerlessness and insignificance in the face of an all-powerful, indifferent landscape. Or, you may shiver on a desolate peak thanks to the violent wind that rips through your soul and threatens to take you off your feet and into the abyss. It could also, like what happens as we finish our adventure later on, lead to running out of food and water, being on the verge of cramping, dealing with significant knee pain, and pushing forward despite all ten toes aching and wishing they were face up relaxing by a poolside instead of being jammed into the front of a sweat-soaked, bacteria-filled shoe, step after step after step. These are all possibilities of the life lived a little farther than most.

But those struggles are counterbalanced by what happens while we are in that untrodden world. Being in a place that is farther, colder, or earlier than where most people choose to venture changes us. It provides space to think about the bigger questions in life, and the solitude to quietly and presently develop some possible answers for ourselves. It pushes our boundaries and develops a meaningful sense of pride in our abilities. We become more resilient, more adaptable, and anti-fragile. We learn that our limits are self-imposed. And that our greatest obstacle is not the landscape or wild animals or the weather but rather our own willingness to persevere and continue forward when the easy thing to do is to stop and retreat back to the mean. The obstacles we face along the way all provide the same lesson that we need to learn over and over again: that *we* are, in fact, the greatest obstacle we face. And if we practice overcoming our doubts, fears, and worries, then we develop the consistent ability to overcome *ourselves* and be reborn on the other side of our old comfort zone. A farther boundary. A new frontier of the self to explore and discover.

Breathing in the clean air as the butterflies swirl behind me, I am keenly aware that I am not storming the beaches of Normandy or taking the first step on some distant planet. Realistically, I am not in danger. I will be home tonight. I will get to down that chocolate milkshake and drift off to sleep in my comfortable bed. Many people have done many more impressive things than Troy and I thru-hiking this trail in a single day. For me, though, this is the frontier of my comfort zone. It forces me to reckon with my own insecurities and beliefs that limit my experience of life. It pushes me to, through, and beyond my physical and mental limits. And *that* is what matters. Those limits may lie far behind one person's and miles ahead of another's. What matters is that I am living among those limits, feeling scared about their presence, and pushing onward anyway.

Because *that* is what leads to a more interesting, more meaningful, and more fulfilling experience of life. Bruised toes and all.

The Meaning of Success

It is amazing how a deep exhale from the Earth creates an explosion of life.

As I cut through the humid air on a warm summer evening, a tickling breeze at my back guides me home. The nostalgic aromas of summertime fill my nose: moisture, flowers, fresh cut grass, grilled meat emanating from homes in the neighborhood, crackling campfires bringing peace in a few backyards, the subtle but ominous clues of a thunderstorm lurking in the distance.

The scents are coupled by a summertime chorus. Crickets chirp in surround sound, accompanied by the more boisterous cicadas who have made their occasional trip up the trees to mate before returning to another seven years of isolation (what a life, eh?). In the distance a group of preteen boys whoop up some mischief by the pond, living a free and feral existence that can only occur without the tyranny of a school schedule. Closer to my ears I hear more boisterous laughter, jokes that can only be told amongst a select few, sarcastic comments aimed in a certain direction but coated with love. I am surrounded by it.

Looking up, the sky is darkening. A magenta sunset is slowly being consumed by twirling, light gray clouds that flash dramatically in the distance. A slight yellow hue remains at their base as they swallow what is left of the sun. Only the residual heat on the pavement below signals the sun's work that day. For now, though, it is gone, lost behind the horizon in an expansive sea of destructively beautiful cumulonimbus. The tree tops lose their color and gradually fade into silhouettes, with the first eager fireflies popping up in the field to my left. I bring my gaze down to street level and smile as my friends come into view, their laughter too much to ignore any longer. Most of us are on bikes, like the world's lamest gang patrolling the suburban street (and who probably couldn't stand up to those middle schoolers who have laid claim to the other end of the neighborhood). One friend, Jake, is left without wheels, but he smiles as he strolls behind us and takes clips for the home movie he plans to make about his summer fun. I look down at my own feet, balanced precariously on top of a scooter purchased just two hours ago for five bucks from a thrift store, a mode of transportation I have not used since my teeth were forced together with braces and my skin was lost in a sea of acne. But muscle memory returns, and I find myself flying down this street on plastic wheels and a thin metal slab.

It is August 1, midsummer, traditionally known in Celtic traditions as Lughnasadh. Today is the midpoint of the summer season, a celebration of the height of life in the Northern Hemisphere. And, beneath the joy, a sober recognition that our half-full glass of summer is being drained, little by little, with each passing sunset. It is a time to gather together and celebrate the warmth, the light, the animals and plants and trees that are bursting all around us with such majesty. And it is also a reminder to savor these moments, as the chances to lay in the grass and feel the warm summer breeze will become a nice memory stirred up on frozen nights before we know it.

For centuries, Lughnasadh was celebrated with feasts consisting of foods from the early harvests and feats of athleticism, often accompanied by dancing and dealmaking amongst the community. For this modern celebration I decided to gather our friends for an evening as close to those traditions as I could. A meal

The Meaning of Success

of fresh fish, local corn, and hand-picked berries nourished our bodies (as did, admittedly, some scallion pancakes and dumplings from Trader Joe's). And, after enjoying the meal together around the table, our own feats of athleticism at the local park were attempted.

Which is why I find myself huffing on a scooter as fast as I can back to the house. We had just ridden down to the park to show off our strength, agility, flexibility, and willingness to be embarrassed. Everything at the park was made for children of the physical kind, not the mental. We struggled to complete a convoluted "climbing" route on the tiny rock wall, engaged in a pull-up competition on the monkey bars, listened as Jake's skin harshly squeaked down the hot plastic slide (only to be met with a murky puddle of water at the bottom), and swung as high as the swing structure would allow us in order to get a bird's eye view of the park and the pond beyond us. It was pure joy and freedom.

Then, suddenly, we heard a rumble in the distance. Thunder. Our time was up.

We are now almost back to the house, my muscles still tired from the pull-ups and my hands wobbling on sketchy handlebars as we race home to beat the storm. I look up once again and breathe in, taking in all the sights, sounds, and smells at once. *This* is summer, I think. The freedom, the camaraderie, the silliness, all wrapped into the sight of five grown, responsible adults hysterically riding their "wheels" back to safety before the downpour. At one point Gab suggests I try to hold her bike handlebars while she pulls my scooter (with me still on it). I almost crash the second we start the experiment. We may be acting like kids, but the urge to avoid a call to my insurance agency triumphs over the impulse to continue this experiment. Still, we laugh at the idea before the conversation shifts to whether Troy would be able to eat twelve large diner pancakes in the span of ninety minutes, and that we will pool together two-hundred dollars if he can. (We complete this challenge about three weeks later. He eats four).

Breathless, we reach our house and fling our wheels onto the lawn. Some of us lay down and feel the Earth beneath our toes. Our friend Sarinah starts doing handstands on the grass, which leads to some hilarious attempts from me as I try to master the skill. The breeze picks up, a sign of the rain to come. Everyone stashes their rides (symbols of a childlike joy that still exists within us) into their cars (symbols of the adult life which we are required to take part in). Promises of indoor games and homemade ice cream outweigh the possibility of being washed by a warm summer rain. It's time to head inside for more shenanigans. While I take a few last breaths of the warm summer air, I come to a concerning realization:

Why haven't we done this more often over the past few years?

* * *

Americans need to chill with their friends more often.

We are in the midst of what the Surgeon General defines as a "Loneliness Epidemic". While we all have those moments of needing to be alone, we are a social species by nature, which makes this trend of loneliness interesting. Thanks in part to our increasingly online lives and fracturing communities, it has become harder for Americans to get out, hang out, and help out beyond the home. Currently, over one-third of Americans either never see friends or only see them every couple of months. This has correlated with a dramatic increase in time spent alone. The average American now spends 24 more hours alone per month than they did in 2003, as well as 20 less hours per month with friends, while our time online has more than doubled in just the past fifteen years.

Our society's loneliness is not just limited to spending time with friends. In 1960 roughly 13% of Americans lived alone; that figure was 29% in 2022. In addition, only 16% of Americans surveyed stated feeling "very attached to their community", which especially makes sense since we are still putting the pieces of our communities back together in the aftermath of COVID. In my own lifetime I have seen town events be retired due to budget constraints and school events getting canceled because not enough students felt like going. Dances, balls, and school celebrations are fast becoming a relic of past generations, replaced by staying home and communicating through screens.

We humans need our tribes, and without them the consequences are harmful. According to the US Surgeon General's office, the benefits of social connection are immense. Which means, conversely, that spending too much time alone has the opposite effect. Social connection greatly increases our odds of survival and provides a sense of meaning, purpose, support, and resilience. A strong social network does not have to consist of five-hundred people you know and talk to. A few ride-or-die friends can be enough to experience these benefits.

Social *disconnection*, however, has the opposite effect. Being ostracized and isolated from a group would have dramatically decreased your chances of survival in an evolutionary context. This is why we are so attuned to social norms and cues, because acceptance is a ticket toward survival (and, more importantly, reproduction) while isolation is a one-way-trip to a hungry tiger and dead-end gene pool. People who report feeling "social disconnection" have double the odds of a depression diagnosis than those who have a strong social network and/or sense of community. This is why one of the worst punishments in historical societies, like ancient Athens, was *banishment.* If you crossed the community badly enough you would literally be kicked out for a period of years, left to wander and figure out how to survive on your own or in a new group.

We need each other. Now more than ever.

Growing up my friends and I got together almost every single day. The time together was rarely formal or carefully planned. It was an era when we'd knock on each other's doors and get up to some mischief around the neighborhood. In addition to feeling the mental health benefits that come with having a tight-knit group of friends, spending all that time together (especially outside) made that time in our lives stretch out and feel more meaningful. Time, quite literally, slowed down.

There are many theories as to why time seems to speed up as we get older. Perhaps it is because each day takes up a smaller percentage of our life compared to when we were young. Or maybe it is because we stop paying such close attention to everything we encounter. Another hypothesis posits that our routines put our brains on autopilot and, after enough days, weeks, or years build up, we can accumulate huge swaths of time that seem like a blur because it all feels the same. Most likely it is a combination of these factors that explains why each year seems to go by more quickly than the one before.

I would argue that, in addition to the disastrous mental health effects of isolation, our tendency to steep ourselves in the same routine for five days a week also speeds up the passing of time. If being with friends on a regular basis makes time slow down, then being with ourselves on dull nights probably speeds it up. What is now common for myself and others in my life is to *not* do anything interesting or fun on weeknights like we did as kids. But this becomes a problem when we stick to the same regimented routine for most of the week and then try to fit in as much fun activity as we can in the fleeting hours between Friday afternoon and Sunday night. We use excuses to avoid social interaction that sound reasonable in the moment, like how we don't want to be tired for work the next day or that we have to prepare our lunches. But the result of rules like "I don't go out or make plans on weeknights" is that we become resigned to bland days focused entirely around our work schedule that all melt together in a gray, amorphous blur, flowing by without much notice or excitement. Rules or routines such as these mean that our only hope for excitement and novelty lies on the two squares at the margins of the calendar. Hardly enough time to live a fulfilling and interesting life. And, when packed too fully, those days go so fast that we blink and suddenly find ourselves in the office on a Monday morning thinking: Man, where did the weekend go?

After the immense stress I faced last year, I was more than happy to do less throughout the week and savor those calm nights with nothing to do. Solitude became a refuge that helped me heal. How long, though, is a refuge useful before it becomes counterproductive? I got into the habit of staying in and staying alone at the start of the year because I told myself I needed to in order to recover and process my feelings. Those same excuses about being ready for work, getting chores done around the house, or making sure I wasn't burned out crept into my vocabulary. But making a habit of doing nothing because I might be tired, or because I have to prepare meals, is bullshit. I'd rather be tired and happy, or hungry in stomach for a few hours but full in memories, than only feel engaged with life on 29% of my days. If I spent more time *out* of a routine in favor of having fun with my friends, I don't think I would be saying on my deathbed, "Man, I wish I had spent less time with my friends and more time preparing for work."

The Meaning of Success

This journey of slow and strenuous living is deeply personal. But the memories that stick out the most are the Imbolc celebration (a great dinner with friends), the initial cold plunge with Troy and Gab on that brisk and clear night, and rock climbing with Troy cheering me on. Each of those memories, I realize, has a common theme:

The people.

It's the people. That is what matters most. Not the thing that gets done or accomplished, but the people are there to experience and accomplish it with me. Sure, the journey of slow and strenuous living is a personal one. But just because not everyone will be into strenuous challenges doesn't mean they won't support me or want to come along for the ride. And, with them by my side, the ride will be slower and more enjoyable.

I need my friends. We all do. *Especially* on a weeknight.

* * *

More than halfway through this year of slow and strenuous living I am seeing more clearly than ever before. I am, on average, calmer and more measured in my approach to life. But I still struggle. Even on this great evening with friends, I am feeling the fatigue of another sleepless night, kept awake once again by lifelong anxieties of not doing enough, not being good enough, not making the most out of my opportunities; that opportunities worth pursuing are those tied to more money, or better status, or a higher living standard. And that I am failing in all of those respects. These are feelings that have haunted me my entire life. And I expect the haunting to continue.

But in this moment, surrounded by community, I realize that I *am* making the most of it all. That the opportunities that truly matter are not those tied to the status-driven standards we are taught to

The Meaning of Success

pursue at all costs. When left to my own devices, without the influence of others, I don't really pine for those things. Instead, I remember old times with friends, navigating life together, and feeling warm and safe in each other's company.

I think back to those incredible summers of my youth, independent and free from the watchful eyes of adults. I remember playing in the woods with Troy and our deceased friend, camping five nights a week in the neighborhood, blowing up soda cans in coals, trying (and failing) to cook a frozen turkey over a campfire, laying in fields watching the Milky Way emerge in the dark canvas above, losing sense of my being in the hypnotic dance of a fire, and feeling so present, so joyous, so *fully* alive on warm, electric summer nights – ones that are increasingly easy to lose and overlook as time goes by, wrinkles form, and responsibilities pile up.

I want them back desperately. How successful I am at making more of *those* moments is the standard by which my life should be measured. This time with loved ones, even on a weeknight, is the true measure of wealth and success.

Once more I summon the present moment and lose myself in it all. The thunder rumbling to the north, the sky periodically lighting up, the chorus of insects, the loud laughter echoing through the walls of a home that Gab and I are building together and making our own with precious moments such as these; each one a memory that gets etched into the walls and serves as a reminder of why we put up with all the real-world pressures in the first place. It is so we can come back here for refuge and rekindle the spark of childhood. So we can protect that flame within us with everything that we have. So those beautiful moments of childhood summers don't get lost in the ether. Instead, they become guideposts for how to live a *good* life. One where I do enough fun things with my friends, one where I am a good person that opens my home to love, one that makes the most of this life by continuing to play and be silly and not worry too much about the point of it all. One where I can still roam the neighborhood with a pack of lifelong buddies, race home for the thrill of fresh ice cream, and be mature enough to appreciate and recognize the importance of these experiences above all else.

    I breathe out, walk into the garage, and close the door. It is starting to rain now. Time is slowing down. And I have more memories to make upstairs.

Slow Food

When was the last time you paid attention to a meal? And I mean, *really* paid attention. No eating while watching TV or driving or chatting with a friend. Just sitting down and tasting every bite, every flavor, every bit of texture on your tongue.

I can't remember the last time I focused on a meal. Most of the time the food on my plate gets devoured quickly and without much thought. It's only when the last bites are being swallowed that I realize how fast the food disappeared and how I didn't even bother to notice how it tasted. Feeling guilty, I usually try to focus on whatever remnants of flavor remain as exhaust in my mouth and resolve to actually enjoy my next meal. But that, of course, never happens. My hunger is strong and my will is weak.

But I can't blame myself entirely for this habit. Because, as it turns out, our entire food system is designed for us to do exactly that: eat quickly, mindlessly, and in great excess.

Despite being one of the most essential parts of human existence, food consumption nowadays rarely comes with a second thought. We are surrounded by endless, delicious options that promise to tame our hunger and tickle our taste buds. Ubiquitous advertising makes us aware of the wonders of stuffed crust pizza, triple-layer bacon cheeseburgers, and the infinite supply of soft drinks that seem to be flowing from some magical spring out in the factories. Food is now cheaper, easier to consume, and more accessible in the West than at any time in human history. And if there is one part of our society that has become the ultimate symbol of speed and convenience, it is what we put on our plates and in our mouths.

In the United States, the average person has almost 4,000 calories per day available to consume at their disposal, double what the human body generally needs on a regular basis. At the same time, we are spending less than ever on food consumption, with the average household spending less than ten percent of their income on groceries (compared to 24% during the 1930s). Over the past generation we have been flooded with cheap, readily available calories. This has led to remarkable outcomes, such as the plummeting global rate of malnutrition. Industrial societies, though, are experiencing some counterintuitive issues as a result of this trend. Too much food, ironically, is making us *less* healthy. It is quite literally too much of a good thing, and it all has to do with the type of food we are producing and how it is being consumed.

During the Great Depression, the United States was at risk of having its entire agricultural economy collapse. There was a vast oversupply of goods, which drove prices down and made it significantly more difficult for farmers to make ends meet. In addition, poor farming practices over generations, coupled with unusual droughts in the Great Plains, turned what was once the most fertile soil on Earth into a dry, thin, barren film of dust. This dust was easily whisked away when the winds whipped up, which became more common during the 1930s, resulting in apocalyptic dust storms that filled homes, suffocated lungs, and blinded vision.

Seeing the crisis at hand, progressive President Franklin D. Roosevelt (with the help of an agreeable Congress and, with some political pressure, a reluctant Supreme Court) set forth a broad series of initiatives as part of his New Deal. In addition to improving natural infrastructure and adjusting agricultural practices to promote modernization and increased efficiency, one of the most impactful programs resulted in government subsidies of certain agricultural products in order to keep prices high and farmers afloat. In particular, in the 1930s and 1940s, the US government chose to subsidize the production of corn and dairy to keep income reliable for farmers and prices stable for consumers. In a time of great crisis, when capitalism was on the brink, this was seen as a necessary measure to ensure the continuation of a strong economy and reliable food supply that could feed a growing, hungry nation. And the programs, for the most part, worked. The supply of key goods was limited, prices of those goods rose, and farmers were able to stabilize their incomes while the grocery shelves remained stocked for consumers. When the country needed it most, intensive actions were taken with net positive results. It was a desperate time that called for desperate measures. Common wisdom would dictate that, once the desperate time ended, so too would the urgent supports put into place. Those actions, though, never ended, even after the economy stabilized in the 1930s, recovered during World War II, and boomed in the early Cold War era. In fact, they have only intensified.

The US government currently spends roughly $30 billion per year for farm businesses and agriculture in order to maintain a stable agriculture sector and keep consumers satisfied with cheap, widely available food products. These programs have led to many unintended consequences as they have grown, greatly complicating the oversimplified narrative of these programs simply helping farmers and feeding consumers. These subsidies, instead of protecting small family farms, tend to disproportionately benefit large, industrial, corporate operations that are able to take advantage of economies of scale. This has led to corporate consolidation in the food industry as profits rapidly increase and conditions become more difficult for small agriculture operations to survive. Smaller farming operations face immense pressure to pay off increasing debt and to ensure that they will be able to stay afloat. This means that producing the most heavily subsidized crops becomes common practice, since a low yield or difficult stretch of weather will not result in financial ruin. This, in turn, reduces the amount of innovation that occurs in the agricultural sector in terms of organic or regenerative farming, as well as operations based on more resilient polycultures. Even if crop rotation, carefully managed livestock grazing, planting cover crops, and reducing fertilizer use are all better for the soil, production yields, the environment, human health, and long-term profit, why risk it when intensively farming monocultures of a safe crop with heavy pesticide use has the smallest economic risk thanks to the backing of the US government? It is hard to blame farmers for not using more sustainable operations when their financial future is more secure with the less healthy, less sustainable option. They need food on their table, too. Unfortunately, this pressure has stripped many rural areas of the United States of their economic diversity, community ties, and broader job opportunities.

Corn is king of the monoculture and is by far the most produced crop in the United States, with over 90 million acres being planted each year. This intense level of production creates a unique problem: what do we *do* with all of this corn? So much is produced that it has to be shipped *somewhere* and consumed by *someone* or *something*. This has led to some imaginative solutions. Thanks to this level of production, corn is now ubiquitous in society in ways we rarely think about. Due to the saturation of the market, companies have to come up with creative ways to use and sell the immense amount of product that is put into the supply chain. In addition to being eaten normally, corn is also used for fuel, animal feed (even though cattle evolved to eat grass, but corn is cheaper albeit less healthy), and as a food additive. Take a look at the ingredient lists on the boxes in your pantry and you are bound to find "corn syrup" or "high fructose corn syrup" in places you would least expect it (for example, I recommend you check your ketchup bottle if you have a moment). As more and more of the food consumed in the US is packaged and ultra processed, corn becomes an increasingly major ingredient in our diet. If we are what we eat, then we are mostly corn.

A similar story holds with another familiar food: cheese. As part of a subsidy program that began in the 1970s, the United States government purchased roughly 500 million pounds of cheese; so much that there are literal caves full of unused wheels stored underground in Missouri. Throughout the 80s and 90s, in particular, "government cheese" became an early meme for those who consumed it as part of social assistance programs, even making its way into certain hip hop songs. Once again, the overabundance of cheese led to the government and food industry needing to create ways for it to be used. This became the genesis for campaigns like the famous "Got Milk?" ads of the 90s, as well as products we don't think twice about today, but are ridiculous when we consider them: stuffed crust pizza, three-cheese roll ups, cheddar melts, cheeseburgers covered with cheese sauce served with a side of cheese fries, 7-cheese pizza, and cheese topped with fries. All of these are insane, but we have become so accustomed to the amount of cheese in our diet that this outrageous level of dairy consumption seems perfectly normal.

In one instance, when I was desperately hungry while waiting for Gab to finish shopping at Target, I hid my face from public view and made my way over to the little Pizza Hut station to order some pretzel sticks. When I received my order, which was somehow both soggy and stale at the same time with just a few specks of salt randomly scattered about, the employee asked:

"Do you want a cup of cheese sauce with that?"

I couldn't understand why I would need a big cup of cheese sauce for two pretzels. And, besides, I have never liked cheese *that* much. So I politely declined with a simple "No thanks".

The employee, though, was surprised.

"You *sure* you don't want cheese?" He repeated this as he filled a cup and held it over the counter.

"Yes, I am sure. Thank you though."

"But . . .it's *free*."

I didn't care that it was free. I just didn't want the damn cheese! I declined once more and walked away before he had the opportunity to restrain me and pour the cheese down my throat because, hey, *it's free* (and also company policy).

This moment exposed a truth about our relationship with food:

We need to eat, and our brain is programmed to get in as many calories as possible, given that it evolved in times of great scarcity. Now, scarcity no longer exists for many of us, but our brains haven't caught up to this new reality. And so the prospect of free or cheap food is so enticing that it is almost impossible to resist. I may poke fun at the insistence of the cheese-loving Pizza Hut employee, but I am admittedly first in line on Sunday mornings for free samples at Costco, and will happily do as many laps around the stations as I can before I am told to lay off and let others get the children get their fair share. Given that our brains see free and cheap food as an opportunity to temporarily guarantee survival, why *wouldn't* we eat as much of the free and cheap stuff as we possibly can?

The food industry, of course, knows this very well. They are

Slow Food

keenly aware of our tendency to seek out extra cheap calories. They also know that, more than anything else, we crave foods that are calorically dense due to being high in sugar, salt, and fat. Foods like this tend to be the highest in calories and signal to our brain that we have hit the proverbial jackpot. This leads to a perfect marriage between the overproduction of subsidized crops and the need for cheap, addicting, and (most importantly) profitable food products from the corporate conglomerates. The supply of subsidized crops is so great that they can cheaply be used in a wide variety of foods, keeping costs down, calories high, and products insatiably addicting. And so corn is turned into a high-sugar syrup and put in everything from soda to crackers to ketchup. It is used to feed cattle to fatten them up as quickly as possible so they can be slaughtered and brought to market in greater quantities. Cheese is ultra processed and put into and onto everything imaginable.

And food, as we know it, becomes *fast*.

On the surface, fast food's purpose is simple: make the company serving it as much money as possible. The more burgers, cheese fries, soda, and corn chips they can sell in a day, the better. Sure, there is a guise that the purpose is to feed the population quickly and cheaply, but that is merely a convenient byproduct of the profit machine that has been created.

We would be remiss to think of fast food as just what we grab in a bag from a tired worker in a drive-thru window. Go into any supermarket and the vast majority of the products available are fast food – think cereals, chips, frozen dinners, protein bars. They are ultra-processed, chemically designed, and full of cheap, profitable ingredients. We can purchase them and immediately dig in before we leave the grocery store without a second thought. Or, at worst, all it takes to enjoy the food is staring at the microwave for five minutes before revealing a sloshy (but calorically rich) dinner. All are designed to be consumed as quickly and cheaply as possible, taste and nutrition be damned.

Besides profit and convenience, there is another, more sinister, reason why these foods are designed to be consumed quickly and in excess: so that we do not consider the unsavory nature of this system that we all have fallen prey to.

When food is provided and consumed at high speed and low cost, we do not allow ourselves time to consider what it is we are eating, whether or not it is good for us, who produced it, how it was produced, and whether that production is a net positive or negative for society as a whole. It is really difficult to consider all of that when we are shoving our face full of french fries in a momentary biological ecstasy that any Paleolithic hunter-gatherer could only dream of. Yet these considerations are of vital importance. Without meditating on these factors over the past generation, we have allowed a food system to develop that is not only fragile but also hazardous to our health. We have devalued food to the point where we try to "fit in a meal" in between more important obligations, with that meal typically being some frozen slop that we toss in the microwave and eat while watching TV. Rather than giving our food (and nutrition) the time, effort, and dedication that it deserves, we often treat it as an afterthought in terms of what we will eat, how we will eat it, and how it was produced in the first place. Somehow, the time it takes to learn how to prepare a good, wholesome meal has become an inconvenience in favor of working longer hours or giving into whatever distraction can grasp our attention for the moment.

But is there anything more human than preparing a wholesome meal out of love to mindfully share with others? To put forth effort together toward a common goal? To use what the Earth has provided

Slow Food

us to the best of our ability? To be nourished from the same pot with loved ones? If so, our current food system has not only devalued our food, it has devalued our humanness.

To devalue our food is to devalue life itself.

* * *

One morning in 1986, Carlo Petrini awoke to another beautiful day in Rome, Italy. We can assume that he began his day like any other. Perhaps he mindfully prepped his daily espresso, grabbed the morning paper, and sat down to relax, enjoy his drink, and catch-up on local events. The news on this day, though, contained information that would change the course of his life, one meal at a time.

It was reported that the Spanish Steps, a jewel in the crown of Roman culture, was being threatened by a foreign invader. This slice of Roman culture was about to be intruded upon, and defiled by, a symbol of fast-paced Western culture that, in Petrini's mind, threatened not just the delicate beauty and character of the plaza, but the entire nature and quality of human existence itself:

McDonald's.

The ultimate symbol of fast-paced living, devaluation of food, and homogenization of culture, had made plans to plant their first flag in Italy. Right in the heart of Rome. Petrini wouldn't take it. And, not surprisingly, neither would others. National protests emerged in the wake of the news in an attempt to block the construction of the blight. But big business usually gets its way. Despite the protests and outcry, the McDonald's opened anyway (and remains an "attraction" as Italy's first McDonald's today). But Petrini's fight wasn't over. He and his countrymen may have lost the battle, however they were determined to win the war.

During the protests against the McDonald's construction, Petrini and others formed a movement they hoped would inspire

Italians not just to oppose the impending fast-food behemoth, but to reclaim control over the increasing pace of life brought on by industrialization as a whole. Their aim was to help our species "regain wisdom and liberate (ourselves) from the 'velocity' that is propelling it on the road to extinction . . . .Appropriately, we will start in the kitchen, with Slow Food." According to the Slow Food manifesto, intentionally slowing down in the kitchen to enjoy local, sustainable, effortful food and meaningful meals would cultivate taste, stimulate progress, protect culture, and improve overall quality of life. Ultimately, it would result in the reclamation of pleasure over profit; of slow, prolonged enjoyment of life over the fast-paced, destructive monoculture created by the industrial food system.

Within three years the movement became international, and beginning in the 1990s there were large events designed to promote and celebrate the local ecosystems, biodiversity, and sustainable production that were supported by the Slow Food movement. Since the initial formation, the group has expanded its mission to not just preserve culture but to also promote environmentally sustainable farming practices as well as social justice, all tied together with the power of food. Whereas our current industrial system exists to maximize production and profits, Slow Food encourages us to support the growth of a system that exists to maximize health, community, and connection to the Earth and each other (notice that *profit* is not part of the equation). These systems, of course, already exist without the Slow Food movement. The organization does not exist to *create* these systems, but rather to bring much needed attention to them so that, as consumers, we have the power to choose which system we would like to support.

Slow Food dovetailed nicely with other movements that arose throughout the 2000s with similar goals, in particular the increase of farmers' markets in the US. Consumer awareness of nutrition is growing, farmers' markets are expanding, and the industry is taking notice. Supermarkets have made more of an effort to source products regionally (and proudly display this initiative to make the shoppers feel good about their choices).

The movement provides an alternative path forward in a broken food system. It encourages becoming aware of the local food ecosystems we exist in, and provides the tools to *support* those systems as best we can. And, not to have their initial purpose lost, it provides a roadmap for indulging in the uniquely seductive pleasure of the slow, intentional, food experience. A pleasure that can only come with savoring a homemade meal, prepped with the freshest local ingredients, amongst a group of friends and family. A pleasure that does not come from scarfing down a fried chicken sandwich in your car before the traffic light turns green.

* * *

While I *used* to care more about where my food came from, the stress of the past year put that concern on the back burner. With more important matters to attend to, I stopped spending time in the kitchen. Less thought was given to what was on my plate or where it came from. I still appreciated food, and theoretically wanted it to come from good sources, but was willing to make the compromise of submitting to willful ignorance in the name of convenience.

Life happens, passions fade, focus shifts. There is no shame in that.

For a while, at least.

That all changed one unusually humid spring morning in central New Jersey. I was sitting in my car on the side of the New Jersey Turnpike, parked outside a bustling rest area. The air smelled like oil, both the gasoline and the food-frying types. I had just escaped from an overpacked barn of travelers all scurrying around trying to get food as quickly as possible in between stretching and peeing (and, I hope, washing their hands). The lines at each food station were ridiculously long and the wait times were remarkably short. Gab and I were seated in the car with our feast soaking through a thin paper bag. My co-pilot on this journey handed me a hot sandwich wrapped in foil: a Chick-Fil-A grilled chicken sandwich with a side of over-buttered biscuit and fried tater tots.

Held in my hand in that sweaty, smelly rest stop wasn't a freshly grilled sandwich made of locally raised chicken from a farmer that I knew. This was a mass produced hunk of slop made in horrid factories with exploited workers; a product that exploited the animal, the farmer, and the citizens who struggled to find healthy food at an affordable price due to the economics that made this sandwich so affordable in the first place.

The sandwich itself was not the only issue; the method of eating it was problematic, too. I unpeeled the wrapper while accelerating into the merge lane heading back onto the turnpike. My first bite came as I sped past a tractor trailer going about eighty miles-per-hour, steering with one hand. Focus on the food was minimal, available only in short stretches of straight road without a crazy driver tailgating me or me having to become a crazy driver to weave through traffic. I do remember, at some point, taking a bite with enough focus to notice the taste. Surprisingly, it didn't really taste like anything. The chicken had no flavor, the bread was all texture, and the only thing that differentiated the sandwich from stale cardboard was the weird amount of tasteless juice coming out of the chicken and the slathering of sauce that soaked the bun. I was eating a condiment. By the time I finished the sandwich and threw away the wrapper, something hit me:

Slow Food

I didn't remember actually eating it.

I *just* ate. I nourished my body with calories and macronutrients (but not with many micronutrients). I, technically, just shared a meal with my wife. But that meal occurred at seventy miles-per-hour, in an unfocused state, and consisted of industrial slop that had no real taste and that came to my hand as a result of a broken food process. In the ensuing stretch of road, while Gab napped next to me, I thought about my values with food and how, once again, my actions were not in alignment with what I claimed to believe. The seduction of cheap, fast, convenient food was winning out over my higher values.

So much of our lives revolve around food. The hours spent grocery shopping. The evenings spent preparing and cooking a meal with love. The actual consumption of our meals, be it alone or with loved ones. And even when we're *not* eating, we are *thinking* about when our next meal is going to be. Always on our mind, more so than the other necessities of water and shelter because those are, for the most part, available without much thought. Food, though, requires attention. It demands presence. Effort. And if we are to neglect the enjoyment, *real* enjoyment, of our food, then by default we are neglecting to enjoy and be present for much of our life. And we will be that much poorer for it.

As I drove down the Turnpike with these thoughts in mind, an apple orchard came up on the right side of the road. I thought about the times I had eaten apples from fast food restaurants, wrapped in plastic and coated with preservatives. An awful experience compared to the apples I had eaten fresh off the trees in orchards just like that. At that moment, I knew that my eating habits needed to be strengthened, slowed down, and made more strenuous.

I was going to join the Slow Food movement.

Slow Food

* * *

The boredom that can be created in five tiny minutes is startling.

I am sitting at the round dinner table in our freshly painted dining room with Gab. A delicious winter melon soup fills a plain white IKEA bowl below me, its scent wafting up into my nostrils and stirring up fond memories of dinners with Gabby's grandparents; this is their recipe we are about to enjoy. But I can't focus on the smell or taste of the soup, delicious as it is. All I can hear is the ticking of the clock across the kitchen in our record room, audible only because the rest of the house is silent. My hand fidgets, my bare foot taps on the wood floor below. Gab and I have been chatting all day, but suddenly we now have nothing to say.

"What do you want to talk about?" she asks, feeling the same urge for distraction that I am.

"I got nothing" I reply, staring blankly into my bowl.

For the first time in forever we are eating without a screen in front of us.

It has become a bit of a tradition: we make a nice meal, then carry it over to the TV trays in the living room and plop in front of the screen for an episode of whatever show we've been streaming. Or, if we are feeling elegant and noble, we will eat in this nice dining room with a computer in front of us while we judge vloggers on YouTube or watch documentaries on the Cuban Missile Crisis. These habits are now off limits for the next month.

As part of my dedication to the Slow Food lifestyle, for the next month I have committed (and dragged Gab along for the ride) to a set of rules that will force me to slow down and savor the pleasure, culture, and joie-de-vivre that food can bring. The first rule, of course, is that I cannot eat in front of a screen. In fact, I

Slow Food

cannot do *anything* while eating. No checking email, no writing down my thoughts, no reading – just total focus on my food. This also means I cannot move while consuming my meals. Since so much of my food consumption happens while I'm walking or driving, for now I must stop and stand in one place while I sit and chew. In addition, each meal must last *at least* thirty minutes to make sure I don't just scarf it down and move on. Finally, I must avoid all fast and ultra processed foods. Everything I eat must be made from scratch or at least *made* (not reheated or "prepared" for me by somebody else). Thus those adulterous bags of Oreos sit unopened in my pantry and will remain so for the foreseeable future.

The anxiety that seeps in while eating without other stimulation is concerning. It makes me wonder how strong these unsettled feelings actually are in my day-to-day life, and whether I have been successfully numbing them with distraction or if my body has just gotten used to being strung out all the time. As my mind swirls, I try to focus on the food in front of me. The winter melon is somewhat translucent, and becomes more so the longer it sits in the broth. The smell of five spice is strong and rises up from the broth into my nose. This meal is, when I think about it, a bit of a miracle. We can afford the ingredients, which is fortunate enough in itself. But we also did not even grow any of this food, and yet here it is in front of me. If anything, this meal is a symbol of both generosity and connection between the generations. It is Gabby's grandparents' recipe that we are enjoying, and it is supported by a winter melon they grew in their small Queens garden. One generation being sustained by the previous – the energy gained from these calories must be put to good use. Not to be forgotten, the taste (when focused on) is sublime, subtle, and bursting with flavor and freshness.

Thoughts like this never seep into my mind when I'm eating

while distracted. Even when I *think* I'm paying attention to my food while we play a movie on our laptop, the delightful experience created by the focus on this meal proves otherwise. Plus, the soup tastes different when it is being paid attention to. Flattered, it lets me in on subtle bursts of flavor and texture that it hides when proper respect isn't being given. That is not to say I no longer feel unsettled – quite the contrary. I finish the first bowl in just ten minutes, which means I have to get (and savor) seconds in order to meet the thirty-minute meal requirement.

Eventually we reach the time threshold and are freed from our self-created dining table prison. And yet Gab and I don't immediately get up to rush on to "more important matters". Instead we linger, slurp the remaining bits of our broth, and chat about how lucky we are to still have family around to help provide for us. While most dinners are quick, tasteless affairs, this one has been special. By the end of the thirty minutes my mind settles down, accepting the slower pace of this culinary experience. I think, with a melancholic recognition of current habits, *Why am I in such a hurry, anyway?*

* * *

If this was a normal summer morning, as I stand with bugs chirping in surround sound while fresh dew wets my sneakers, a large, smelly sheep would not be galloping toward me at full speed. It emerged from its hiding spot in a massive red structure once it noticed me, and now it is gleefully lifting its head through a wire fence with one purpose in mind: a nice scratch of the head. It follows my every movement with excitement, and appears to be personally offended when I walk away. I don't want to hurt its feelings, but there is so much else to see on this farm, and there are other animals whose heads await a nice scratching.

We find ourselves on the Nettle Meadow Farm Sanctuary in

Slow Food

the Adirondacks. Nestled into the valley beneath the mountains, the sanctuary is home to dozens of animals who need a safe home due to mental or physical impairments. This includes a duck with a broken wing, peacocks whose previous owner did not know where to put them (which begs the question: why get peacocks in the first place? Also . . .*how*?), a goat on the mend from a broken shoulder, and what is described to us as a "mentally disabled llama", which also comes with the caveat as being the only animal we should *not* approach to pet (message received). The goal of the farm is to give these animals a safe, delightful place to live out their days with plenty of space, food, healthcare, and other luxuries denied to them in more exploitative agricultural operations.

The farm also is a working cheese production facility, which is what brought us here in the first place. Nettle Meadow has a regular stand at our farmers' market, and we often buy their cheese because it is by far the best around (and, as we learn on the property, it has won multiple awards in national competitions). We are on a self-guided tour because of something the worker at the farmers' market said when I went to pay a few months prior.

As I put my cheese on the stand, I grabbed my wallet and instinctively reached for my credit card. The worker, a tall man in his thirties, outfitted with a tie-dye t-shirt with the farm's logo, aviators, and a hat that held together a long mane of hair, immediately interjected:

"Hey man, do you have cash by chance?"

"I do."

"If you could pay with that," he explained, "that'd be great. Chase takes 3% of every sale, *and they haven't even milked a single goat.*"

That line stuck with me. At first I felt guilty. How much money is actually taken from small operations by payment processing companies so I can get my reward points? I've heard that these precious rewards, which have paid for multiple getaways and overnight trips through the years, are funded primarily from these "transaction fees" charged to businesses each time I swipe the card. In my mind, I always thought this was a fair trade-off. Target and Wal-Mart have enough money, so if I can get a night at a hotel in Vermont every now and again just from shopping there, what's the harm? Yet here I was struck with the reality of the system's impact on small, barebones operations.

Since then I always pay cash for local joints and save the rewards card for the big businesses. But that interaction lived rent-free in my mind. As time went on, I thought less about the card companies not milking any goats and more about how *I* have never milked any goats. How I have never actually taken care of an animal or raised one for the purpose of eating it, or its byproduct, at any point. During my job at a soap shop in college (which also doubled as a small farm) I fed lots of chickens and cleaned lots of shit, and occasionally gathered some eggs. I've had small gardens through the years and would, by the end of summer, have a few bits of produce to enjoy. But that has been the extent of my authentic experiences with the food I eat. While shopping at farmers' markets I have shaken the hands that feed me, but never saw what those hands do to get the food from their farm to my plate. How could I be so indignant about payment processing companies being detached from the process when I was, too?

When we go into the grocery store we are completely removed from the environment that our food is produced in. Much of what we see is produced in massive factories and scientific operations that look nothing like the pristine farms printed on the packaging. Take milk, for example. Instead of a happy cow grazing in a pasture like the logo implies, much of our dairy is produced in massive operations that have little-to-no regard for animal welfare, are riddled with disease, and exploit both the animals and the farmers. While images of "grass-fed beef" conjure up misty mornings on rolling meadows, the reality is that most of our meat is produced in Concentrated Animal Feeding Operations (CAFOs) that pack insane amounts of animals into small areas where they are physically and mentally abused, tortured, and treated merely as product before being brutally slaughtered and processed by exploited workers in dangerous conditions that foster both physical and mental health ailments for little pay. That image, while more accurate, doesn't sell when put on the packaging.

The further removed we are from our food, the less we care about it. And the less we care, the more we believe that the animals are being treated well, that the operations are sustainable, that the farmers are fairly compensated, and that the ridiculous health claims that come with ultra processed foods are true. In our blissful ignorance, we can go on buying over-processed, unsustainable, unhealthy foods that harm us, the animals, the workers, and the planet without a second thought other than, "This looks nice, and it's so cheap!" Food becomes an abstract concept instead of a tangible reality that we need to confront if we want to live a healthy life in a healthy society. It becomes something that needs to happen fast and cheap, in spite of that being at odds with the reality of food production. We hoist unrealistic expectations of speed and efficiency on one of the most important aspects of our society and individual lives, and we pay the price because of it. Not in dollars, but in health. Which is *far* more valuable.

And that is why Gab and I find ourselves staring at a massive,

Slow Food

hideous pig sunbathing in a large pen. We know that this Slow Food experiment cannot be complete if we don't connect with the process of what we eat, from farm to table. It is important for us to see where our food comes from and to develop a deeper appreciation for the process that nourishes and sustains us. And, while the pig will never have a hand in either of our meals, just being here with it and enjoying the late summer sun together increases the sense of connection we have with the whole system.

Near the bird sanctuary, which houses a few chickens, three peacocks, and a couple of random rabbits, the co-owner of the farm saunters over to greet us. Lorraine and her business partner, Sheila, opened the farm in 2005 after moving to Upstate New York from Oakland, California. They had a dream to make the best possible cheese while also providing a sanctuary for injured and at-risk farm animals. Lorraine has a presence about her: warm, welcoming, tough, and attuned to the needs of the animals. While chatting she breaks her train of thought multiple times to crouch down and feed some clover to the birds. The peacocks, she tells us, came from a man just a mile down the road who, for some bizarre reason, acquired a small flock and then realized he did not know what to do with them. She gladly took them in, and the original couple has since reproduced. Most importantly, she tells us, they all get along with the rabbits. "It's a motley crew," Lorraine admits, "but they all interact and love each other."

It's obvious she cares deeply about the animals and the process of cheese-making. One would think that, when arriving on an award-winning cheese-making farm, there would be a bit more glitz and glamor. Perhaps some signs advertising their winnings, or a structured tour with a paid guide speaking into a small microphone as they move hoards of people around a semi-industrial, picturesque operation. Not here. The tour is self-guided, the farm almost silent except for the occasional short conversations between workers discussing their projects. The animals seem thrilled to have visitors, as each sheep, goat, and cow (but *not* the sun-bathing pig) run right up to us in hopes of snacks and scratches. Lorraine is very firm with telling us that the one rule of the farm is to pet everyone you see (except the workers and, of course, the llama).

Our chat is brief, and Lorraine thanks us for visiting, caring, and donating before shuffling back to the main house, hands behind her back. As she walks away, I realize how different the pace of this farm is than the regular pace of food shopping. Going to a supermarket usually involves driving on a busy road, averting death with each left turn, circling for parking, managing cart traffic, muttering ill-will toward the person who left their cart in a parking spot, and being funneled in-and-out like the cattle in we're about to eat. The only chance we have to think about where our food comes from or how it's processed is our assessment of the promises made on the packaging. Speed, efficiency, and profit rule our food production system – from CAFO to microwave.

That's not the case here. When Gab and I pause our conversations, it is quiet. Occasionally we hear the sigh of a horse or the sound of hay crunching underneath the feet of a goat. The workers are doing everything manually, to the point where we don't even hear a power tool. Lorraine seems serene for the owner of an award-winning farm. The whole area just feels . . .peaceful. As if the mindful process of creating an exceptional product generates a confidence that profit, even if modest, will come as a result.

Gab and I take one more look around the farm before hopping in the car and heading a few miles south to the farm's restaurant and new cheese-making facility. It is here where the farm's harvest is sent to be processed and made into some of the most delicious cheese in the country, and where you can eat an authentic farm-to-table meal.

Walking into the modified log cabin, we immediately feel the same sense of slowness that we encountered at the farm just twenty minutes earlier. We are greeted with genuine hospitality and are seated immediately next to a large charcuterie station. On the board is a variety of products, including the farm's famous sheep cheese.

As I place a chunk on my plate, paired with some fresh berries, I think about the sheep that ran right up to me during our visit. She was thrilled to be scratched and did not want me to leave. I know that when many people think about where their animal products come from (myself included) they feel a sense of guilt. We know intuitively that CAFOs and slaughterhouses are a moral stain on our society; that the animals there are tortured most of their lives unnecessarily; that the whole system is cruel and unusual and repugnant. It's why many people swear off factory-farmed meat (like I try to, often unsuccessfully) or animal products entirely.

Staring at this cheese feels different. I literally met the sheep who created this product. And they live in a calm, quiet, happy little oasis. They are given a chance at a new life, safe from the horrors of other agricultural operations, and as a result help to nourish and sustain me and thousands of other people. They *experience* joy and *create* joy for others, directly through the thrill of bounding up to them like a puppy or indirectly with the taste of their cheese. And the people profiting off of this are not part of some multinational corporation hell-bent on obscene profit generated through blood money. They are good, honest folks who do their best to make a difficult operation work, even if it requires saving a few random peacocks and housing a neurodivergent llama.

Slow Food

This is what food should be. Slow, genuine, in tune with the seasons. Sure, it's a bit more expensive. If the whole system worked in this way, there wouldn't be as much supply. And profit margins will be slimmer. But food isn't a new phone or operating system or a fresh line-up of fall fashion. It is a necessary component for the health of all life on Earth. We *should* be willing to spend more to do it right when we are able. And we should support subsidizing healthier food options so that those struggling to make ends meet can have nutritious food available to them instead of empty calories and excesses of salt, sugar, and fat (a civil rights issue that is often overlooked). The reality is that cheap food is not cheap. It equals expensive healthcare. It fuels more frequent, expensive environmental disasters. And it results in the costliest effect of all: a deep sense of apathy from us about the systems to which we are all still an integral part of. Right now, saving a few bucks here and there costs us dearly. But it doesn't have to be that way. We can have healthy, affordable options available to everyone *if* we choose to advocate for that path forward.

I understand the immense privilege it is to be able to bite into the insanely delicious, farm-to-table pot-pie that gets plopped onto our table after we finish our free cheese samples. In it I see the love, care, and dedication of a group of people fighting to make a better, more just, more humane food system. I see our local culture and ecology embedded into the meal, completely in tune with the season. I see nutrient-dense food that is going to nourish my body and improve my health. And when I look around the restaurant, I see a little safe haven from the fast-paced world, and food system, that exists outside these doors. This meal becomes my most appreciated in quite some time, as Gab and I savor every delicious morsel, making it take much longer to finish than usual.

With each bite, I dream of what our world could be when brought together by food like this. It is a dream I hope can become a reality one day.

And maybe it can, even if it's just around a single table.

The experience gets me thinking as Gab and I finish up our meal. So far, this Slow Food experiment has calmed my mind, expanded my palette, and fostered a greater appreciation for where our food, *real* food that is, comes from. Now I think it is time to tie it all together. I decide quietly, as Gab makes sure to get the last bits of melted cheese from her sandwich, that I will combine everything I can about the Slow Food movement into one final, meaningful experience centered around delicious food and great company.

And the perfect time for this idea is near: Mabon, the Fall Equinox, the official start of the harvest season.

* * *

On a brisk September afternoon, with oak leaves swaying in the breeze and the hickory tree beginning to burst into a full dress of yellow, I smile as grill smoke enters my nostrils and a beach ball gets batted around in the yard below me. I look up at the smoke wafting upward into the crisp blue sky as the sounds of laughter and off-color jokes provide the soundtrack for the scene.

Today is the end of my Slow Food experiment. Together with our regular group of friends, we are celebrating Mabon, the autumn equinox, embracing the themes of balance and letting go in line with the changeover from summer to fall. Once again we have gathered to bask in the sun and each other's company. This time, though, the priority is our meal.

As I near the end of this year-long journey, one of the more profound lessons I've learned is the importance of community and how it is lacking in today's world. We are more isolated, more alone, more distant than ever. A year of deliberately being a kid again with a group of friends has shown just how lonely and bottled up I became throughout my twenties. The sweet release of playing outside with friends, no matter how stressful life is, provides comfort regardless of circumstances. Even if a week at work is dreadful, demoralizing, and makes me question my worth in society, knowing that the week will end with a made-up game, dirt on the knees, and a stomach sore from laughter provides a light at the end of the tunnel.

These thoughts pass through my mind as I flip the chicken spiedies (a hometown delicacy) on the grill with a cheap but effective metal spatula. Right now, I feel a deep sense of connection between myself, my tribe, and my food. This is a meal that gave me comfort throughout my entire childhood, and continues to do so as my skin begins to wrinkle and my eyes drop ever-so-slightly in the first signs of life's inevitable tolls. I've eaten spiedies around campfires, at graduation parties, and at countless birthday parties. When I visited my family last year in the midst of the gauntlet, my parents knew to have a plate ready to soften the gnawing in my soul. Together that night, Gab, my parents, and I shared a meal that provided relief amidst the storm. Around the table, with plates below our tired minds, the world made sense for a few moments. Sometimes that's all we need to heal enough to continue forward for another day.

Food is the biggest missing link in today's world that heals our body, our minds, our souls, and our relationships. There is no simpler and more powerful way to break the epidemic of loneliness than to share a meal with loved ones. The easiest solution to heal our broken relationship with the environment is to make sure that meal is cooked with local ingredients from towns and people we know. The best defense against the endless noise of the outside world is to engage the senses in a meal full of meaning and purpose, surrounded in a circle by loved ones whose laughter, stories, and shared experience provides a shield that blocks out the negativity that swirls outside. Eating with, and from, our community strengthens ties, deepens roots, forges connection, and helps to build a life of purpose – one where we are no longer at the center, but instead where we recognize our integral part in a greater, more important, whole.

"Pete, catch!"

A tight spiral slices through the air toward me. Without a thought I snap my right hand up into the sky and snag the football thrown in my direction.

"Go long!" I shout, tossing the ball below to nobody in particular and enjoying the swarm as everyone attempts to catch the pass. It's a good thing Sarinah threw that pass to snap me back to reality, because the spiedies are fragrant, perfectly cooked, and ready to be plated.

For this meal I did my best to source everything locally, and with as much meaning as possible – much more deliberately than our Imbolc celebration earlier in the year. The chicken comes from a local butcher I researched who has his own farm, freeing me from the prison of CAFO-sourced meat. The corn, squash, and peppers that add a natural sweetness and fragrant aroma to the kitchen were grown just three miles from our house in a field that sways with amber waves in golden sunsets, watched over by purple mountain silhouettes in the distance. The buns are baked in the next town over, delivered fresh to a local grocer each morning. And the dessert, fresh and gooey chocolate chip cookies made by Gab, may not have local ingredients, but it *is* made with flour we milled ourselves after sourcing the wheat from a family farm out in Washington. Even our friends partake in the theme, as Troy's farro salad is filled with fresh tomatoes grown in his backyard. This is a celebration of community, balance, and meaning. It's a perfect way to end a month of reconnecting with myself, my community, and an oft-neglected environment.

* * *

Our food system is unbalanced. This is a problem that impacts all of us. And it is one that threatens to disrupt our physical health, our community ties, and our societal well-being in one fell swoop. Without a balanced, healthy, *slow* food system, our society cannot survive. And we cannot possibly live our best lives, if we define "best" as being a life of balance, a strong and supportive community, good physical health, and a thriving, diverse ecosystem. Unfortunately, we currently define "best" in terms of profit margins, efficiency, and economies of scale. When quality of life is measured in those terms, it's no wonder our system is broken and unhealthy.

Because of this, we need to shift our perspective when it comes to how we nourish ourselves. Industrial agriculture has created incredible wonders. I, for one, love being able to buy raspberries in Upstate New York in the dead of winter. That being said, an over-reliance on efficiency and profit leads to unhealthy monocultures, dangerous chemical use, unsustainable soil treatment, poor working conditions, and a less nutritious diet. Sure, we are producing more calories than ever. But they are not high-quality calories coming from high-quality food that supports high-quality experiences. Like much of our other consumption (i.e. goods, media, content), they are junk. And we are suffering the physical, mental, and communal consequences because of it.

I don't believe that fixing our food system, at this stage and scale, is possible. At least not for this generation. And I don't think doing so will solve all of our problems. However, I *do* think reshaping how we interact with it is the single-most impactful change we can make as individuals. This entire project is dedicated to the argument that much of our lives will improve when we take aspects of our culture that are too fast and convenient and intentionally slow them down and make them more challenging. After this experience, I can strongly confirm that applying this process to our food system has immense benefits that spread way beyond our plates. And it is also the simplest to apply.

First, buying whole foods over ultra-processed junk food immediately improves our nutrition and health, hands down. Whenever a new study comes out about health indicators in relation to nutrition, the theme is clear: eat more real, whole foods. Regardless of the percentage of animal products to plant-products or types of proteins or amount of carbohydrates, starting with real food is non-negotiable if we want to improve our health and nutrition. This first step is powerful and breaks those initial bonds to our broken food system that we are stuck in.

Next, we all need to eat locally (or regionally) whenever we can. Again, this may not be often. But there is power in meeting the people who grow what we put on our plate. There is a sense of responsibility to the environment when we visit the farms that produce our calories. And what better way to develop a sense of community than by knowing the hands and minds and sweat that went into our meals? In this sense, our community isn't just made up of who is at the table with us. Instead, it includes who brought us together in the first place. Spending our precious dollars on this community makes a strong statement about who, and what, we value. Plus, if we're being more realistic and less philosophical, I'll take an apple I picked straight from an orchard over a waxed, store-bought apple any day of the week. The taste comparison is unmatched.

Unlike ultra-processed foods, whole foods require time, care, and attention. They need to be *cooked*. And that's the next step. Making time to cook real food is essential. Meals we cook ourselves are almost always healthier than fast food and take-out in general (as long as you're not frying your own chicken night after night), which means our physical health will improve over time. The attention and care that cooking requires removes us from our devices and the constant, swirling noise of the outside world. It provides a few minutes of refuge alone in our kitchen. We improve our competency and agency, which are essential to our self-esteem. Cooking, even if just for ourselves, is a radical act of self-care. And, all things considered, it's pretty cheap.

Of course taking time to cook meals more frequently is inconvenient. It negatively impacts our productivity in other areas of life. It takes time away from keeping up with the news and social media and the demands of our inbox. It requires us to be patient when we are at the end of a long work day, to use energy when we are exhausted, and to take time in our increasingly-packed schedules.

Good.

Because spending time cooking wholesome meals isn't like other areas of work or productivity. It doesn't *take*. It *provides*. Spending time prepping, cooking, and eating isn't time lost that could be used "better" for more "productive" activities. No. It is *time well spent* and creates a life well lived. Doing this reaffirms that our health, sanity, and the nourishment of ourselves and others takes precedence over endless loops of production and consumption. Pausing to watch soup bubble in a pot, and to later share it with family or friends, is an act of rebellion against a fast-paced world of convenience and "more". It is proof that we are still *living*. Not for profit or production, but for its own sake. And that's enough.

Finally, even if our meal isn't home-cooked and made up of real, local food, there is nothing stopping us from putting down the screens, taking a few deep breaths, and enjoying whatever it is we fuel our bodies with. We are too distracted and don't pay enough attention to our food. Many meals are consumed at forty-five miles per hour, without a single thought about the taste or texture riding our tongues. The common phrase "I can't even remember what I ate for breakfast today" says less about our memory and more about our inability to pay attention. Our meals take up so much of our life that, if we forget to notice them, then we forget to live. Whether it's a fast-food burger or a homemade feast, each meal deserves our undivided attention, if only for a few bites. Maybe then we would recognize whether something is worth eating, or if we actually feel *good* after eating it, or whether there is an alternative that is better, more flavorful, more steeped in meaning.

* * *

Food is complicated. Throughout this experience I examined my food from a variety of perspectives, including health, nutrition, culture, cost, economics, morality, emotion, tradition, locality, and environmental impact. There is no single factor that can determine our choices, even if some are more influential than others. To say we should only eat based on a single principle, or that we are even capable of that, is naive. I understand that many people can't just slow down and cook a good meal often, if at all. There are folks who don't have a healthy grocery store around for miles. There are others who are on economic assistance and need to stretch a processed meal as far as they can. Our food system, like many of our bodies, is not healthy. And to expect everyone to make the "right" choices is impossible when there is no single "right" choice, and decisions that are objectively healthy are made more difficult by circumstance.

Having worked in the nutrition coaching world, I recognize the shortsightedness of judging people for their food choices based on a single factor. I frequently encounter the world of extreme diets. These claim to have the secrets to health, youth, and longevity, but they are nutritionally unsound and impractical to follow. I see people who judge others' eating choices based on ethics alone, while neglecting the equally valid factors of culture, tradition, and economics, among others, that often leave people with impossible food choices. Demonizing others for eating a certain product that's steeped in their culture and sense of identity, or for having a bit of oil on a salad, or for using a supplement, is counterproductive. This does nothing to fix the problems we face with our systems or our health. Instead, it leads us down a path of further polarization and tribalism that is all too prevalent in other parts of society. To turn food into such a sludge-pit would be a travesty.

What I *have* learned, and what I can say with certainty, is that we should all make our best effort to eat real food whenever possible. It may not be every meal, or even every day, but the benefits that come from the simple act of eating real food are too powerful to ignore. In addition to improving our health, it also fosters a sense of connection with our environment and the systems that sustain us.

Food is life. And, like our modern lifestyle, it succumbs to the pressures of infinite growth, profit, productivity, and efficiency. This is a great shame and creates a series of problems that certainly won't be fixed within this generation. But in this truth lies the path forward. Our food is a reflection of our values and our culture. Therefore, if we slow down and focus on the quality of our food and the company it is shared with, then our life will naturally be slower, of higher

Slow Food

quality, and shared with better company. This is an internal path that we can work toward regardless of our constraints. It is a path that is not only necessary for a life well-lived, but it is also one that is almost universally accessible and enticing.

As my friends begin to load their plates with the colorful feast on the table, I make a silent pledge:

From here on out, I will give my food the time, attention, care, and respect it deserves as often as I can. Whether it comes in a wrapper on the highway or takes all day to cook in the comfort of my own home. I will be there for it. Wholly present. Always mindful. Genuinely appreciative. Respectful to the core.

Just like I should be for my life.

The Magic of Forest Bathing

Breathing in, I feel the sweet air fill my nostrils and circulate into my lungs.

Breathing out, I sense the energy and power of the forest around me.

Breathing in, I stare at the full moon hovering through the trees above me.

Breathing out, I take in the sun's final light, reflected off the moon that is guiding my path.

It is mid-October, a perfectly brisk night in the middle of fall. Leaves are changing and a large percentage of my blood is diluted with apple cider. As I stroll through the forest on this serene evening, I can't help but think about all of the incredible experiences I have had this year, and how much growth the experiments from these past few months have created in me. I feel a sense of calm, confidence, and acceptance that, truth be told, I have not felt in quite some time (if ever).

I am in this forest under the Hunter's Moon, named for the deer hunt that traditionally occurs this time of year. The purpose of this experience is to bathe under its light. And no, this does not mean I am about to strip naked and wade into the murky, stagnant, leech-filled pond that lies next to the path. I am here to forest bathe, a practice that has gained notoriety and popularity over the last decade. And one that, over the previous two weeks, has cleansed me in a variety of ways. This bath just happens to be extra special, being under the light of the full moon. It marks the halfway point of my forest bathing experiment, the final challenge of this slow and strenuous year, which will continue for a complete moon cycle.

Just two weeks in, the profound effects of this meditative practice are being felt. I am already convinced of its need to be more widely adopted in society. And I am calculating ways I can do this more during my normal work days.

For now, though, I remember that I am here to be present. I bring my focus back to my breath and the soft Earth beneath my feet. The crickets provide the soundtrack as a light breeze with crisp autumnal undertones guides me further down the path, illuminated by the mirror above.

* * *

In the 1980s, a young Japanese doctor noticed that something wasn't quite right with modern society. The pace of life was increasing dramatically. More and more people were moving into Tokyo, which was already one of the most densely populated cities on the planet. "Commuter Hell" began to form as workers pushed and squeezed their way into overstuffed trains that would rocket them to a job that, more than likely, required that they work an unhealthy amount of hours. And, if they missed the train, the most convenient solution was to be stuffed into a capsule hotel, lie on a bed, and watch TV until they fell asleep and continued the unnatural routine early the next morning.

The young doctor was confused. How could a country that was mostly covered in forests, and that had such a deep, rich tradition of being connected with nature, so quickly turn into a society disconnected from the natural rhythms and landscape of the Earth? How was it that a population whose traditional spiritual beliefs reflected presence in the beauty of nature had that mindset replaced with a rushed, overworked dogma of increasing production in sterile urban landscapes? And was there a relationship between the literal "death from overwork" (known as *karoshi*) and this fast-paced, urban lifestyle?

By this time, the term "technostress" had been coined to describe the unhealthy results of too much time spent with technology. Whether it involves watching too much TV, checking your phone every few seconds, or spending endless hours online, technostress can result in symptoms such as anxiety, headaches, mental fatigue, short temper, and even depression. Couple this with fast-paced urban life and the chance of developing health issues compounds. Stress levels are higher for people in urban areas compared to less populated ones, in part due to the overstimulation that comes with loud noises, crowded streets, polluted air, and visual stimuli. And we are now an urban, technocentric species; more than half of us live in urban areas while access to the internet and smart-devices increases each year. Even in the 1980s, doctors were noticing the impacts of increased urbanization coupled with technostress. Which is why that young doctor, Qing Li, sought ways to help people alleviate this stress and find a method to help people live more present, calm, peaceful lives in spite of the increasing industrial and technological stressors they were facing.

His solution was simple: get people into the forest.

And it worked.

Dr. Li is known as the founder of a therapy called Forest Bathing (*shinrin-yoku* in Japanese). The premise is uncomplicated and accessible: spend time mindfully exploring the outdoors while engaging all of your senses. Whether it involves slowly walking through a forest, camping under the stars, having lunch in a park surrounded by wildflowers, or even sitting at the base of a solitary tree, forest bathing simply requires the practitioner to find a natural space and engage with it using as many senses as possible, without distraction. The key is to leave your work, phone, and concrete environment behind in order to spend meaningful time surrounded by the natural world (regardless how big or small that patch of natural world may be). And while this started from a deep intuition that time in nature is beneficial, it took a few decades for science to catch-up with our own inner wisdom.

In 1990, a preliminary research group in Japan led a forest bathing expedition in order to determine the mental and physiological effects of spending an extended time slowly walking through the forest. While the trip can't be considered as a rigorous study, it did conclude that the participants experienced improved mood and increased energy after the expedition; a promising start. Fourteen years later, in 2004, Dr. Li helped to found the Forest Therapy Study Group and conducted a more rigorous study on the effects of forest bathing. What they found was that, primarily due to a decrease in the release of cortisol (otherwise known as the "stress hormone"), participants in the forest bathing experiment (as well as subsequent ones conducted in the years since) experienced lower levels of stress, adrenaline, and blood pressure. Results also found that participants had increased heart-rate variability, better sleep (about an extra hour per night), less anxiety, and overall improved emotional disposition. To put it simply, spending a few hours to a few days wandering in a forest chills us out . . .a lot.

Intuitively, this makes sense. While we may not realize it, we have become accustomed to constantly elevated stress levels. How often do we actually sit and do nothing but stare out the window? Instead of letting our brains relax, we are constantly shifting from one "crisis" to the next, be it checking our phone, catching up on email, seeing if anyone liked our post, watching the world go to hell on the news, thinking about our endless to-do lists, or just doing *one more thing* before we stop working and attempt to go to sleep. This may be normal, but it is not natural. And so it is not surprising that disconnecting from these habits, especially for an extended length of time, would allow our brains to finally breathe a sigh of relief and calm down. Staring aimlessly into swaying branches while listening to birdsong and babbling brooks is what we evolved to do in our spare time; not check our email ten times an hour to see if anyone wants to chat.

The idea of forest bathing is especially pertinent as the pace of life continues to quicken and become more disconnected from nature. Journalist Richard Louv, in his book *Last Child in the Woods*, coined the phrase "Nature-Deficit Disorder" as a way to describe the mental and physical ailments that come from spending too much time indoors and on screens. His review of the research on the impacts of this lifestyle led to similar findings as the Japanese teams who were inspired to successfully attempt forest bathing as a treatment. The effects are especially apparent on children, who, according to the Children & Nature Network, spend 44 hours per week in front of a screen and merely 10 minutes per day playing outdoors. The constant stimulation that comes from our devices, paired with a lack of time outside to let the brain relax, may result in increased cases of Attention-Deficit Hyperactive Disorder (ADHD), behavioral problems in schools, and stunted development of linguistic, social, and emotional regulation skills. Whereas time spent in nature, in particular unstructured play outdoors, can alleviate many of these issues and result in more positive outcomes.

As we spend more time indoors and in front of our screens, we become less connected to the natural world in which we evolved. In

The Magic of Forest Bathing

Reconnection: Fixing our Broken Relationship with Nature, Professor Miles Richardson argues that, as our society has become more reliant on industrial technology, we have lost the "spark" that makes us connect with, and care for, the natural world. Whereas just a few hundred years ago most people saw nature as a magical place worth connecting with, many of us now see nature as something that is other, separate, a nuisance at worst or merely a background at best. Part of this is due to us having less need to interact with the environment, while we have also fallen prey to the attention-seeking behaviors of companies desperate for a bit of our focus in order to advertise to us. The oak tree across the street does not care whether or not you pay attention to it. The social media app that just sent you a notification does, and will do anything it can to steal your attention. And so we fall into the trap and let our attention be diverted from notification to notification, unaware of the calm rhythms of nature that surround us and don't require our noticing to continue onward.

Over time this leads to a destructive feedback loop: lack of attention results in lack of noticing, which leads to lack of awareness, which fosters a lack of caring. And when we don't care, we don't love, which means we don't even attempt to protect or preserve. Why watch the leaves change when I could see if my crush liked my newest photo or if my boss approved of my presentation? Why care about the trees being torn down for a parking lot when I never notice them anyway? My personal army tank needs more room. And besides, there are more important matters at hand. At least that is the lie we tell ourselves.

Thankfully, this apathy toward nature can change very quickly. Richardson found in his research that spending time in nature was not enough to forge a connection with it. Oftentimes, we use nature as a setting to *accomplish* something – some goal like a hike, paddle, or run. When doing this, feelings of nature connectedness do not increase in any meaningful way. Instead of performing, to experience true nature connectedness we need to slow down and consciously observe our surroundings and attach value to them. This could mean taking photographs of natural scenes we find to be pretty or writing down three things we thought were beautiful and interesting while going on a walk. Simply acknowledging that something in nature moved us in an emotional way is enough to forge a deeper connection. Suddenly the breeze isn't an unnoticed phenomenon that ruffles our hair while we respond to a text; it becomes a refreshing moment on a warm day. Or a tree is no longer an unseen feature in an overlooked landscape; it morphs into a beautiful ecosystem of its own with strength, wisdom, and merciful shade. These value-adding exercises turn nature from "other" to "ours". It's amazing how fast we can begin to care if we just give it a chance.

I tested this theory with an impromptu experiment involving my high school students. Earlier in the year, my sunrise morning routine came up in conversation and they were shocked. *Wait,* they protested, *you're not checking social media? Or email? How early do you wake up?* And then, my favorite question:

You seriously just sit outside and do nothing for thirty minutes?

I responded that, yes, I have been doing that. And that it was delightful and they should all try it. One student raised her hand and protested:

"I don't even have 10 minutes in my day to just stare out a window. I'm too busy."

Knowing I could push a little with this class, I responded quickly:

"Really? What's your screen time? A couple hours, maybe?

You're telling me you can't spend 10 minutes less on your phone and use that time to watch birds?"

A quiet realization settled on the classroom. I knew it was not their fault – their minds have been manipulated by attention-seeking companies since they were children. But I saw an opportunity to forge a connection. At that moment, I told my class to come to the window and look at the scene outside. Scattered across the ground were about *fifty* robins, all hopping around trying to find delicious worms to munch on. They scuttled about in patterns underneath the pine trees. I stood in the back and watched as my students became transfixed on the birds. A group of boys began commentating like it was a sporting event. Another student noticed a woodpecker on a tree, which led to others trying to find it. Here, in just a few minutes, a room of twenty-five apathetic sixteen year-olds became transfixed by the simple beauty of nature. Afterward I told my students that, when they finish work, the best thing they could do would be to stare out the window for a minute and let their brain rest. Sure, not everyone followed this advice. But as the year went on I noticed more and more students stare at the trees while they waited for their next assignment. Some students began spending their break-time at the window instead of on their phones. And as the weather became more pleasant toward the end of the year, the question, "Can we have class outside today?" became more frequent. I always obliged to this request. I felt it would have been cruel to deny it. Over time behavioral problems became less frequent, I made connections with students who were previously distant, and a stronger sense of community developed amongst classmates. A small sample size, sure, but a powerful one.

* * *

My own history supports the benefits of forest bathing, even if I was partaking in the practice unknowingly. I grew up in an area surrounded by forests, tucked into the bottom of a glacial-cut valley in Upstate New York. Just about every day I would venture out of the house and stroll through the hardwoods toward the rushing creek in my backyard. Or, if I was up for an adventure, I would climb the large hill that I lived at the bottom of and explore the ancient paths of a forgotten ski resort and sneak up on the hunting blinds that scattered the landscape. During summers in high school, my friends and I would camp out for multiple nights in the neighborhood woods completely on our own, as if we had created our own little society hidden from adults. If I was ever stressed out, worried, anxious, or had a problem to work through, a long walk in the woods *always* did the trick. My parents learned that, when I said I'd be going out for a walk, I could return in fifteen minutes or four hours, depending on how I felt. Eventually they stopped asking how long I would be gone for – they realized that not even I knew the answer. I didn't *know* that these walks (or "forest baths") were inherently lowering my blood pressure, reducing my chances of developing depression, or improving my sleep. I just knew that, when I walked in the woods, I always felt better. It was a part of my identity and my life. And that was all that mattered.

As I grew older, predictably, my time in the forest waned. I moved into apartments surrounded by more fast-food chains than white pines. I was housed in complexes surrounded by private, strictly managed land instead of the relaxed meandering landscape of my youth. As responsibilities and expectations piled up, jetting off on a spontaneous four-hour walk with no communication became unrealistic and irresponsible. My walks had to be timed, scheduled, and worked around more important matters. *Especially* since I could no longer just step out my front door and immerse myself in a pristine Northeastern woodland. Plus, trespassing is not as cute when you are a thirty-one year old man as it is when you're just a teen wandering aimlessly about. Being caught at my age would result in me becoming the latest source of unnecessary anxiety peddled on the local town Facebook page. Anonymity is preferred.

With each passing year, as my connection to nature has waned, I have become more stressed, worried, and anxious. Maybe it's because I have more to lose now that I've built up a life and family. It could also be the weight of responsibility that comes with being relied upon by so many people. And, of course, the events of the past year have compounded upon the little daily stressors that I already face each day.

When we moved into our new home, the opportunity for walks in the forest suddenly became available again. There are patches of woods all around the neighborhood, and there is even a pond just a few minutes away that I could walk to every single day. Since it is new, though, my house does not feel like home; I am still a bit disconnected from it. As I read more about forest bathing I thought that, perhaps, more time in the forest could cure what is ailing me. What if the prescription to my disconnection, frayed attention, and constant stress is simply more time in the woods? Even if that time has to be scheduled, condensed, or compromised to accommodate Gab (who is decidedly *not* an outside person), returning to a daily ritual of sauntering through the woods would do more good than harm. And, hopefully, it could help me reconnect with who I am at my core.

Deep down I feel a gap between my current self and my younger self. It does not feel like there is a continuous path that brought me to where I am today. Instead, it almost feels like there's a blank spot, where suddenly I appeared in my current form having forgotten who I was in my youth. I often sense a nagging feeling of being "someone else" instead of my true self, which follows me around each day. It's as if I forged the identity of a "successful and productive adult" who does "successful and productive things" instead of living authentically. At certain points throughout the past few years, everything from my lifestyle habits, emotions, and even my haircuts and clothing style have felt like I have been putting on the costume of someone I thought I *should* be, not who I actually am. This has led to an unavoidable sense of hollow-ness that keeps me from being wholly happy and fulfilled with my sense of self.

Before the responsibilities and expectations and bills and global pandemics began piling up, I always figured myself out while mindlessly wandering in the woods. And if there is one thing that has fallen by the wayside in my adult life, it is that. Not necessarily the occasional, longer hikes that I have continued to do (when carefully scheduled on the calendar). What matters most to me are those spontaneous strolls with no goal or mindset or target in particular. Those have the largest impact. So when I think of who I am deep down, *that* is the image that comes up: puttering through the forest with no goal to accomplish other than being alive and enjoying my precious life in nature. It is the image that resonates more than any other with my soul.

Without this practice, though, that "gap" persists and I feel a bit lost on a daily basis. Heck, if I wasn't lost, I wouldn't be on this journey in the first place. I wouldn't have put off those things I wanted to do for so long. I wouldn't have been taking my life for granted so frivolously. I wouldn't have slipped into the seductively convenient and comfortable (but less fulfilling) habits that make up my days. I would feel like my own person again.

Which is why this is the perfect way to conclude my slow and strenuous year.

Somewhere out there little me resides, waiting to be remembered and nurtured into a whole person. He is waiting to feel less like a "productive and successful adult in society" and more like Peter just continuing to live his life as best he can. At this point, it's dawning on me that maybe this was the point all along: to find him once again, and bring him back into my being.

And he can only be found in the forest.

* * *

The sun peeks through the labyrinth of trees like golden swords slicing to the ground as I take my first steps into this new terrain. It is nothing special – just a small patch of woods with a path at the edge of my neighborhood that borders a creek. For months I have driven, biked, and walked past this without a second thought. As I begin my forest bathing experiment, though, I need to find a regular location that I can access easily. It may not be the large forest that surrounded my childhood home, with endless trails, cliffs, and a roaring creek, but it's something.

Stepping into the path feels like being transported into another world. Behind me is a cliché, bland suburban neighborhood. In front now lies a magical, whimsical forest that is sure to house fairies and gnomes in its hidden crevices. Walking onto the path feels like being hugged by the Earth, as if the trees are saying, "It's okay. You're home now." As I move along I spot a massive mushroom exploding with growth on the edge of a decaying oak stump (a black-staining polypore, I find out later). Beyond that, reeds sway in the breeze as they emerge from the mud, exposed from low water levels due to lack of rain. Through the reeds a movement catches my eye and I freeze in place: a great blue heron is perched on a rock in the middle of the mud. It is seeking out its breakfast, carefully moving in the shallow water, its gaze focused on potential menu items below. I gasp, and it hears me. Without even turning its head, its wings spread to show off its massive span; it gracefully levitates off the ground and floats further downstream, away from my prying eyes. I am disappointed before remembering that I too would not like to be stared at by some stranger in the diner booth next to mine. I'll be more subtle next time.

Further down the path, a mist gathers along the wider part of the stagnant creek that, when mixed with the low-angled light of the golden sunrise, twinkles and reminds me that the space filled by mere air is not actually vacant, but full of matter and its own characteristics. I swoop around the bank and reemerge further down the road, once again brought back into the standard suburban landscape.

The whole walk takes a mere thirty minutes. The landscape is ordinary and overlooked. I don't see another person the entire time I am there (a trend that continues as I frequent this path almost daily throughout the month). For the first time, though, I *have* looked deeply at it. I notice as many plants, trees, animals, mushrooms, and characteristics as possible. New plants are identified, I have a run-in with a gorgeous bird, and now there are familiar lifeforms that deserve a daily check-in to see how they change as the season begins to turn. In a way, I feel like a true local. Someone who is connected to this little plot of land in a meaningful way. All it took was noticing the habitually unnoticed.

* * *

Slow strolls in the woods on sunny mornings are pleasant and easy. As the month goes on I begin to love my new morning routine, which now couples a slow walk meant to foster intentional attention paid to my surroundings with my previous ritual of watching the sunrise every day. While sitting on the deck and watching the golden light slowly work its way down the trees is fulfilling, watching the same process while under the canopy of a forest is a much more immersive experience. My days feel like they take longer when they begin with this ritual, and I look forward to seeing my friends each day: the black-staining polypore, the Virginia creepers, the reeds, the oaks, maples, and elms, and occasionally, if I'm lucky, the great blue heron. While slow, these forest baths are anything but strenuous.

Until the rain comes.

It is a dark, gloomy late afternoon as I sit in my car with the remnants of a tropical storm pounding on the hood. The sun is going to set in an hour, but it is impossible to tell since it is hidden behind a thick mass of clouds sweeping across the entire Northeast. While Gab is out at a friend's house, I decide to check out a large nature preserve on the north-end of town that I have driven by many times but have never stepped in. At first my laziness almost got the best of me. *Why do I have to go when it's pouring?* I thought in an attempt to justify my unwillingness to venture outside. *I can just wait a day and go in the sunshine.* But, due to the rain, I did not embark on my usual morning forest bath. And a commitment is a commitment, even when it rains.

When I was younger this would not have been an issue at all. My friends and I played outside when it was pouring, snowing, a hundred degrees, or five-below-zero. It didn't matter. The desire to play outside triumphed over all conditions. Now, my desire to be comfortable keeps me in more often than not, and I have grown to hate that about myself. *Besides*, I think as I put on my hat and prepare to step out into the rain, *I might as well have a true forest bath.*

Immediately soaked, I venture down a dark path that provides some slight relief from the rain, thanks to the canopy of leaves above. The path is wide and soft; beautiful for walking and perhaps skiing come winter time. While the trees are not old-growth (this was clearly farming land a generation ago and has since been left to rewild), they are of sufficient size to immerse me in their embrace. As the path continues the sound of the road fades into the distance, and I am left with the comforting sound of rain bouncing off the millions of leaves above.

When forest bathing, it is important to engage all the senses. Sure, walking around and looking at the scenery is great. But the full effect comes from intentionally creating a more intentional sensory experience. This requires not just looking, but listening mindfully to the sounds of the forest. It means feeling the breeze and perhaps the trees themselves that we share the space with. It invites us to literally stop and smell the roses (or the pines) and, if we are brave enough, to taste the world around us. For me, this involves closing my eyes, thrusting my head upward, and sticking out my tongue to catch the rain drops falling from above. It's a pretty meta experience to realize I'm drinking rainwater that has traveled halfway across the globe, in a storm that originated off the West African coast a couple of weeks ago. *That* is what it feels like to have a connection with the world, not the empty promises of imagined connection made by social media companies.

Drenched to the bone thanks to my old raincoat alerting me in the worst possible way that it is no longer up for these types of jobs, I begin my exit from the forest once it becomes too dark to make out individual features on the ground. I realize that on a dark, rainy night like this I could have easily stayed inside and comfortable. It would have been a reasonable decision to make. And yet I am the only unreasonable adult out here in the wild, sopping wet, with a huge grin on my face. The wind begins to pick up and the darkened trees start swaying above me. Mercifully it is a warm breeze that sweeps across my face and dries a tiny bit of the rain dripping down from my cheeks.

I feel *alive*. All of my senses are connected with the Earth. My sense of time disintegrates and any anxieties or worries or unfinished "to-dos" slip beyond my consciousness. Inside this forest, just a short drive from my home, the child inside me awakens. This is his favorite thing to do: romp around the woods with no real purpose and no concern for outside conditions. I toss a lifeline to him that he examines for a moment before smiling, giggling, and crouching down to pick it up. Holding my end, while he holds his, for the first time in years I feel a true connection between the two of us. And it's one I promise to hold dearly as I catch a glimpse of my wet, dirty, glowing face in the rearview mirror upon my return to the car.

* * *

"I'm tired," Gab says between heavy breaths. "Can we rest?"

"Of course!" I reply, trying to remain as upbeat as possible in hopes that today works out.

Gab is not an outdoors person by any stretch of the imagination. Whereas I grew up wandering in the woods, camping on school nights, and swimming in lakes, Gab was raised in a packed Long Island suburb surrounded by highways that cut off any chance of childhood adventuring. She grew up primarily indoors and comes from a genetic pool that gets horrible reactions to mosquito bites (I've seen her ankle swell up like a balloon from just a tiny bite in the past. Her reluctance to sit outside for fires in buggy evenings is understandable). But she is also a thoughtful and supportive person, and has put great effort into at least tolerating the outdoors so that she can occasionally join me on my pursuits. Today is one of those days, as I have dragged her along for one of my more intensive forest bathing sessions after promising to arrange a pick-up of some craft supplies she wanted from Facebook Marketplace; supplies that happened to be located near a small mountain. Marriage is all about compromises.

My hope is to foster a love of the outdoors, and forest bathing in particular, in Gab (to the extent that it's possible). At this point in the experiment the results are profound. My days are stretching longer, my sleep is improving, and a peculiar sense of calm is seeping inside me. I feel less productive, and more importantly less *need* to be productive, which is resulting in longer stretches of staring out the window or napping on my deck. I now track my observations in a small nature journal, where I mark the times of the sunrise and sunset, the moon phases, and any interesting sights that appear on my walks. Internally, I am developing a sense of becoming both an amateur naturalist and a whimsical forest wizard. Plus, what better way to round out the year than by sharing a slow and strenuous experiment with my wife?

It is a perfect day to trudge up this steep but manageable mountain – cool, a slight breeze, not humid enough to break a sweat. Gab and I stop to rest frequently, chatting about work, meal prep ideas, drama she saw online, and our new CrossFit habit as we work our way up. Near the top we pass by two happy families who are on their way down from the summit. A young boy is well ahead of his father and grandfather, and he precariously hops from rock to rock, attempting not to touch any soil as if it is made of lava. As a seasoned veteran of this imaginary game I offer him a few footwork tips along his descent. He smiles and continues to hop down the little rock slide masquerading as a path. Moments later the older generations catch-up and, in typically polite-hiker fashion, they smile, wave, and tell us "It's *so* worth it" at the top. This validation is critical for Gab, who usually doesn't believe me when I say how worth it the hike is and that we are getting close to the top (and with good reason – I'd be lying if I said we haven't had some mishaps in the woods before).

Soon after our encounter with the family the sky starts to clear up and to the right, which is a sign of the approaching summit. As we ascend up the final bit of the trail we see an older woman resting at the base of the fire tower that dominates the summit area (the Adirondacks are known for such fire towers, most of which are climbable for exceptional views from the top). I ask if she is okay.

"Oh, yeah," she explains with confidence, "Just taking a rest. You should go up the tower. My husband says the view is exceptional."

Climbing an Adirondack fire tower can be a dizzying experience. The staircases are long, narrow, and open-air, which means you can see all the way to the ground with just a quick glance down. While stable, the amount of swaying in a strong breeze is always concerning. Gab, having never been up a tower, states that she'd rather not go up and see the view. This is fine with me, as my purpose is to enjoy time outside with the love of my life and to make sure that *she* is enjoying herself as well – it's not about me. I take a quick trip up the tower and soak in the expansive mountain views in every direction, with a few small lakes speckled about in the valleys of the landscape.

When I return, Gab is posted up on a rock underneath a tree canopy. I plop down and begin pulling lunch out of my bag: dried mangoes, trail mix, pretzels, grapes, cup noodles, and a small stove. Gab's eyes widen when I pull out the ramen and a couple cans of soda.

"You carried that all the way up the mountain?" she asks, surprised at something that is routine for me.

I crack open one of the cans and proclaim, "I wanted to make sure you eat and drink well up here!" Her smile serves as a silent "thank you".

Together we sip an icy cool Diet Coke and munch on our snacks while enjoying the warm breeze that begins to stir up the summit. A few puffy clouds begin to appear overhead, but none appear threatening. The songs coming from birds swooping about provide the soundtrack as we sit and take it all in.

"This is nice," Gab says, as if she doesn't want to admit it. "I get why you do this."

From behind we hear the older couple we met approaching the other end of the trail. We strike up a short conversation about their travels and how the wife, Carol, used to be afraid of climbing mountains. Now she is a proud Adirondack 46er and makes sure her husband, Scott, knows that he wouldn't be one too without her.

After playfully whacking Scott's rear end with her hiking pole, she turns to Gab and asks point blank:

"So, did you make it up the fire tower?"

Gab smiles and giggles a bit. "No. It's not for me."

"That's what I used to think," Carol says with the tone of a matriarch who is ready to expand the horizons of someone's comfort zone. "Until I did it. Go on. Get up there and do it. You already came all this way."

"Yeah!" Scott chimes in. "It's so beautiful up there. You can't be the only one that doesn't see it!"

Gab looks at me with a face I intuitively know the meaning of, thanks to reading it for almost a decade. Without speaking a word out loud, she explains that she wants me to speak up and politely RSVP "No" to this invitation by saying something like:

"That's okay! She gets a bit dizzy with heights. Just not for her. But we're enjoying this lunch and the view from here. Maybe next time!"

Knowing that this is exactly what Gab wants me to say, I do the opposite.

"Yeah, come on! You'll feel accomplished once you get up there."

Her mouth flattens and her eyes expand as she glares at me. It may be the wrong call, but a little playful peer pressure from a supportive audience might just help her create an experience for herself that she'll always remember. If *I've* benefitted so much from pushing my comfort zone this year, she will, too.

Sensing that defeat is imminent, Gab gets up and starts walking toward the fire tower. Scott and Carol march along to the trail and begin their descent while Gab and I watch from above as we ascend the staircase. She requests that I stay behind her. With each precarious step on a seemingly endless climb of thin wooden boards, I keep my hand on her back and speak aloud whatever pops into my mind to serve as a futile distraction.

After every five steps the platform does a 180 degree turn before continuing up the next set of stairs. The turns are the hardest part, as we are confronted each time with a view that displays how high we've climbed. Eventually, Gab has enough.

"I can't go any farther. How much is left? Let's turn around at this one."

What she doesn't realize is that she is saying this at the top of the tower.

"We're here!" I shout from behind. "Just duck your head and

crawl into the room."

Together we enter a tiny tin box that stands at the top of the staircase, with open air views all around. Gab grabs my arm with her left hand and grips the railing with her right, her knees bent in a slight squat to prevent her from standing straight and embracing the freedom of the environment. Her breath slows as she looks around the panoramic views of endless colored mountains and deep blue lakes all the way to the horizon. It lasts only a few seconds before she says that she is ready to come down. While she doesn't see it this way, she is triumphant right now. She worked through a serious fear and was rewarded with a spectacular view and the pride of knowing that yes, in fact, she *can* climb up an Adirondack fire tower. It's what this year has been all about, and sharing this moment with her is icing on the cake.

After a careful descent we emerge at the bottom of the staircase victorious. Our ultimate goal achieved, we head down the trail to complete the loop and return to our car. Gab has a sudden spring in her step; an extra boost of confidence, joy, and endorphins that come as a result of the experience of climbing the fire tower. She doesn't admit it, but I can see that she is really *enjoying* herself out here. No screens, no thoughts of work, no social pressures (besides what Scott and Carol provide). Instead, we are hand-in-hand, frolicking through the forest together, not a care in the world.

Then the sky darkens.

Without warning, a rumble of thunder shakes the mountainside above us. Just twenty minutes ago, in the fire tower, I did not see any clouds that were of concern. They were white, puffy, and sparsely populated. Apparently, in our frolicking, we didn't notice their rapid descent into madness. The forest is now dark. In an instant the faucet turns on and rain starts pouring down in buckets from above. The trail quickly floods and becomes a fast-moving stream, leaving us to try and traverse the muddy outskirts of the footpath. At one point, in between rumbles of thunder, I hear what sounds like a massive suction cup. Turning around, I see Gab's shoe stuck in the mud, completely soaked. She looks up and frowns like a kid whose ice cream fell off the cone and onto the pavement. She has never been caught in a storm before. A bit of fear and uncertainty is in her face, and she looks to me to make it all better (which I secretly have always loved, and always will).

I yank on her leg and jostle her foot out of the mud with, thankfully, her shoe still attached. Immediately I pull off my shirt and begin cleaning her goopy, muddy leg with it as my torso gets soaked in the downpour. In my mind I envision myself a sexy action hero saving the day for my damsel in distress. Gab's face says otherwise. Once her leg is clean I yank and pull my skin-tight shirt back on, rolling its soaked fabric down my stomach as it sticks to my wet skin with every movement. This is not what I intended for our lovely day out in the forest. I always get anxious when plans go awry and I feel like Gab is not having a good time. Especially now, when we were connecting over the beauty of the outdoors together (which is not a common thing). Seeing that I need to right the ship before it sinks, I grab her face with my soil-speckled hands and move close.

"Hey, it is what it is. Everything is perfectly fine. We're safe. We're already soaking wet and dirty, so we might as well laugh at the situation. Freaking out isn't going to make us any drier."

She chuckles.

"I guess the Universe doesn't want your scheme to turn me into a hiker to work at all."

We both start cracking up. She's relaxing, so I grab her hand

and we begin to trot down the trail with vigor. After just a few minutes the rain lightens up and we both calm down, no longer distracted by the roaring of thunder or rushing of water beneath our feet. In the distance a crimson figure appears through the trees.

My car.

If we had started this adventure just ten minutes earlier we would have avoided the whole storm. But, to be fair, we also would have missed Scott and Carol, Gab would never have gone up the fire tower, and we would have had a pleasant but far less memorable experience. The apparent mishaps along the way turn out to be blessings. Without them, we would not have grown closer, tougher, and more resilient together. Maybe all of this was part of a plan.

At the car I pull out a clean shirt and pair of socks for Gab to slip into, while I sink my soaked ass into a car seat that is sure to chafe on the drive home. Finally comfortable in the passenger seat, Gab chuckles and turns to me:

"It was pretty nice . . .until it *DOWNPOURED!*"

I smile and grab her hand.

"That was nice too," I respond. "It's all part of the experience. I love it all. Plus, now we have a funnier story to tell."

"True," she says, looking out the dashboard window while squeezing my hand. "If nothing else, it's good content."

As we begin to pull out of the parking lot, we see two figures approaching from the end of the trail. It's Scott and Carol. They must have taken the short detour to look at the reservoir nearby, even in the rain. They are both soaked to the bone, Scott is barefoot, and they have huge smiles. I roll down the window.

"Hey!" I shout, leaning my head over the side of the car. "She made it up the tower!"

"Atta girl!" yells Carol. "I knew you could do it, hun!"

The Magic of Forest Bathing

We wave as the window rolls up and our tires roll out, leaving muddy tracks behind us.

It's on the ride home, on some lonely country road in between random bouts of rain underneath small puffy clouds, when I realize that some forest baths are more satisfying, and more meaningful, than others. They do not have to be epic or adventurous. Sometimes, the simple and familiar are the most beautiful. While Gab dozes off in the passenger seat, rocked to sleep by the swerving asphalt and the sight of farmhouses in the distance, my plans change. This experiment will not end the way I planned, I decide. But it will be perfect.

* * *

Being my final challenge of the year, the grand vision for this forest bathing experiment was to end it (and the year as a whole) with one final, epic, forest bath deep in the wilderness. I planned on taking two days to hike and explore the wilderness alone, isolated in rugged terrain. Then, I thought, I could experience the *true* power of forest bathing and transmit that knowledge to others. Plus, it would also be a rather strenuous expedition, thus adding another feather into my cap in the name of doing hard things. A great way to end. Not perfect, but great.

But plans are fickle. Life happens. And weeks before the planned backpacking excursion I find myself sitting in my childhood bedroom on a crisp, misty fall morning. We are on a spontaneous weekend visit to the motherland. Per usual, I awake before everyone else and embrace the coziness of the early sun. Looking out the back window toward the woods, a siren calls me to tie my shoes and venture out the door while Gab, my sister, and my brother-in-law still lay asleep in bed. Untied to the mast, I cannot resist.

The Magic of Forest Bathing

Something has called me toward a more meaningful place to reflect on the power of the forest, slow living, and doing strenuous things. It is the home of my original forest bathing practice, the place that made me fall in love with nature all those years ago. Where I lived slowly, did hard things, and dreamed big dreams before life got in the way.

I have returned to the forest of my childhood.

Alone, my thin sneakers step through the dew-soaked grass as I cross through a portal to another world. *This*, the simple, unremarkable return to where it all began, is meant to be the final experience.

Traversing down the steep hill toward the meadow I catch a convergence of scents: the sweet, flowery smell of summertime hits the high notes while the undertones consist of the first fallen leaves of autumn beneath my feet. The Earth is in transition.

At the edge of the meadow lies the entrance to the forest, which looks like a beckoning fairy-land full of whimsical creatures and magical spirits. As soon as my feet enter the green tunnel a strong sense of place washes over me: I am home. I spent most of my years on this planet exploring this little patch of land, protected by its solitude. This is where I rambled, rode my bike, built forts, played games, got covered in dirt, tasted true freedom (away from adults), mended broken hearts, planned futures, and thought about life, God, and the universe. The ancient trails traversing the woodland are riddled with my footsteps, fossilized underneath fresh soil. I don't come back here as often as I'd like, and it currently has been the longest stretch of time I've *ever* gone in my thirty-one years without being here. But returning always feels right, especially given how I've rekindled my connection with the woods.

Beginning on the path, I spot some twisted metal debris high up in an oak tree. It's a tree-stand. One that belonged to my deceased friend. He used to hunt back here on occasion, which was super illegal but also a good excuse for him to find some much-needed solitude. The pegs in the tree leading up to the stand still feel sturdy, but the seat itself is too high, rusty, and decrepit to be trustworthy. While a memorial climb up to the top seems nice, it is unwise. Maybe his spirit is still up there, watching me from above.

"I miss you, man."

The leaves are in their finest colors, exploding with hues of yellow, orange, and red. Down a slight hill I come upon the Lightning Tree, named in honor of a legendary summer day from adolescence. Troy, our friend, and I were throwing the football in the street. When we grew tired it was decided that we would all stop home for a quick bite to eat before heading back to my house to continue the activities. While making these plans, though, something surreal happened: the sky turned green. Storm clouds began closing in and turned the sky a color the likes of which none of us had ever seen. We knew this would be a big one.

We all sprinted home, hoping to eat and get back together before the storm hit. We were, inevitably, too late. Within minutes of our separation the heavens opened up on our neighborhood and thunder rumbled with violence. I watched the carnage from the window in my basement, with sheets of rain coming down so heavily that I could barely see my own backyard. Suddenly, a flash. And, instantaneously, a roaring crack of thunder. Something close was hit, most likely in the back woods.

The next day I wandered down the path for my usual walk when I saw it: the lightning tree, the source of the noise. A large pine had its bark stripped away in a spiraling pattern from the top of its trunk all the way to the roots. Next to it, another tree had a similar pattern, this time going *up* from the bottom to about halfway up the tree. Shredded, burned bark was scattered about the crime scene. It was a moving display of nature's power.

Staring at the scar, which is now more than a decade old, I wonder if I am the only one left around these parts who even notices it, let alone knows the lore of its creation. Many of the paths are slowly growing over. Not the main ones frequented by dog-walkers, but the side trails that my friends and I blazed and maintained during our feral youth. One of these forgotten paths is covered by bright white asters popping up in their early autumnal glory – the same ones that I have been seeing around my house. Finally, a connection between my two homes.

I brush through towering bushels of root-weed and emerge at the creek, which is low and trickling after weeks without steady rainfall. Many of the rocks on the shore are bright white, temporarily exposed after the dry spell. They look like my skin the first time I'm exposed to warm summer light: blinding.

The creek is a hotbed for fossil activity. It's impossible to go a few steps without finding some fossil etched into one of the stones that catches my eye. Many of these rocks are probably new and unseen thanks to the ever-shifting shoreline of the creek. Others might have been sitting here for my entire life. I will never know. But I do take a few as keepsakes, breaking the "Take only photographs, leave only footprints" advice found near forests around the country. The rocks I select are colored, patterned, and riddled with fossils. One looks like an ancient explosion of primordial shells and plant life. Another, a red hue reminiscent of rocks found in Glacier National Park in Montana, is covered in lines that look like a topographical map. I have no plans for these rocks, but I gather half a dozen anyway and keep them in my grasp. Here I have spent the past few years diving into the ultralight hiking world and trying to *shed* weight in the name of speed, and now I'm slowly sauntering through a small forest carrying large rocks that tire my forearms and smaller finger muscles. Why? I'm not sure. I'll blame the serenity that this forest bathing experiment has created in me.

During my struggle to find the right position to hold the six rocks in a way that doesn't burn out my hands, I see the remnants of a walnut shell ripped to shreds by some hungry animal. While I have violated the former part of the Leave No Trace principle ("Take only photographs") this anonymous little critter has shown no regard for the latter ("Leave only footprints"). Further down the trail I balance this cosmic karma of my rule-violation by picking up a coffee cup lid and sliding it into my back pocket to be disposed of back home.

While the Leave No Trace principle is vital for the health and well-being of our fleeting wilderness, I find it to be incomplete. Don't get me wrong: it is an important philosophy that protects the environments we love. And yet, in the end, leaving *no* trace shouldn't be the goal; just the opposite, in fact.

If we truly connect with a place in nature, spend a lot of time in it, and allow it to provide healing and rest and insight, then we cannot just leave without a trace. While our physical presence can (and should) be unseen, our *psychic* traces should remain all over the landscape. If we go to one distant place and consume it on a time-crunch for the sake of pictures then sure, the psychic trace will be minimal. A place experienced in that way can impact us, as some of my hikes in faraway landscapes certainly have, but not in the deep-rooted way that a lifelong connection with a specific place is capable of. Truly connecting with a place must result in psychic traces being scattered all about the landscape. Because what is the point of traversing through a landscape, grand and majestic as it may be, if we don't allow it to imprint something on our being?

Even a small, run-of-the-mill natural area can be more profound than a grand, sweeping environment when given the opportunity. It's impossible for me to look around these woods and not see my younger self romping around, playing, and healing under the sway of the trees. Everywhere I look there are ghosts of seasons past running on trails, building forts, going off jumps on my mountain bike, staring into the creek looking for answers to life's toughest questions, lying on the ground and staring up at the fractals in hopes of one day being loved and starting a family. Hoping to be the person I am now. Dreaming of living the life I now get to live every day when I open my eyes. I *can't* look at these woods without feeling a love for them and a desire to protect them. My stories, my being, my sense of self are all steeped in this little plot of land nestled beside a quiet creek in Upstate New York. My trace is deeply embedded in its story, and vice versa.

This is the lifeline between who I was as a child – authentic and free – and who I am now. It's the through line of a lifetime, where I can look at my inner child, smile, and acknowledge his continued presence. Reconnecting with him in the forest takes the label of "successful and productive adult" off my shoulders and replaces it with a quiet sense of wholeness. We are together again, one being, proud of each other for everything we are and have become.

Our inner child exists inside all of us. All the time. Just waiting to be seen. We are just too disconnected and move too quickly to recognize him.

* * *

Weeks later, as I watch a maple leaf slowly float down into my backyard, the true impact of forest bathing becomes apparent to me.

The Magic of Forest Bathing

I think back to the very beginning of spring when I gasped with joy at the first tiny buds beginning to sprout from the ends of formerly barren branches. This being my first year in my home, I was curious to see the landscape change as spring became summer. Through the summer months I spent endless hours sitting on my deck becoming immersed in a green canopy that brought me peace. And now, as my forest bathing experiment has ended in its official capacity, the first signs of change are once again apparent. It is beautiful, the cycle of nature. And I'm happy to be sitting here to experience it. Besides, without this experiment, I probably would have missed it.

Returning to the forest without an objective has reinvigorated my spirit. My days have begun with exercise and golden rays tickling my face. My lunch breaks at work are spent feeling increasingly cool breezes instead of stale air pumped out of a vent. My evenings have been filled with sunsets, stars, crickets, and slow strolls hand-in-hand with Gab. Each day *feels* new and different because I am observant enough to notice the differences in the landscape, however subtle. I have watched that black-staining polypore mushroom burst into existence in a dramatic firework then slowly decay back into humus, and only I know its story and current whereabouts. I've listened to the birds prepare for either migration or the lean times, as their songs have dwindled in frequency while the nights cool and sunsets come earlier. I've watched the asters and fungi populate my property as a reminder that, no, we are not alone here, and that these life-forms will persist here long after Gab and I are gone. Now, thanks to this habit of observation, my *new* home feels like an *actual* home. I am becoming rooted in this place, *invested* in its health, in love with its cycles. It may not be where I spent my formative years, but who's to say we can't be formed in the years well beyond adolescence? Perhaps I am just beginning.

The Magic of Forest Bathing

 I can't speak to the health benefits of forest bathing. Unlike some more robust experimenters, I didn't bother to check my heart rate, blood pressure, or other health indicators beforehand – it seemed unnecessary. I don't know if I'm more or less likely to get cancer or if my cortisol levels have actually lowered. The point of forest bathing is to slow down and be present in nature, which is hard to do when I'm pouring over minuscule metrics. Besides, too many wellness practices now obsess over optimized metrics. As if success is determined more by what we produce (or what we don't) than who we become. While I certainly *feel* better, and would guess that some metrics somewhere have improved in my body, I don't need to get a blood test to justify the validity of the practice. And neither should anyone else. Forest bathing, while it began as a health practice, is as much about mental and spiritual health through philosophical development as it is about increasing cancer-killing cell content – more so, in fact. While the lessons I am taking from this experiment are ethereal, they are far more powerful than anything a scientific study with an "*n* of one" can determine.

 In addition, time now passes much slower. Especially when I'm feeling too busy to bother, making the effort to get out and appreciate the natural world stretches my days in ways that other habits simply can't match (except, perhaps, spending time with friends). Spending twenty minutes to an hour each day sauntering, breathing, and looking around in wonder provides my brain with more unique stimuli to process which, in turn, slows down my perception of time. By noticing subtle changes in the landscape I can track them bit-by-bit, and so there are no longer any sudden, dramatic changes in my local environment. Fall doesn't just "happen", leaves don't just change, and animals don't just appear. Like our own terminal case of increasing wrinkles and graying hair, each change happens daily, subtly, *almost* without notice. Making it noticeable changes everything. It allows us to grow and age *with* our environment. It helps us embrace the seasons of our lives just as we embrace the seasons of the year. Eventually it helps us to not feel so alone, because our friend the forest is going along for the ride with us.

Finally, my journeys into the forest continue to make me a bit sad. Just about every time I venture out I am the only person in the woods. Whether it's a dark, rainy afternoon or a beautiful sunny morning, encounters with other people enjoying the Earth's stunning beauty are rare. I'm fortunate to live in a place with many natural areas to enjoy. But I know this is becoming more and more of an anomaly. As our society continues to develop its foolish, unwise disconnection from nature, more trees are being cut down and turned into strip mall parking lots. More marshlands are being drained for luxury apartment complexes. More parks are becoming bordered by landfills. And, as a result, more and more of us face increasing stress, worry, anxiety, and speed, coupled with a tragically limited perspective of life on Earth. When we disconnect from nature we are not just engaging in a damaging physical process. We are damaging our mental state as well. Worst of all, our spiritual health suffers the most.

There is power in the practice of engaging with a landscape larger than ourselves. There is wisdom in understanding that life will continue to exist with or without us. When we aggrandize ourselves and our "progress" and our problems too much, we fall into the trap of thinking that we, as a species, are fully in control. But if there is anything we have learned in this era of industrialization it's that, the more we meddle with nature, the more we *should* realize that the Earth almost always has a better system in place. It's why neighborhoods flood when built near manmade lakes that can't handle sudden, increased rainfall. Or why the destruction of a forested landscape leads to an increase in certain diseases due to more frequent contact between humans and nefarious carriers. It explains how, after centuries of destruction, we are finally approaching the realization that maybe *we* were the problem in the first place, and that restoration is the key to a healthy future. But without a deep knowledge of, and appreciation for, nature's processes, no one will care enough to notice.

Not only does the infinite universe not revolve around our individual, petty problems, but the comparatively microscopic Earth doesn't either. The migrating birds pay no mind to an upcoming election. The mighty oaks do not care when or where or why missiles have been launched. The winding bank of a wild creek does not change course due to congested traffic patterns. These things exist, always, regardless of whether we are there to appreciate them or not. And they will continue to long after we are all dead, buried, and decomposing into rich humus that will support another generation of life.

As a species, we can no longer afford not to notice, not to care, not to experience. In this age of rapid destruction and all its negative side effects for the individual, the population, and the ecosystem, the first and greatest act of resistance must be to slow down, leave the human world, and enter the real one, if only for a moment.

We will all be better for it.

Epilogue: A Life Worth Paying Attention To

My hands, calloused and scraped from continued rock climbing, shake in my lap. I am now far more anxious than at any other point in the year. Perhaps even my life.

I am sitting in a stiff chair that is much too small for my long frame. The air is stiff and stale and fluorescent lights shine down harshly on my sensitive eyes. My breathing is inconsistent and my chest is tight. In my right hand lies Gab's left hand, and I look at her with an air of feigned reassurance. It was only one year ago that we sat in an office just like this, unsure of what the future would bring. At that time a doctor poked around on a scan while I came to terms with the potential reality of our "forever" being cut far too short – there was no guarantee that her illness *wasn't* terminal at that time. After months of pain, a brutal operation, and weeks of waiting on test results that would determine our future, she mercifully came out the other side okay. There haven't been any signs of regression since. We have been, as far as we were told, "in the clear". Now, though, we are back in a sterile doctor's office holding our collective breath. The last place we want to be.

Gab looks at me with both hope and concern, her mouth slightly curled and her beautiful eyes wide. She is quivering ever so slightly. The doctor, in her white lab coat, doesn't make eye contact with either of us. Instead, she continues her analysis with a focus and determination so intense that I can't decide if I should feel confident or terrified. I look down at my white shoes, dirtied from weeks of forest bathing, and begin to tap them rhythmically as if I'm playing on an invisible drum kit – my go-to habit when anxiety pulses uncontrollably through my veins. The phone stays in my pocket, its hold on me finally broken after almost a year of effort. My stomach nervously churns the homemade pancakes, berries, and local maple syrup we shared for breakfast. Once again our future hangs in the balance, entirely dependent on whether this woman we have just met does, or does not, find *something*. Can we really go through a major event like this again? Am I strong enough, even after a year of trying to become so?

*　*　*

One year ago I plopped my pale body into a frozen lake to prove a point:

Life gets better when I slow it down and make it more challenging.

As my toes numbed in the depths of the black lake that evening, I wasn't sure that idea was true. It was just a hunch. Deep down there was something lacking in my soul, as if part of me had gone missing, swept up in the frenzied pace of daily life. Time had become a blur in the years prior, my sense of confidence waned with each new convenience that promised to take away my agency, and activities that made life meaningful were experienced less often – a victim of the seductive convenience that we are all faced with. The hollow, empty feeling all of this created became so uncomfortable that the thought of immersing myself in shock-inducing water seemed like a more desirable alternative. As if the temporary pain could spark my soul back into motion. Or, counterintuitively, that the cold water could be the trick to living life on full boil.

After taking care of Gab, surviving the car accident, managing our wedding and house purchase, enduring the death of my friend,

Epilogue: A Life Worth Paying Attention To

and reflecting on Nanny's final words, to say I was overwhelmed would have been a great understatement. Every day there was a deep wound in my chest that I carried around, dragging me down even in the brightest of moments. My main emotion was exhaustion. So much happened in such a short period of time that I didn't even know where, or how, to begin picking up the pieces. When everything starts crumbling at once, and you expend every thought and ounce of energy you have to save what you can, how do you begin to move on once the dust settles and your heavy breathing slows?

On a sunny Tuesday morning in our apartment I logged onto a call with a virtual therapist – something I had never done before. At this point I didn't know where else to turn, and I needed a neutral party to see the situation clearly and, hopefully, inspire next steps. The therapist on the call sat in his living room. I could hear the happy sounds of three little children running around in the background and the occasional, hushed threat from the mother trying to get them to leave and calm down while their daddy was on a call.

"So, Peter. What brings you here today?"

After taking him through everything that happened, he sat back and put his hands on his head.

"Holy shit, dude" he responded. "That's a lot."

For some reason, that particular reaction coming from a professional was validating. It proved, to me anyway, that I wasn't just being dramatic.

We spent the next hour discussing how each event impacted me and how I was managing with the complex swirl of emotions. My body began shaking at times. Tears flowed. Emotions I couldn't put a name to were identified. Slowly, even in that short amount of time, I began to feel lighter as I provided myself with some much-needed love, which I often neglect to do.

Epilogue: A Life Worth Paying Attention To

Toward the end of the call the therapist told me something I didn't realize I needed to hear. While putting his hands together in a way that all therapists on TV tend to do, he leaned forward and said:

"Pete, you were there for everyone who needed you. You stepped up. You met your responsibilities. You cared for others even when you were hurting yourself. You did something really, *really* hard. And you're better for it. Give yourself some credit, man. You can rest now."

My eyes welled up and it felt like a weight was lifting off my shoulders. I never did give myself any credit for holding strong and taking care of my loved ones, even though I needed to be taken care of, too. All the emotions, phone calls, paperwork, and meetings I managed in spite of my feelings or grief and anxiety never elicited a single pat on the back from myself. That being understood, I did have one point to protest:

"But how can I actually rest? There's still more to do. I feel like I need to get away for a while, disappear, heal. Then I can come back better than before."

The therapist smiled.

"Why can't you relax right now?" he said with that look people have when they know they're about to hit a home-run. "You're at home, talking to me. No one needs you. Nothing is required. People always think they need a big adventure or vacation to relax. But do what your Nanny said: enjoy every moment. Find those pockets of peace in your day to breathe and heal. You'll find that, over time, it all adds up. And you'll be much better for it."

He knocked that one right out of the park, that's for sure.

When this slow and strenuous year first came to mind, the initial idea was to do something big and epic. Taking a summer to drive around the country and live out of our car. Spending a month

Epilogue: A Life Worth Paying Attention To

hiking the Appalachian Trail. Flying to the other side of the world. Walking to Canada. Escaping. All ideas that would have stoked and inspired the younger version of myself.

"If I could just get away from it all and go on a big adventure," I thought, "then I'll come back and everything will be okay.

While that is a seductive idea, it isn't true.

Our society often dreams of, and glorifies, the idea of ditching all of our responsibilities to go live on the road in complete freedom. This is especially true for Millennials and Gen Z, where YouTube channels chronicling the lives and adventures of people who are doing just that rack up millions of views and inspire others to try and live the same way. Comment sections are filled with dreams of leaving life behind and traveling indefinitely. Videos that complain about the constraints of responsibilities like jobs, families, and mortgages are met with acclaim and encourage those in their 20s and 30s to rid themselves of such dead-weight.

At first, ideas such as these *did* provide the main inspiration for this project. But upon further inspection, their inherent shallowness was brought to the surface.

I'm all for big adventures. The ones I've gone on have been life-changing and have made me a better person. Grand adventures can be a catalyst for real, true change and have ripple effects that last for years. But that's *only* if two conditions are met:

First, the adventure must allow us to run *toward* our problems, not away from them.

And second, most importantly, they must end.

At a certain point, indefinitely globe-trotting, hiking, running, or road-tripping just becomes just another way to avoid dealing with our issues; it's no different than scrolling or binge-watching TV. When the solution is always "out there", when happiness comes "once I do this", when peace lies "at the end of this trail", we step on an endless treadmill that never gets us to our desired destination. And so we keep searching, traveling, and moving *outward* instead of doing the necessary introspection to heal and grow into a better person.

This led to the realization that my year of slow and strenuous living couldn't be done in an isolated, one-off challenge or adventure. If it was going to be truly impactful, then it needed to be integrated into my daily life within the responsibilities and constraints I face. Sure, I could go off-grid for a month and "find myself". But upon my return, my job, my family, my phone, and my internet connection would all be waiting for that "found" self to return and get back to work. And realistically they couldn't be ignored forever. Whatever lessons I learned from that adventure would have to be applied to a normal life – how I live 99% of the time instead of that magical 1% spent in far-off places doing incredible things. Even Walter Mitty had to fill out a new resumé when he got home.

An epic experience is not required for the slow and strenuous life; nor do we have to quit our jobs and move to a cabin in the woods. Thinking that way is just an excuse for continued inaction, as we mock those with the privilege, finances, or time to go do the big things while we kick rocks with hands in our pockets and complain that "we could never do that", when deep down we know that's bullshit. We are all capable of slowing down and living more strenuously; it will just look different for everyone.

For me, keeping the challenges from this year reasonable in scope, domestic in circumstance, and accessible in nature allowed for it to happen in a way that was more impactful. In the end, I couldn't make excuses like I could with a bigger, more complicated plan. It would have been easy to put off this experiment by convincing myself that the mundane can't be beautiful. I could have bought the lie that only grand experiments and epic adventures create lasting change, and that they must happen *outside* my normal, day-to-day routine. From there, it would have been so simple to bail on a big plan due to lack of time, resources, or freedom.

Instead, the choice was clear: either I would keep my promise and step-up to the challenge, or I would retreat from my plans like a coward and continue living as a poor, timid soul on the sidelines. With each circumstance I was faced with that choice. It's convenient to pretend that a decision to live better is never sitting right in front of us, waiting for our response. But deep down we know that's a lie. That decision is *always* available for us to make, whether we want to admit it or not.

Plus, running away from our issues on some meaningless grand adventure implies that the life in front of us is incapable of beauty. The reality is that I, you, all of us are needed in some form or another. We are relied upon. We need to show up, take responsibility, and do what needs to be done to make a better life for ourselves, our friends, and our family. We can't run or hide from this responsibility without harming others. But this reality is not a ball-and-chain. It's a blessing. And it's not something we should try and escape from. The therapist made this clear for me.

"Responsibilities", much demonized in our culture today, are a sign of a life well-lived. As I age, I realize the inherent value that these responsibilities have. A life where no one counts on you, no meaningful work is completed, no deep connections are made, no roots are developed, and no one misses your presence is a sad life indeed. Being "tied down" by responsibilities that prevent you from doing whatever you want, whenever you want, isn't a sign of a dead-end life. It means you are valued, that you matter, that people *rely* on you. You are wanted, needed, and important. That's what life is all about: our impact on others. Isn't it?

This is why the challenges I embarked on became more subtle and easily integrated into my normal, routine, "boring" life. Managing a healthy relationship with technology is essential regardless of our personal circumstances. Facing our fears can help us even if we're in the drudgery of a nine-to-five. Committing to cultivating deep, meaningful friendships makes life more fun and provides a safety net for ourselves and our loved ones. Pushing our limits, even if just for a day, shows us that we can still live an extraordinary life in ordinary circumstances. Appreciating the little things, like a home-cooked meal or a beautiful forest, makes life worth living. And all of this makes us better versions of ourselves for the people who need us.

There were no guarantees that slowing down and inserting meaningful challenges into my life would make a huge difference. But it did. This has been the longest, most impactful year of my entire life, with more growth, insight, and joy than I've ever cultivated before. This little idea that spawned while scribbling in my journal on a thrifted table in the middle of our apartment blossomed into a new way of life; one that I will hold onto for the rest of my days.

Slowing down has exposed the absurdity of our current pace of life. Constant motion, wearing "busy-ness" as a badge of honor, and cramming an unreasonable amount of tasks into an already packed schedule is no way to live. We are promised that making everything faster will inevitably make our lives better. And this story, of course, is told to us by those who stand to profit from this trend. But speed has consequences.

Epilogue: A Life Worth Paying Attention To

It's impossible to appreciate our short time on Earth when we're caught up in an endless, frenzied to-do list. The most important parts of life deserve to be slowed down. They deserve time, attention, and care. Fast-paced food has broken our agricultural systems, compromised our health, and devalued one of the most important experiences of life itself. Prioritizing speed with our information has led to infinite, addictive scrolling through mountains of brain-dead garbage in the names of attention-harvesting and profit. A calendar that prioritizes pointless activity ignores a slower-paced calendar of cosmic beauty that reminds us of our insignificance and how precious our life on this tiny little rock actually is. Ultimately, a fast-paced life does not encourage a deep, examined, intentional life. And so, without taking a breath and slowing down, we resign ourselves to a shallow existence that washes by without noticing until it is inevitably, tragically, too late.

And if we never challenge ourselves with the time we gain by slowing down, we fail to realize our great potential. The promises that come with a life of immense convenience are hollow and unfulfilling. We shouldn't be striving toward endless ease and comfort when the price includes our competence, confidence, agency, peace, and self-esteem. A racing heart and sweat-soaked brow are indicators of an experience worth having. Pushing our comfort zone beyond our perceived limits, and believing in ourselves enough to succeed, is life-affirming. It puts us in the arena, boils our water, and turns us into a vigorous soul making the most of the random, fleeting, and precious time we have. Whether it's a test of physical endurance, making things from scratch instead of buying on impulse, facing our fears head on, fulfilling a promise, stepping up for those we love, or bearing a burden so that others may live lighter, anything that adds intentional friction to our life leads to personal growth and a better existence. Imagine going through an entire life without ever having tried. Without knowing what you're capable of. With promises unmet, limits untested, and dreams not pursued.

Worst of all, imagine not enjoying every beautiful, fleeting moment.

* * *

"Oh!"

Suddenly the doctor makes a slight noise, as if it squeaked out of her larynx by accident. She begins typing with urgency. My head shoots up through the stale air and I fixate my gaze on the pixelated screen to my left. Gab squeezes my hand a little too tightly, testing the integrity of my finger bones. There is a glare from the fluorescent lights beaming from above. But they are a mere inconvenience. The image on the screen is clear. For the first time, I see it:

A heartbeat.

"There it is!" the doctor exclaims. "The heartbeat! 138 beats per minute. Eight weeks. Due date: May 1st."

Tears obscure my vision. A lump in my throat hampers my voice. I look at Gab and smile, then bury my face into her side. We weren't sure if this day would ever come. We didn't know if, after everything we went through, it would be possible. And yet here we are, together, looking at our baby for the very first time.

I am going to be a father.

* * *

There was no way for me to know beforehand, but everything I went through this year, every struggle I endured, every demon I faced head-on, every moment I doubted myself, was for him. In retrospect, the timing was perfect. Without the challenges of the past

Epilogue: A Life Worth Paying Attention To

year, I would not be this stronger, calmer, capable, more present, and more confident version of myself. Instead, my son would have been raised by a tech-obsessed, easily distracted, anxious man who never had the guts to truly know himself or the presence to appreciate the millions of precious little moments that make up parenthood. Now, thanks to the slow and strenuous lifestyle, it doesn't matter what life or fatherhood throws at me: I'm ready. It's hard to feel anxious with this level of competence.

When combined, a slow and strenuous life lets us savor the fleeting moments of silence and peace that fill the margins of our lives. It helps us prove that we are capable of more than we imagine. It etches memories so deeply into our mind that they can never be forgotten. And, before we know it, life becomes rich and densely populated with warm memories, day after day.

This journey began as a selfish one. It was meant to fill holes in my psyche and soul; ones that were only made visible through a series of significant events. The main goals were to follow Nanny's advice and to live like the person I dreamed of as a young man. By the end of the year, I was hoping to be calmer, stronger, and more capable. Most importantly, I wanted to feel *alive* in a world that tries so hard to deaden our souls and distract us from what truly matters with work, consumption, and content.

* * *

One hot summer afternoon when I was seventeen, my deceased friend and I were hanging out in his driveway doing nothing in particular, as seventeen year-olds tend to do. After some less mature conversations, the topic eventually switched to dreams of love and family. Looking at the cracks in his driveway to avoid eye contact, I told him that one day I'd get married and have kids; that all I *really* wanted in life, deep down, was to love, be loved, and raise a loving

Epilogue: A Life Worth Paying Attention To

family. That was it. Career, accolades, location – none of that mattered as long as I could fulfill that dream. My friend, also avoiding eye contact, said the same for himself. We had just defined what success looked like. That day we promised that we'd find a way to make it happen and, if fate allowed, we'd live on the same street so our kids could grow up together. Such are the naive dreams of lonely teenagers. And while I may be the only one still able to fulfill this vision, he'll be in my heart every step of the way, cheering us on. I'm sure of it.

* * *

What I now realize is this journey was never meant for me. And it's why it couldn't be done in some far-flung adventure on the other side of the world: because I love, am loved, and have a loving family. This year was really meant for Gab, my family, my friends, and now my son. Its purpose was to make me a better version of myself for *them*. Together, throughout this year, we strengthened our bonds and committed to a more fulfilling way of life amidst the current state of chaos. We made our own little corner of the world better, kinder, slower, more interesting. None of this growth would have been possible without all of them supporting me, going along with weird ideas, and being present to enjoy life with. And now, with a fresh perspective, this little village can share our slow, meaningful, beautiful life with our baby boy.

And, hopefully, he will enjoy every moment. I know I will.

Bibliography

BBC News. *"Facebook Emotion Study."* BBC, 29 June 2014, www.bbc.com/news/technology-28051930. Accessed July 2025.

Bogard, Paul. *The End of Night: Searching for Natural Darkness in an Age of Artificial Light.* Little, Brown, 2013.

Children & Nature Network. *"Benefits of Time Spent Outside by Kids."* www.childrenandnature.org. Accessed July 2025.

Food, Inc. 2. Directed by Robert Kenner and Melissa Robledo, performances by Michael Pollan and Eric Schlosser, Magnolia Pictures, Participant, and River Road Entertainment, 2024. 94 min.

Gallup. *"U.S. Depression Rates Reach New Highs."* Gallup, 17 May 2023, news.gallup.com/poll/505745/depression-rates-reach-new-highs.aspx. Accessed July 2025.

Harvard Business Review. Waytz, Adam. *"Beware a Culture of Busyness."* Harvard Business Review, Mar.–Apr. 2023, hbr.org/2023/03/beware-a-culture-of-busyness. Accessed July 2025.

Huberman Lab. *"Using Light for Health."* Huberman Lab Newsletter, www.hubermanlab.com/newsletter/using-light-for-health. Accessed July 2025.

Li, Qing. *Forest Bathing: How Trees Can Help You Find Health and Happiness.* Viking, 2018.

Lieberman, Daniel E. *The Story of the Human Body: Evolution, Health, and Disease.* Pantheon Books, 2013.

Bibliography

Lifehacker. "Why Time Feels Like It's Flying By—And How to Slow It." *Lifehacker*, 2015, lifehacker.com/why-time-feels-like-it-s-flying-by-and-how-to-slow-it-1745852093. Accessed July 2025.

Louv, Richard. *Last Child in the Woods: Saving Our Children from Nature-Deficit Disorder.* Algonquin Books, 2005.

Mabon House. "A History of Mabon." *Mabon House*, www.mabonhouse.co/new-blog/a-history-of-mabon. Accessed July 2025.

Military.com. "New Pentagon Study Shows 77% of Young Americans Are Ineligible for Military Service." *Military.com*, 28 Sept. 2022, www.military.com/daily-news/2022/09/28/new-pentagon-study-shows-77-of-young-americans-are-ineligible-military-service.html. Accessed July 2025.

Office of Disease Prevention and Health Promotion. *The State of Physical Activity in America.* U.S. Dept. of Health and Human Services, 2019, odphp.health.gov/sites/default/files/2019-11/The-State-of-Physical-Activity-in-America.pdf. Accessed July 2025.

Olmstead, Grace. *Uprooted: Recovering the Legacy of the Places We've Left Behind.* Penguin Random House, 2021.

Outside Online. "Teddy Roosevelt Walk 50 Miles." *Outside*, www.outsideonline.com/outdoor-adventure/hiking-and-backpacking/teddy-roosevelt-walk-50-miles/. Accessed July 2025.

Psychology Today. "Subliminal Ads, Unconscious Influence, and Consumption." *Psychology Today*, 2014, www.psychologytoday.com/us/blog/sold/201406/subliminal-ads-unconscious-influence-and-consumption. Accessed July 2025.

Richardson, Miles. *Reconnection: Fixing Our Broken Relationship with Nature.* Pelagic Publishing, 2023.

Bibliography

ScienceAlert. *"The Science of Why Flow States Feel So Good, According to a Cognitive Scientist." ScienceAlert*, www.sciencealert.com/the-science-of-why-flow-states-feel-so-good-according-to-a-cognitive-scientist. Accessed July 2025.

Slow Food. *"Our History." Slow Food*, www.slowfood.com/our-history. Accessed July 2025.

Slow Food. *"Slow Food Manifesto." Slow Food*, Oct. 2023, www.slowfood.com/wp-content/uploads/2023/10/slow-food-manifesto.pdf. Accessed July 2025.

Space.com. *"Full Moon Rises Tonight: February 2024 Snow Moon Lore." Space.com*, www.space.com/full-moon-rises-tonight-february-2024. Accessed July 2025.

United Nations. *"Cheese Caves and Food Surpluses: Why the U.S. Government Stores 1.4 Billion lbs of Cheese." UN News*, 2022, news.un.org/en/story/2022/12/1131637. Accessed July 2025.

USC Applied Psychology. *"Thinking vs. Feeling: The Psychology of Advertising — Ads Per Day." USC Applied Psychology Blog*, appliedpsychologydegree.usc.edu/blog/thinking-vs-feeling-the-psychology-of-advertising. Accessed July 2025.

USDA Economic Research Service. *"Chart Gallery: Daily Calories per Capita." USDA ERS*, www.ers.usda.gov/data-products/chart-gallery/gallery/chart-detail/?chartId=58376. Accessed July 2025.

USDA Economic Research Service. *"Feed Grains Sector at a Glance." USDA ERS*, www.ers.usda.gov/topics/crops/corn-and-other-feed-grains/feed-grains-sector-at-a-glance/. Accessed July 2025.

Wikipedia contributors. *"Imbolc." Wikipedia*, en.wikipedia.org/wiki/Imbolc. Accessed July 2025.

Wikipedia contributors. *"Poy Sang Long." Wikipedia*,

Bibliography

en.wikipedia.org/wiki/Poy_Sang_Long. Accessed July 2025.

Wikipedia contributors. *"Rite of Passage."* Wikipedia, en.wikipedia.org/wiki/Rite_of_passage. Accessed July 2025.

Wikipedia contributors. *"Russefeiring."* Wikipedia, en.wikipedia.org/wiki/Russefeiring. Accessed July 2025.

Wikipedia contributors. *"Wheel of the Year."* Wikipedia, en.wikipedia.org/wiki/Wheel_of_the_Year. Accessed July 2025.

Made in the USA
Middletown, DE
31 August 2025